BECOMING BRITISH

UK CITIZENSHIP EXAMINED

THOM BROOKS

Biteback Publishing

First published in Great Britain in 2016 by
Biteback Publishing Ltd
Westminster Tower
3 Albert Embankment
London SE1 7SP
Copyright © Thom Brooks 2016

ISBN 978-1-84954-976-9

10 9 8 7 6 5 4 3 2 1

A CIP catalogue record for this book is available from the British Library.

Set in Arno Pro by Adrian McLaughlin

Printed and bound in Great Britain by
CPI Group (UK) Ltd, Croydon CR0 4YY

CONTENTS

INTRODUCTION

Citizenship matters. Only a country's citizens can enjoy the full rights of their shared political membership. To be a citizen is to have the most fundamental rights – or, as the philosopher Hannah Arendt said, 'a right to have rights'. The right to live in a state permanently, the right to vote and the right to run for elected office are a small handful of wide-ranging privileges that individuals have as citizens. But it is even more than that. Being a citizen is about belonging to a community.

It can be easy to overlook how important our citizenship is to us. Emily is a young woman living in London and building a successful career in the media industry. I asked her what being British meant to her and she said, 'I'm afraid I take British citizenship very much for granted.' Emily understood its significance and she is 'hugely grateful' for it. However, it is not something you merely *think* about; it is just something you *are*.

Her reply to my question is what most citizens born British say to me. Becoming British is something that just happens – and something we might not notice about ourselves. It's an achievement of birth to British parents on native soil. No application, no tests and nothing more – and easy to take for granted. Emily's path to becoming British is a simple one. A journey made by no more than showing up. Being British requires little effort for the great majority of British citizens.

Not everyone is this lucky. Tracy is a solicitor in the southwest and came to the UK from the United States. Tracy faced several hurdles in her path. She told me that British lawyers at her firm didn't know the answers to the British citizenship test she was required to pass. Tracy thought some of the obstacles she confronted served no purpose other than to make the process of her becoming British look legitimate and it was 'a relief to get it over with'.

Migrants like Tracy are part of a growing number of people who become British through *naturalisation*. But don't let the name fool you – there's little 'natural' about it. Naturalisation is a process where migrants are forced to jump through increasingly difficult hoops. These can change so quickly they challenge the most learned lawyer and politician. And the only thing growing as fast as the hurdles is the application costs. Naturalising is becoming British the hard way, where some of the rules may seem 'unnatural' and maybe a touch un-British as some migrants find they have more hurdles to jump than others to become fellow citizens.

Citizens are equals. But how they become citizens can vary enormously. The UK is made up of many citizens like Emily who are British from birth and a growing number like Tracy who had to pass several tests as a migrant. This means there can be no avoiding the significance of immigration, and different ideas about who should and who should not – or must not – be able to become a British citizen are central to any discussion.

British citizenship is no less controversial for the fact that defining what 'Britishness' is has proved so difficult. You need only turn on your telly or see tabloid headlines to confirm that how citizens are *becoming British* is a crucial issue of our time. Migration is about crossing territorial borders, but British citizenship is about crossing civic boundaries, recognising others as equals. This raises some fundamental questions about being British. What is Britishness? Can it be tested? Should new citizens integrate with current citizens? How important is knowing English? Does any of this matter?

This book explores the big questions the public often asks but which are rarely answered by politicians, their special advisors or anyone else. UK citizenship has undergone substantial changes, and a clear, up-to-date examination of what it involves, of who can become British and on what terms, is long overdue.

I explain the immigration problems that modern UK citizenship law and policy were meant to solve, what the major challenges are today and how they should be met. While immigration of both temporary and permanent residents receives widespread attention, much less time is devoted to the major increase in the number of British citizens and how this might be managed better. This book fills this crucial gap and redresses the balance.

I know about becoming British for a simple reason – I did it. I became British. Been there, done that, got the T-shirt. Like Tracy, I am also an immigrant to the UK. Originally from the US state of Connecticut, I spent two years in Ireland before moving to the UK in 2001. I've called Britain my home for fifteen years and became a UK citizen in 2011. I do not merely know how Britain's complex immigration system and citizenship rules work; I experienced them first-hand from applicant to citizen. I know about becoming British because I became British – with a lot of paperwork and receipts to prove it.

A few words about the chapters that follow. *Becoming British* covers the main issues – from the background to Britishness and the citizenship test, to the EU, family life, asylum and much more. This book begins with the crucial background so often neglected concerning where we are today and how we got there. Chapter 1 looks at rising immigration to the United Kingdom, providing an overview for the growing numbers becoming British and the challenges successive governments have faced to manage access to citizenship. Chapter 2 examines the shift from subject to citizen that has revolutionised how becoming British works, with lasting – and surprising – effects as a once global power began to shrink. Chapter 3 considers the question of Britishness and the many frustrated attempts at defining what it is. These chapters set the scene for the rest of the book.

Next, the book reveals the facts behind the myths and misunderstandings. Chapter 4 discusses how to test for 'Britishness' and focuses on the UK's citizenship test – which I liken to a bad pub quiz. Sample questions and answers are provided that will make you the envy of any dinner party or social gathering. Chapter 5 is about the English question, or, more exactly, the question of how much English new citizens are expected to know and why. Chapter 6 addresses the free movement myth regarding Britain's membership of the EU, and how the UK could restrict the movement of EU nationals better if only the government knew how. Chapter 7 is about marriage and the right to family life as pathways to British citizenship. Chapter 8 concerns asylum seekers and refugees and their experience of becoming British. Chapter 9 considers the powers of the Home Secretary to end the citizenship of British nationals and deport them. The final, tenth chapter sets out my recommendations for how British citizenship can be improved and how we can begin the kind of national conversation we need urgently.

This book is informed throughout by the latest research, the current immigration rules and my observations through personal experiences. Immigration is a complex topic and the official guidance can change daily. But this doesn't mean a book about it must be unreadable or outdated as soon as it is printed. I believe that British citizens deserve a clear guide that lets everyone see the challenges of British citizenship for what they are in a way most readers can understand – especially if they have not thought much about these issues before. This goes too for people thinking about becoming British: this book is for you both.

I have benefited enormously from speaking to people – hundreds of British citizens past, present and future – across the United Kingdom over the past decade. They come from all walks of life, a myriad of backgrounds. Their stories are messages of the hope, aspiration and belonging as well as the confusion, discrimination and alienation that citizenship in modern Britain means for everyday people. They say much about the Britain we want to be and how we want to get there. Unless otherwise stated, I have disguised the identities of people interviewed out of respect for their privacy. Many of their stories raise deep concerns about the problems current immigration policy brings to bear on real people. I am thankful to them for sharing these often painful stories with me so that they might get the attention of ministers and the wider public about what is actually happening in our country.

I am also very grateful to the ministers, elected MPs, peers and policy advisors who gave their time generously to share insights into key decisions and events that have shaped the evolution of current policy. They have helped broaden and deepen the discussion here by helping to flesh out the thinking behind many of the policies we have today. References for each chapter can be found in the 'Further reading' section at the end of the book, where supporting evidence for claims made can be found. Those wanting to look into the details should look there.

I began by saying citizenship matters. It does – citizenship is hugely important to everyone from the British citizen wanting to welcome new members to those in favour of tighter restrictions, as well as to those hoping to become British citizens in the future. It's now time to start our journey to see why this is, how it all works and what we can do to improve the system – before it is beyond repair.

CHAPTER 1

IMMIGRATION RISING

———

I t was like any other spring day in Rochdale. But a general election was on the horizon that morning in 2010, and Prime Minister Gordon Brown had come to Rochdale to speak to voters and help promote local Labour Party candidate Simon Danczuk. It was an ordinary day that became extraordinary for a chance encounter with a local grandmother named Gillian Duffy.

Gillian was selected by one of Brown's aides to speak with the Prime Minister. The aim of his campaign team was to show Brown engaging with local citizens and win positive coverage in the media. But that's not how things turned out. In front of the cameras, Gillian voiced her concerns about the economy, but it was what she said about immigrants – and how Brown reacted to what she told him – that made the headlines.

Gillian briefly mentioned her worry that immigration was too high. Brown replied by changing the subject of their conversation. He reminded her that the three big issues she had raised with him – education, the NHS and helping people – were his priorities, too. They parted with a handshake and a smile, but the laughs were soon over.

Brown hadn't removed a microphone used for the cameras when he spoke with Gillian. Oops. As his chauffeur drove him away, taking him off camera, Brown's voice remained audible and every word was recorded. 'That was a disaster,' Brown says, before criticising his aide for choosing Gillian. 'She's just a sort of bigoted woman.' For many people, these seven words neatly summed up the problem: political elites were taking too little notice of important issues like immigration. To raise a worry was to be branded bigoted and racist.

Brown had his words played back to him soon afterwards during an interview with the radio host Jeremy Vine and was understandably quick to apologise for his comments. He promptly went back to Rochdale to apologise in person to Gillian – and to make clear that he understood her concerns about immigration. I'm sure he did after that second meeting. But the damage was done.

This was more than an interview that went badly wrong. It touched a nerve. The public had concerns about immigration that they dared not express for fear they would become demonised.

Voice worries about immigration and others may wrongly suspect it is based on mere prejudice. Should anyone want to discuss this with their elected leaders, the conversation would be moved on to some other issue. Better to bury any talk of immigration concerns and avoid awkward moments than discuss the worries on people's minds. Or so it went in 2010. Not much has changed since.

*   *   *

A year before sweeping to power as Britain's first and, to date, only female Prime Minister, Margaret Thatcher said something that still resonates with many people:

> If we went on as we are then, by the end of the century, there
> would be four million people of the new Commonwealth
> or Pakistan here. Now, that is an awful lot and I think it
> means that people are really rather afraid that this country
> might be rather swamped by people with a different culture.

Swamped. Floods. Tsunami. Besieged. Marauding. And worse – you get the idea. It's raining immigrants. A shower without end. This is the alarmist language that is used regularly to describe immigration. People who come to live in Britain are not seen as neighbours or potential citizens, but like hordes of locusts that are not merely different but dangerous, which must be curbed before they destroy everything in their path. Immigration is not an opportunity, but a threat – and it must be stopped.

In 2004, one in eleven people normally resident in the UK were born abroad. Only ten years later this had risen to one in eight. Over a quarter of all births in 2014 were to mothers born outside the country. The most common non-British countries of birth for UK residents are Poland, Pakistan and India. Between 2001 and 2011, migration accounted for 56 per cent of the population change in England and Wales. Britain has a population of about 64 million – and five million were born abroad. These are important demographic changes that some understandably find to be increasingly a problem.

It comes as no surprise that immigration is the number one issue of concern for voters today, overtaking the NHS and the economy. A recent poll run jointly by *The Economist* and Ipsos MORI concluded that 'we have never seen concern about immigration this high', and it shows no signs of letting up. Pensioners and the skilled working class are most strongly concerned, but far from alone. Worries about immigration outstrip concerns about schools, housing and terrorism combined. What the public want – or say they want – is less of it. Much less of it. And they don't have much faith in politicians to deliver, either.

It's not difficult to uncover statistics that fuel deep concerns about immigration by the public. The problem is knowing which numbers to count – and this is where the government is getting itself into trouble.

The government has responded to public fears over immigration by playing the numbers game, committing itself to reducing net migration to fewer than 100,000 people annually. Despite their best efforts, they are achieving the opposite result. Rather than falling, net migration has risen to 323,000 – only slightly off the record high of 336,000 reached in the year up to June 2015. The 100,000 target has more recently been downgraded to an 'aspiration', but it remains a goal despite the government's inability to come close to it. I have spoken to several former ministers – including former Home Secretaries like Charles Clarke and Jacqui Smith – and have not met anyone who thinks a net migration cap is a satisfactory policy.

Net migration is a crude way to measure people leaving or coming to live in Britain, bringing together different things. Net migration is about outflows and inflows without regard to their composition. We count the total number of people leaving the country and contrast it with the total number coming in. Net migration is calculated by subtracting the roughly 294,000 people who left the country from the circa 617,000 who entered it. Together this gives us a net migration total of 323,000. That's roughly the population of Coventry in one year.

The numbers certainly sound like a lot – although it amounts to about half of 1 per cent of the total UK population of 64 million people. But the story of net migration is about more than the numbers of people who come to Britain – it's also about those who leave. In fact, it might surprise a lot of people to know that when it comes to immigrating, Britain does it best. A recent report by the Organisation for Economic Co-operation and Development (OECD) found Britain has a greater proportion of its citizens living abroad than any other European country. If high numbers of people leave each year, this can bring down net migration overall. British citizens leaving the country to work elsewhere may help the government get closer to its 100,000 net migration target.

The big problem for the government is that fewer people are choosing to leave the UK as its economy slowly improves. According to the Office for National Statistics, this slowdown is to blame for high net migration today. About 87,000 British citizens returned to the UK last year. Roughly half came for work-related reasons. Nearly 10 per cent came back for formal study. Net migration might appear to be a measure of non-British migrants, but it includes British citizens too, a fact which is rarely noticed. If you're looking to assess the numbers of non-UK citizens, net migration isn't it.

As one former immigration minister told me, net migration is not a target: 'It's a nonsense.' Net migration figures can vary sharply not only in the numbers that come to the UK, but in the numbers that leave – whoever they might be. Net migration takes no notice of nationality. Each person counts the same whether from Britain, Europe or North Korea. Nor does it matter whether people have come to the UK for work, study or an extended visit. Consider a few examples that show why net migration targets don't work. If 300,000 people enter the UK, the government has failed its target – even if every one of them is a British citizen. Should 250,000 people want to leave the UK to find work and pay their taxes elsewhere, this would then satisfy the target and it would not matter whether everyone who left was British, French or Chinese. While you could have a target for managing immigrants coming to the UK, a net migration 'target' makes little sense when it can be met or missed almost entirely by chance. And it takes no notice of the potential harm to the economy or our society, either.

Michael Howard demonstrated this point when he was leading the Conservative Party during the 2005 election against Tony Blair. Howard stood by manifesto pledges to reduce immigration and to ensure cleaner hospitals, among other policies. But the obvious question, which caused enormous damage to his campaign, was simple: who is going to keep our hospitals clean if migrants are kept out?

Cutting migration has consequences. The Migration Advisory Committee is an independent group of five economists who advise the government. They found that one way to reduce net migration would be to set a salary threshold of £18,600 for anyone wanting to sponsor a family member coming to the UK who was not a European citizen. But the consequences are that these income hurdles can create new problems by hitting hardest people working in the public sector and others in less well-paid work – in addition to the likelihood that it would split families up. Most migrants to the UK come for work: 167,000 have a job offer in hand and another 104,000 come looking to find employment. About 31 per cent of migrants come to the UK to study and 14 per cent either accompany or join their family. These examples reveal a gap between what the public expects from reducing net migration and the reality of how the measurement is used – and that gap risks further undermining public trust in politicians to control immigration.

Dr Scott Blinder, the former director of the Migration Observatory at Oxford University, suggests that we should 'mind the gap' between popular perceptions about migrants and who they actually are. His research confirms that most people thought of migrants as asylum seekers rather than fellow British citizens or international university students – in fact, asylum seekers account for about 10 per cent of net migration, far fewer than the public believes. This gap between perception and reality is a problem for citizens and policy makers alike. Even the controversial Tory MP Enoch Powell, who described British immigration in the 1960s as 'like watching a nation busily engaged in heaping up its own funeral pyre', believed that students 'are not, and never have been, immigrants'.

It is difficult to fathom a modern government taking a harsher line on international students than a politician like Powell. But then again we live in interesting times when it comes to immigration. Clear thinking can be hard to find and in short supply.

I regularly give lectures and interviews at universities. I visited one university campus recently and spoke briefly to the porter at the security gate named Brian. He was a white British man who lived locally and appeared to be in his early sixties. Brian seemed curious to learn a bit more about this stranger with an American accent. He asked me about what kind of research I was working on at the moment. My reply was easy – immigration policy – and I explained that I was writing this book.

With a puzzled look on his face, Brian asked, 'So do you know any immigrants?' A long pause followed. He seemed genuine. Couldn't he hear my voice, my clear New England accent? Somewhat stunned, I said, 'Yes, I am one!' 'No,' Brian replied promptly, 'you are not an immigrant – *you* are *an American*.'

There's a serious point in this story. I'm not the only person born in the US and living in Britain who has experienced similar treatment. My American friend Tracy, introduced earlier in this book, told me that often people would start sharing their very negative views about immigrants with her. Taxi drivers were notorious for this in her view, but work colleagues little better – and it would happen frequently, even casually. Tracy made a point of challenging this behaviour, and rightly so. She would remind them that – ahem! – *she* is an immigrant and hope this would at least temper the awful comments about immigrants she often heard. But this rarely worked. A common response was, 'But you're not *that type* of immigrant.' Graham, another American who recently became a British citizen, told me that 'people see us as less foreign than the French'. How right that is; it perfectly sums the American exceptionalism in the eyes of some British citizens.

Brian the porter would probably agree with this too. When I found myself having to convince him that Americans who live in the UK are immigrants, Brian replied with perfect sincerity, 'Yes, but you *look* just like *us*.' No doubt he had a specific idea in mind about what British citizens look like – probably referring more to my being white than my being bald.

It's common for people to have flawed views about how many migrants there are in Britain and why they are here, such as believing most migrants are asylum seekers when they are actually a minority. It doesn't mean that an immigration problem doesn't exist. When Ed Miliband's campaign team produced Labour-branded coffee mugs with the pledge 'controls on immigration' ahead of the 2015 election, it sparked angry criticisms from the left, who viewed it as reactionary, right wing-style campaigning.

But Miliband's critics got this one wrong. Immigration controls are necessary. Recognising this fact does not make someone bigoted or racist. This is not to say that no one who supports immigration control harbours such views – there are plenty of people who think anyone British must 'look just like us'. The issue is not that controls exist, because we must have them; the issue is their fairness and their purpose.

In his autobiography, former Prime Minister Tony Blair gets right what many get wrong: 'When people in Britain used to say they were against immigration, a goodly proportion would really be against a particular type of immigrant, i.e. black or brown face

... the tendency for those on the left was to equate concern about immigration with underlying racism. This was a mistake.'

Blair argues that immigration 'can cause genuine tensions' by straining limited resources if not properly controlled. It's wrong to assume that everyone concerned about immigration does so because of prejudice. Blair is correct to see it for the mistake it is. Gordon Brown might have benefited from this advice when he met Gillian Duffy in Rochdale.

Some worry that uncontrolled immigration damages the British economy. This can be a product of the genuine tensions that Blair refers to. These tensions are especially understandable at a time when the economic recovery is slow and fragile. People are under a lot of pressure to find decent work and affordable housing, while the squeeze on public finances heaps extra pressure on public services. Many can feel the strain, hoping relief is around the corner. Migrants can be perceived as a problem, especially when money is tight.

Migration has not damaged the economy, but its benefits are modest. The respected Oxford economist Sir Paul Collier found that immigration's effects on the UK labour market were positive but small: 'The net effect of immigration on the rest of us has effectively been zero.' This is supported by a joint report by the Home Office with the Department for Business, Innovation and Skills published in 2014 that found little evidence that migration caused any significant displacement of Britons from the labour market when the economy is strong. While the report found limited evidence for when there is a recession and for those in low-skilled labour, migrants help create jobs and expand the economy, not shrink it. This is not unique to Britain: US President Barack Obama commissioned an economic report in 2013 that concluded: 'Immigrants add to the labor force and increase the economy's total output.' The fact is the job market is not always a zero-sum game where any job for you means one less for me.

An in-depth report on immigration on the British labour market by Jonathan Wadsworth for the LSE Centre for Economic Performance found 'no evidence of an overall negative impact of immigration on jobs, wages, housing or the crowding out of public services'. Wadsworth confirmed that, on average, 'UK immigrants are more skilled than those in the United States', with likely favourable effects for the British economy. This is supported by the Treasury, which says annual GDP growth is 0.25 higher thanks to immigration. The Office for Budget Responsibility claims that immigration has led to a smaller national deficit because of the taxes paid by immigrants. So, while the effects are modest, immigration has brought greater economic benefits than drawbacks overall.

The current Tory government has tried to act by restricting the ability of non-EU citizens to work in the UK. In autumn 2015, the Home Office refused permission to the Newcastle upon Tyne Hospitals NHS Foundation Trust to hire eighty-five foreign nurses from the Philippines. As a result, the trust was one of ten to call on the Home Secretary to ease the immigration rules to avoid putting patients at risk.

The effects of immigration on the economy do not affect every part of the labour market equally, though. Low-skilled labourers are more likely to oppose immigration, and this can make sense since migrant labour has affected that sector more negatively than others. In fact, these labourers can feel some degree of alienation as they witness wealth creation in other sectors that doesn't seem to trickle down far enough to reach them. Given the more direct and intense competition they can face, it is unsurprising that these labourers hold the views they do.

There is a similar logic that helps explain why many UKIP supporters hold stronger anti-immigration views than supporters of rival political parties. Sir Paul Collier found that they were more likely to be dependent on benefits than most other voters, and this may be part of the reason for their holding anti-immigration views. If you believe immigrants are coming to take a share of welfare support, then this can lead to fears there may be less for those already on benefits. Collier says that the opposition to immigration by UKIP supporters may be explained by their 'entirely rational fear of a meaner future'.

But, however rational this fear may be, it is also predicated on an assumption that immigrants are more likely to seek welfare benefits. The government has found precious little evidence of so-called benefits tourism and only occasionally are the anti-immigrant lobby called out on it in Parliament by anyone, whether Labour, Liberal Democrat or Tory. In a recent Parliamentary Question, the former Conservative Party chairman

Chris Patten asked the government about what assessment they had made of whether new European migrants of working age settled in the UK were more or less likely to claim benefits than the national average. The official reply was that this information was 'not available'. Two words that say so much.

The economist Jonathan Portes, who is the director of the National Institute of Economic and Social Research and a former chief economist at the Cabinet Office, has argued that the level of the minimum wage is more of an attraction than any in-work benefits for EU migrants. With the government introducing a higher 'living wage' in April 2016, Portes suspects this may undermine their efforts at reducing migration from Europe. This seems likely now that Britain has one of the highest minimum wages in Europe.

Another cause for public concern about immigration is culture. The United Kingdom has become a more multicultural society over the last few decades because of rising immigration. For some of the people I spoke to in the course of researching this book, the problem was not learning about other cultural traditions or even celebrating them. No, the issue was a concern that native British traditions had a second-class status in relation to others. Few objected to young children being taught about Diwali, but there were stronger feelings about ensuring nativity plays are performed at Christmas.

Indeed, during a panel interview programme I took part in for a local television channel, it was the threat to nativity plays that drew the biggest concerns about immigration – not jobs, housing or health care. They didn't harbour anti-immigrant views and did not seem to notice I was a migrant, but they were concerned that well-intentioned efforts to accommodate cultural differences left an unprotected space for local cultural activities that were important to them. Such a view is neither jingoistic nor culturally protectionist and it is easy to see how parties trading on these fears can be attractive to many people concerned about immigration – even if the fears are misplaced or exaggerated.

This worry about the culture shock Britain is experiencing through increased immigration may be the most important factor in the debate. It's not the abstract net migration statistics or the job market that strikes a chord with most people, but the perceived changes in a local community and a heightened sensitivity to anything deemed to be 'foreign' gaining a foothold. People will have greater confidence in the government's handling of immigration when they are less anxious about the rapid sense of societal change that globalisation can cause, not when a statistician decrees net migration is under 100,000 people.

Four years ago, I was asked to speak on a panel at Sunderland's Civic Centre by the independent Labour organisation Progress, a group originally launched by Peter Mandelson. The other panellists included the Labour MPs Hilary Benn, Julie Elliott and Phil Wilson. We were asked to provide our views on how the Labour Party might win the next general election in 2015. If only we could have seen into the future.

I argued that the main issue is insecurity – and I still say this now. The economy was likely to remain weak. The choice is either to play to anxieties with a politics of fear or to respond with a politics of hope. But the danger, I predicted, is that immigration could explode as a top public concern if general anxieties about employment, housing and other issues were stoked. This was because immigration so easily speaks to fears about each topic: any squeeze on jobs is because the migrants have them, any problems finding affordable housing are because the migrants have it and so on. Hope is a powerful friend, but it can struggle when fear begins to take root. My analysis was not unique and others came to similar conclusions. But it convinced most in the audience: to combat insecurities, there are fears that must be put to rest.

Facts and figures are a crucial part of this effort, but it's a change of heart rather than a change of mind that counts most. One recent study found that about 70 per cent of the current UK population is directly descended from people that inhabited Britain in pre-Neolithic times, before 4,000 BC. If true, this may suggest that it's how citizens view societal change that matters more than whatever demographic changes there have been – as these changes may have been relatively slight over the past 6,000 years.

It is unsurprising to see how little influence the facts about immigration have on the debate. When former US President George W. Bush accused the fact-slinging Vice-President Al Gore of resorting to 'fuzzy math', liberals were outraged. But the majority of Americans watching the television debate got it. Loud and clear. Numbers can be useful for providing supporting evidence for the values or views a person has, but they are often unable to bring about a change of heart by their own power. So, facts and figures are important, but not in the ways we might expect, and it's crucial we grasp this point.

Research by Bobby Duffy, the managing director of Ipsos MORI, has found that migration levels have had little effect on public concerns about migration. Up to 70 per cent thought Britain was 'being swamped' by other cultures in 1978 when net migration was zero. So, reducing the official migration statistics to the tens of thousands is unlikely to get you very far. The public tends to overestimate the numbers of foreign-born people in the UK. One poll found the public believing it was 31 per cent when it was actually 13 per cent. But, while perceptions can be wildly off track, the point is the public thinks there is too much immigration. It is important that the facts are better known, but winning over minds won't win hearts – and that more difficult task is what must be done.

Often the places that have the smallest foreign-born population have the greatest anxieties about immigration. A few years ago I was asked to take part in an hour-long radio programme on immigration at BBC Newcastle. The format was simple. I would give a few facts about immigration in the area and then we would take questions from callers live on air.

The first caller was John from Amble, a small fishing town in Northumberland with a population of roughly six thousand.

John phoned to say that immigrants were utterly changing his town for the worse, to the point that it had become unrecognisable. Before I could respond, the radio presenter asked him how many immigrants lived in Amble.

I'll never forget John's answer: 'None.' That's right. There was not one person he knew or had met – no one at all – who was an immigrant in Amble. The presenter was curious: 'That's very interesting, John. Tell me: have you ever spoken with an immigrant?' The answer was the same. None at all. Nul points. Nada. Zilch. Of course, the presenter had to correct him: 'Well, that's not quite true. You're talking to Thom Brooks, our local immigration expert!' I was the first immigrant John had ever spoken to. Or so he said.

Needless to say, John seemed confused – and I was bewildered. The north-east of England has the lowest foreign-born population in the UK. It's difficult to believe a small north-east town has been so utterly transformed by immigration when a local resident has neither seen an immigrant there nor ever spoken to one. And yet he firmly believed this.

But he didn't get this idea from nowhere. John was quick to point out that things like this must be happening, even if not really in Amble, because the newspapers say it all the time – and newspapers wouldn't tell porkies, now would they?

Before the call was over, John also believed in all seriousness that because I was an immigrant in Britain I must have entered the country illegally, hidden in the back of a lorry travelling from

Calais through to Kent via the Eurotunnel. Really. He sounded somewhat relieved when I told him I had taken a flight from New York. I've still not set foot once in Calais. How did he come to have such a sincerely held belief so utterly divorced from all reality? Simple. He claimed to see it in the papers all the time. The media has much to answer for.

*   *   *

Immigrants are all around us. Some choose to become British citizens. Fifteen years ago, then Leader of the Opposition William Hague MP said that 'our nation is a nation of immigrants. Celts, Picts, Saxons, Angles, Normans, Jews, Huguenots, Indians, Pakistanis, Afro-Caribbeans, Bengalis, Chinese and countless others. These are the British people, all of them. It is what makes our country such an exciting and varied place to live.' How right he is and how many individuals who became British have contributed to making Britain truly great.

In 1859, Michael Marks was born in what is now Belarus to a Jewish family. He moved to Leeds about twenty years later and set up a successful market stall. Michael wanted to expand his business and was introduced to a cashier named Thomas Spencer. Together they created the now famous Marks & Spencer department store. A British institution founded by an immigrant who became British himself.

He is not alone. The composer George Handel left his native

Germany for Britain, where he wrote his most famous work, 'Messiah'. He became a naturalised British subject in 1727. Two hundred years later, the celebrated American poet T. S. Eliot moved to the UK and took up British citizenship. He went on to win the Nobel Prize for Literature.

Perhaps the most famous immigrant today who became British is the Queen's husband. Prince Philip was not always the Duke of Edinburgh. He was born on Corfu as the Prince of Greece and Denmark, but gave up these titles and became a British citizen before marrying Queen Elizabeth II. Prince Philip and the Queen have been married now for over sixty-five years.

Michael Marks, George Handel, T. S. Eliot and Prince Philip are only a small handful of famous immigrants who became British citizens. Ever since there was a Britain there have been people who became British by birth and those who immigrated and became British later in life. But, equally, there have always been public concerns about rising immigration. These worries continue today and have perhaps never been greater.

The link between the need to restrict migration and the need for greater restrictions on citizenship has been made before. Lord Green of Deddington, the chairman of Migration Watch, has said the tens of thousands becoming citizens each year is a clear outcome of 'mass immigration' for nearly twenty years, and highlights the need for clamping down on too many migrants becoming British citizens. In 2013, over 200,000 migrants became British citizens. This was about 20 per cent of all new citizens in

Europe during that year. Countries like Germany and France had only half that figure. That's roughly three new British citizens for every 1,000 individuals resident in the UK. Only 3 per cent of all applications for British citizenship were rejected.

This is a huge change from a few decades ago. Fewer than 25,000 migrants became British in 1965. The number of naturalised British citizens, stable at between 50,000 and 70,000 as the millennium approached, saw a steep rise from 1998, when new citizens leapt from about 50,000 to over 200,000 in 2013.

The government's commitment to reducing net migration has had a knock-on effect of fewer immigrants becoming British citizens. Since the coalition government of 2010–15, there has been a sharp fall in successful applications for British citizenship. There were 118,152 people granted citizenship in 2015, down 40 per cent from 207,989 two years earlier. This is the lowest annual figure since 2002. The main reason is a change in the requirement that applicants prove knowledge of English, introduced in October 2013, making the standard more difficult. This led to an increase in applications immediately prior to its introduction. Similarly, the number of people granted permission to live permanently in the UK fell by 12 per cent to 104,690 – a level not seen since 2001. Roughly half of all successful applications for British citizenship are accepted on the basis of the person satisfying residency requirements, typically a five-year period for most applicants. The rest are divided fairly evenly between applications based on marriage or as children.

So where does this leave us? Immigration has been rising – in terms of both numbers and public concern. Current government aspirations to reduce net migration to under 100,000 have only led to it moving in the opposite direction and crossing above the 300,000 mark. As immigration has risen, so too have the numbers of migrants applying to become British citizens. These issues of citizenship and immigration come together. But before we turn to what might be done about them, we need to understand the relationship between them.

The United Kingdom has a unique experience as a global imperial power that came to the modern citizenship game late as its empire waned. The significant shift from subject to citizen has had a profound effect in shaping ideas about British identity, dramatically altering how citizenship has been defined and regulated. The next chapter explores that transformation – and its consequences for Britain's immigration policies today.

CHAPTER 2

FROM SUBJECT
TO CITIZEN

Rising immigration has changed Britain and what it means to be British. This isn't because migrants come and go whenever they please. They can't. The British government, and not immigrants, makes the rules – as it should be. Nor is there any right to become a citizen wherever you want. Becoming British is subject to rules – and these laws have an important history.

The legal commentator Gary Slapper has called Parliament 'a formidable law factory' churning out meaty products of variable quality. In ever greater quantities, too. Nowhere is this truer than in the realm of immigration law. The relevant rules and guidance change virtually every day and are expanding at such a rate that many immigration officials are struggling.

This has been a problem for British citizens and migrants alike. I've heard countless stories of government ministers, immigration officials and personal lawyers getting it badly wrong. The consequences can be profound for the people affected by these needless errors.

Melanie was from Canada and came to Britain on a spousal visa with her husband. Their relationship went downhill and they were soon divorced – a difficult and painful experience that will be familiar to many. Melanie's lawyer advised her that she could continue working and only needed to decide whether to gain a new visa or leave the country when the spousal visa expired. But it ended from the date of her divorce and Melanie ran into serious difficulties with the Home Office, who accused her of overstaying. She was threatened with deportation despite having sought legal advice to avoid it.

Furhan applied for a visa permitting him to work in the UK from his local British High Commission in Pakistan. Furhan paid his application fee and received his passport a few months later. However, the High Commission made a mistake and granted a visa for six months shorter than requested. The High Commission admitted their error, but it came at a price. Furhan was given a choice. He could accept the incorrect visa allowing him to start work and return much earlier than planned, or he could cancel his request and resubmit his application to receive the visa he applied for in the first place, but he would lose the full, hefty fee paid on the first application – thanks to the High Commission's error – and he must then pay the same fee a second time so his second application could be considered.

Welcome to immigration in the real world. These are not the stories of sly individuals eager to engage in criminality or wrong-doing to enter and stay in the UK. They are law-abiding citizens trying to play by the rules and do the right things, but those in positions of trust have let them down, leaving them out of pocket, sometimes out of a job, and at risk of being sent out of the country through no fault of their own.

Talking about immigration is like trying to hit a moving target. Such rapid changes might be born of the best intentions in attempting to reassure the public, but they are increasingly unfit for purpose. A system that splits families and fails to meet the basic needs of its citizens is nothing to be proud of.

These problems did not happen overnight. They evolved over time. Much of the migration to Britain today has its roots in past decisions on citizenship and immigration now forgotten, as we shall see. British citizenship has been an experiment that once united peoples around the world under a global empire now in retreat, and the experiment has had long-lasting effects that can be seen to this day.

This historical context helps explain how Britain came to have the immigration policies it does, which is crucial to under-standing our current situation and the key drivers behind the migration debate today. At its heart, this is about a fundamental shift from recognising British citizenship in terms of being a *subject* to becoming a *citizen*. This move has had a significant effect on how immigration works – and the challenges Britain faces.

For any other country, this might be a story about how successive governments managed migration flows of citizens moving from one state to another. However, Britain is not like any other country in the world. It has a different past that has shaped its distinctive present that can be summed up in one word – empire. The United Kingdom was the heart of the world's largest global empire. At its peak, it had about one-fifth of the global population under its umbrella; about 450 million people worldwide. The UK was, in the words of the eighteenth-century British statesman George Macartney, 'this vast empire on which the sun never sets'. The empire may have ended, but its influence on how citizenship and immigration works today has not.

A key starting point is in its name: Britain is the *United Kingdom*. It is a collection of different nations under the Crown with a monarch as the head of state. This role is currently held by Queen Elizabeth II, who has been on the throne since 1952, making her the longest-reigning British monarch. The monarchy is an important part of Britain's historical roots. It is easy to forget that while we may talk about *nationality* as a kind of political and legal status conferring special rights and responsibilities on its members, it was not always so. Before there was nationality, there was *allegiance* to the ruling monarch, and this defined political and legal membership and rights for the UK and many other European countries.

Centuries ago, local communities would swear an oath of allegiance to a feudal lord, and that lord would swear his allegiance to the reigning monarch. This grew to become a general allegiance for everyone to the monarch, in a tradition that continues today. An individual only becomes British through naturalising once they take an oath of allegiance to the Queen.

When I received my 'citizenship invitation' when applying to become British in 2011, my letter from the UK Border Agency clearly stated:

> To complete the process of becoming a British citizen, you will need to attend a citizenship ceremony to receive your certificate. In the ceremony, you will take an oath or affirmation of allegiance to the Crown and a pledge of loyalty to the United Kingdom. This is a formal promise to Her Majesty the Queen and the United Kingdom.

The ceremony was held at Gateshead Civic Centre. All of us approved for citizenship had to declare that 'on becoming a British citizen, I will be faithful and bear true allegiance to Her Majesty Queen Elizabeth the Second, Her Heirs and Successors according to law'. Oaths of allegiance to the British monarch have been an ancient rite of passage for centuries, with no end in sight. Some things never change.

Anyone who swore allegiance to the monarch became the Crown's subjects. This included virtually everyone born in the Crown's territories, and anyone born on a ship in service to the Crown, which is important given Britain's major naval presence at home and abroad. There was nothing like an official immigration policy at this time. What probably passed for the prevailing view is that of a Chartist commentator writing in 1848: 'The exile is free to land upon our shores, and free to perish of hunger beneath our inclement skies.'

So what mattered was being a subject. Today, many countries follow one of two models. The first is to grant citizenship on grounds of a 'right of the soil', called *jus soli*. This links a citizen to a particular place, such as by birth. The United States is a good example of this: anyone born in a US state can become an American citizen. The second model is the 'right of blood', called *jus sanguinis*, where citizenship comes from parentage. Britain brought these two together: place of birth and parentage both have their place. Being a British subject has historically been about being born in the UK to a British father, although much has changed more recently.

Of course, prior to 1707, British citizenship did not exist: English and Scottish subjects each bore allegiance to their respective monarchs. The Act of Union between England and Scotland forged a new individual: the British subject. Being British was neither exclusively English nor Scottish, but a status that encompassed both. A new form of citizenship and identity was born.

British citizenship grew slowly, but surely. The year after the Act of Union, Parliament passed an Act that would naturalise 'Foreign Protestants'. Its aim was to provide support and refuge to Protestants facing religious persecution in Europe. It was short-lived and was repealed in 1711 because it was viewed as a threat to national identity.

Before 1844, it wasn't easy for migrants to become British – each naturalisation required a special Act of Parliament. These were expensive and were rare because most could not afford to do it. After 1844, naturalised migrants were more often approved to become British by the Home Secretary. However, these special Acts of Parliament continued, albeit very infrequently, as late as 1975, which saw the passing of the James Hugh Maxwell (Naturalisation) Act.

So gone are the days when you can have your own personalised law; now, the process for becoming a British citizen has become transformed into a complex hurdle-jumping exercise increasingly difficult for migrants to pass. I clearly missed my chance for a Thom Brooks (Naturalisation) Act – and no chance we will see a Kevin Spacey (Naturalisation) Act or a Madonna (Naturalisation) Act for these American entertainers with homes in the United Kingdom. Instead, anyone seeking to become a naturalised citizen must gain approval by the Home Secretary. That's more complicated than it might sound, as we will soon discover.

Being British meant different things depending on where a person came from in an expanding global empire. There were two classes of British subjects at this time in the nineteenth century. The first were imperial subjects from the United Kingdom. The second were local British subjects based outside the United Kingdom. Only imperial subjects from the UK could travel freely to any part of the empire. Non-imperial British subjects had greater restrictions on their travel.

The second-class status of non-imperial subjects became an increasing problem as the British Empire expanded between 1870 and the start of the First World War. While a young lawyer in South Africa, Mahatma Gandhi said, 'I felt that, if I demanded rights as a British citizen, it was also my duty, as such, to participate.' So began Gandhi's efforts to help his fellow Indians first in South Africa and then in India to exercise their rights as British subjects, which would lead to his spearheading India's successful independence campaign. The British Parliament in Westminster governed the nationality for all British subjects throughout the global empire. As dissatisfaction grew with the special privileges afforded to only persons from the UK having imperial status, the British government took what seemed like a bold move by extending the status of imperial British subjects beyond the UK to include Australia, Canada, New Zealand, South Africa and later Burma. This was enacted through the British Nationality and Status of Aliens Act in 1914, made law under H. H. Asquith's Liberal government. The Act neatly divided the world's population into imperial subjects, local subjects and everyone else – 'everyone else' being 'aliens'. This built on the Aliens Act 1905.

Originally targeting the settlement of Jews from Eastern Europe, it established the first immigration officers at all ports of entry to the UK with the power to refuse 'undesirable' aliens unable to support themselves or their dependants. Anyone who had been expelled or convicted abroad of a serious non-political crime could be denied entry.

These changes represented another significant shift in how British citizenship was understood. It meant that being British no longer required being born in the United Kingdom or setting foot on British soil. An Australian was as much of an imperial British subject as someone from Yorkshire. What started as the forging of English and Scottish nationalities into a shared British citizenship had grown much further. Being British became more than being from Britain. And border controls were becoming a permanent fixture of British immigration law and policy, as well as an area of frequent change.

One example is how the process of becoming British was revised. The 1914 Act made clear specific hurdles that migrants must leap to naturalise. These required their residence in the UK or another 'dominion' of imperial British subjects for at least five years. Migrants needed to have the intention to stay permanently if granted citizenship. They must also be of 'good character' with 'an adequate knowledge' of English or a language 'recognised as on an equality with the English language' in dominions that recognised other languages. This 'equality' exception on English gave equal recognition to the Welsh and Scots Gaelic languages.

If the Home Secretary or his representative approved an application for citizenship, the individuals only became British if they swore an oath of allegiance taking the form of 'I, [name], swear by Almighty God that I will be faithful and bear true allegiance to His Majesty, King George V, His Heirs and Successors, according to law.' While these requirements of residency, intention, good character, common language and formal declaration of allegiance to the Crown largely remain, their uses and interpretations have changed over the past century.

Thus, British subjects continued to exist in countries spanning the globe. Then as now, Britain was a major exporter – of people. British subjects left the UK to populate colonial territories from North America to the Far East – not always voluntarily, as in the case of convicts sentenced to transportation to places like Australia. But the subjects in these colonies, whether convicts or free residents, lacked the full rights of their colonial masters. While imperial status was extended to some, it did not apply to most. The effect was that imperial subjects in the more prosperous parts of the British Empire were able to freely travel to set up their livelihoods and pursue opportunities, while the poorer majority faced more restrictions.

By the start of the First World War, the UK still had an immigration system that placed Britain at the centre of a large empire – and this created a unique problem. Britain's empire soon began to decline in the aftermath of the world wars. In 1946, Canada decided to create its own brand of citizenship, separate from the status of a British subject. The system now risked collapse as other countries in the Commonwealth considered their next moves.

Then something extraordinary happened. Asquith's 1914 reforms had extended imperial British subject status only to some. A new British Nationality Act in 1948 went one giant step further and created a new status: the citizen of the United Kingdom and Colonies, otherwise affectionately known as 'CUKC'. All subjects were recognised as citizens, even where their countries had become independent with their own nationality laws. That's right – *all* subjects. Everybody. This was the last gasp of a receding global power that it would come to regret. CUKC soon became a shared form of citizenship some might find cuckoo.

The British government even encouraged people to migrate to Britain in order to take new jobs. Indeed, such facts are included in an earlier version of the UK's citizenship test to highlight that Britain has tried to import migrants to support its economy. To quote an example: 'In the 1950s, centres were set up in the West Indies to recruit bus drivers for the UK.' A second illustration points out, 'After the Second World War the British government invited people from Ireland and other parts of Europe to come to the UK', while textile and engineering firms sent agents to India and Pakistan to find workers. Encouraging people to immigrate to Britain was an important part of the UK's economic strategy in the post-war years.

If the 1914 Act extending full British citizenship to subjects in dominions like Australia and Canada was a great expansion of what it was to be British, then the new citizen of the United Kingdom and Colonies form of citizenship represented more of the same – but at full throttle with bells and blinkers on. 'Being British' now meant being a subject in any one of nearly fifty different territories around the world, including the Bahamas, Belize, Christmas Island, Cyprus, Mauritius, colonial Nigeria, the Seychelles, Singapore and colonial Sierra Leone.

And then the unravelling started to happen – and fast. British citizenship began its retreat soon after it made its furthest reach. Independence was in the air and soon India, Pakistan and Southern Rhodesia were gone. These former British dominions and colonies launched their own separate nationalities, such as the Republic of Ireland, ending British citizenship for many in their countries. It sometimes remained possible to still be a British subject and non-British citizen concurrently, but things were clearly moving in one direction.

Britain's global empire was receding and its newly expansive ideas on who could have British citizenship shrunk accordingly. Since the Act of Union joining England and Scotland, British identity had rapidly stretched to include people the world over. Now that process went into reverse.

The great contraction of British citizenship began in earnest with the passing of the Commonwealth Immigrants Act 1962, which brought to an end the free movement of citizens of the United Kingdom and Colonies throughout the Commonwealth.

This was a change ushered in by events: Britain's hand was forced to some degree by the increasing number of Commonwealth countries declaring independence and establishing their own nationality rules. People in these countries could remain British although they usually chose the citizenship of their new free state. If the decision to launch a new citizen of the United Kingdom and Colonies was the last gasp of a receding empire, the move to taper off this global view of British citizenship was its final groan.

Consider the enduring legacy of these legal changes. Since 1914, many British subjects living outside the United Kingdom held the same right of movement as British subjects in Britain. Not only could they travel for work or study in the UK at will, but they could enter as fellow citizens. In tightening restrictions, the UK tries to move to the kind of British citizenship it had in the early eighteenth century. In doing so, the door has been closing not merely on nationals of states formerly part of the British Empire, but on many other people who had rights to full entry only a relatively short time ago. When critics accuse British governments of opening the door to migration, they regularly overlook the importance of this historical legacy.

But another enduring legacy is regulatory. As immigration legal scholar Gina Clayton notes, the 1962 Act formalised 'the heavy reliance on formerly unpublished instructions, guidelines and concessions'. These sometimes informal sources had previously provided internal guidance on how immigration officials should exercise discretion, unbeknownst to the people seeking entry. When the guidance was formalised, the rules grew in their size and complexity. Yet, the Act also made what was a somewhat mysterious process for some applicants more transparent – and it was an important step towards different migrants receiving equal treatment and avoiding racial prejudice.

Seneca, the great Roman philosopher and statesman, famously declared himself to be 'a citizen of the world'. He was a national of no single state – his citizenship was shared by humanity. Probably the closest this ideal has come to being realised in practice is in the British citizen of the United Kingdom and Colonies. To that extent, it has historical importance as a real achievement that has never been matched.

The first seeds were laid by Tory governments, the first led by Edward Heath and the second by Margaret Thatcher. Heath's Immigration Act 1971 replaced existing border controls and established the new concept of 'the right to abode' in Britain. This right is still in place today. The right to abode is simply the right to live, work and settle in the United Kingdom. All British citizens have this right and are thus free to return to the UK at any time after travelling abroad. The 1971 Act neatly divided the world into those who had a right to abode and those who did not.

However, British citizenship as we know it is a child of the Thatcher years and is enshrined in the British Nationality Act 1981. The Act modernised citizenship legislation, bringing it much closer to what most other European countries and the US had had in place for decades. The long transition of British citizenship from a *subject* to a *citizen* was complete. At last, modern UK citizenship was born and Britons became British. Taking effect on 1 January 1983, the Act came a mere 917 years since William the Conqueror led the Norman Conquest, fully embedding a status of citizens and discontinuing use of the term 'British subject'. By contrast, the United States set out its first laws on citizenship in legislation like the Naturalization Act of 1790 – but better late than never.

The British Nationality Act was a major break from the past. But this transition came with several strings attached. What was once a simple system now became much more complex – and it created a very British problem.

The new law made anyone born in the UK prior to 1983 a British citizen. Not a subject, not a 'citizen of the United Kingdom and Colonies', but a *British citizen*. It did not matter if they were a citizen of somewhere else in 1983 – they now had a right to recognition as a British citizen.

For everyone born in the UK after 1 January 1983, individuals were British citizens only if their father or mother was also UK-born. This was an important change because previously British citizenship could be passed down only by the father, and was not passed down to children born out of wedlock. Now, citizenship could be handed down by either mothers or fathers, to children born in or out of wedlock.

The Act sounded the death knell for the British subject status that had been a hallmark of citizenship since 1707. Only thirty-six people became British subjects between 1983 and none since 1991 – the difference is that they lack the full rights and duties held by the then new status of British citizenship. We're all becoming British *citizens* now.

The British Nationality Act also set out the fundamentals for becoming British by naturalisation. Anyone wanting to become British must possess *full capacity* and be able to understand the importance of the decision to take on a new nationality. New citizens must have an *intention* to live in the UK if citizenship is granted. Most are required to satisfy a *residency* requirement of at least five years. These are all governed by guidelines that allow for exceptions and discretion.

It has long been expected that new citizens should demonstrate a knowledge of English and of 'life in the United Kingdom'. Later chapters explore how these requirements have changed into formal hurdles to be passed, including the introduction of the 'life in the United Kingdom' citizenship test in 2005. Finally, there is the wide-ranging 'good character' requirement that demands that anyone applying today has no unspent convictions or serious offences in the UK or abroad, that all British taxes are paid, that they have not been bankrupt while in the UK and that their presence in the country is not contrary to the public good. These ideas about good character are discussed further in the next chapter, where we look at Britishness.

The newly established rules were confusing. The right to live in Britain was not restricted to British citizens alone. Commonwealth citizens born before 1983 from former dominions and colonies and who had a parent born in the UK also retained a right to enter the UK without immigration controls. This makes sense only given the new rules: the law recognised that anyone born previously in Britain had a right to British citizenship and so qualifying Commonwealth citizens with a British parent would meet this test. But there was a twist. Some countries, like Pakistan and South Africa, were suspended and then readmitted to the Commonwealth. However, their renewed membership did not revive a right of abode for their nationals. So, these countries were back to 'normal' in the Commonwealth, but their citizens held a different status.

That was not all. The right of abode could also be held by people deemed 'British overseas territories citizens', previously known as 'British dependent territories citizens'. These were people connected to the dependencies from the empire like Bermuda, British Antarctic Territory, the Falkland Islands and the Virgin Islands. Isles exotic and distant. They need not have a parent born in the UK to possess British overseas territories citizenship. All such citizens were granted British citizenship in 2002.

There were also 'British overseas citizens', who were different from 'British overseas territories citizens'. This was largely a catch-all category covering individuals who were citizens of the United Kingdom and Colonies in a colony that gained independence, but were unable to acquire citizenship of their new country. This was true for people of Asian origin living in former British colonies in east Africa. This category of British citizenship continues, although it applies to a small few. Between 1983 and 2000, there were 1,062 people who became citizens through this route.

A regular feature of statutes concerning immigration over the last few decades is the wide discretion they afford to the Home Secretary. This has increased legal complexity through the back door – and has contributed to immigration becoming one of the fastest-changing areas of law.

Successive Home Secretaries have expanded the immigration rules to help structure the exercise of discretion by officials presented in what has been called 'the language of the administrator rather than the lawyer'. This is supposed to improve the advice officials give to the public concerning immigration queries and avoid similar cases being treated too differently. To some degree this has worked.

While these rules are binding on immigration officers, the Home Secretary can depart from the rules in appropriate circumstances to permit a migrant to stay in the UK who might normally be refused. Should someone fail to convince officials to decide a case in her favour there is always the *hope* – although in practice it is rarely satisfied – that this might be swiftly reversed should the Home Secretary be persuaded to intervene. It's doubtless many will try, no matter how small the odds of success. Hope does that to people – as any chance is better than none.

The guidance issued in the immigration rules can be lengthy and complex. For example, the Home Office's official guidance on grounds for refusing applications for leave to remain runs to over fifty pages and has changed six times in less than a year. That's a change every other month on the official guidance for refusing one particular type of visa application. The full text on refusals is about 350 pages long. Margaret Phelan and James Gillespie's *Immigration Law Handbook* containing all relevant statutes and rules is currently 1,912 pages – and it's about 140 pages longer than the previous year's edition (without including any relevant case law). That's a lot of rules covering a lot of complexities. With the current Immigration Bill now at more than 200 pages, the rulebook looks set to grow further. Welcome to the world of immigration law.

Every facet, from pre-entry requirement to deportation and appeals, is covered. For almost a decade this has included an Australian-style points-based system used for granting visas. Points are earned based on salary, savings, satisfactory knowledge of English and other factors to determine whether a threshold is reached permitting entry, subject to qualifications and exemptions that are under review.

Possibly the biggest secret in British immigration policy is that this points-based system has been alive and kicking for several years now. I worked with Phil Wilson on his 2015 re-election campaign as the Labour Party's Member of Parliament for Sedgefield, previously held by one Tony Blair. Phil and I were speaking to voters on the doorstep in his constituency and immigration issues would routinely come up. We would hear people ask why only

Nigel Farage and UKIP were calling for a points-based system. The answer was that the points-based system had already been phased in, beginning in 2008. But there are so many rules, which are changed so frequently, that the public has a near-impossible task understanding it, not to mention navigating its increasingly complex web. It's hardly any wonder that many who have experience of the system claim, 'It is a *lot* more complicated than I had expected.'

Nigel Farage has said there is a 'flood' of migrants coming to Britain, but the real flooding is found in the rule books, which are now spilling over with statutes, official guidance, regulatory orders, European protocols and much, much more. Hundreds of pages have been produced spelling out ever more restrictions and complications. If only they were more comprehensible. Immigration lawyer and leading expert Sophie Barrett-Brown says the law is 'horrendously complicated, with rules being made just for their own sake. There were a dozen major changes to the rules last year, often hastily drafted and trickling through in dribs and drabs. And there are updates issued virtually every day.'

When I prepared my own settlement application, I completed the application form and put together additional paperwork requested in the form's guidance notes, such as past payslips, bank statements and proof of address covering at least five years – and I was advised to bring everything going back to when I first moved to the UK in 2001. This decade of documentation literally filled a small suitcase that I brought with me.

The issue was that not everything I needed in my application was mentioned in these notes that I had followed so carefully. I also had to have further paperwork, such as a statement from my then employer confirming that they would continue hiring me if my application for permanent settlement was allowed. This was only picked up by a brilliant solicitor and thank goodness it was – while I was not, in the event, asked to show any of my payslips, the employer statement was requested when my application was considered. This could have been overlooked easily. Another immigration lawyer remarked to me that, however useful official websites like gov.uk might be, the webpages were not always well organised and important information could be missing. Such is the result of a system changing more quickly than frontline staff or many lawyers can keep up with. While I had used allegedly 'current' documents provided online by the then UK Border Agency, there is a clear problem where the official documents and websites available are inconsistent, incomplete or outdated. It's not only citizens who are left confused but, worryingly, those entrusted with implementing the rules.

If the purpose of this proliferation of rules is to lower migration and raise public confidence, the effects have been the opposite. The United Kingdom has long exported its citizens outward. Net migration in 1964 was minus 50,000 – i.e., more people were leaving than entering. A whirlwind of new legislation and rules later, by 2015 we had 212,000 more coming than going. 'Policy is being driven by the matter of perception,' one senior advocate said to me, 'so that the government can claim it is clamping down even though in real terms the impact on numbers is absolutely marginal.' This is not a recipe for success or for inspiring public confidence. And the government needs to hear this message loud and clear.

A sign that immigration policy was in flux can be seen in the swiftly changing ministerial posts covering immigration issues under the Home Secretary, who is directly responsible. In the beginning the post was called the Parliamentary Under-Secretary of State with responsibility for the Immigration and Nationality Department. The name was not by any means elegant, but it remained unchanged from 1979 to 1997. So far, so good. But things were to change, and fast.

It started under New Labour. Michael O'Brien got the ball rolling as Parliamentary Under-Secretary of State for Immigration. He was succeeded in 1999 by Barbara Roche and then Lord Rooker in 2001 as the newly renamed Minister of State for Asylum and Immigration. After starting as the Minister of State for Citizenship, Immigration and Community Cohesion, Beverley Hughes was rebranded Minister of State for Citizenship, Immigration and Counter-Terrorism from 2003 to 2004. Des Browne, Tony McNulty and Liam Byrne each served as what was now called the Minister of State for Citizenship, Immigration and Nationality. This changed again, while Byrne was still in post, to the Minister of State for Borders and Immigration, as it remained under Phil Woolas. In 2010, the coalition government renamed it once again to Minister of State for Immigration, a post held by Tory MPs Damian Green and then followed by Mark Harper. Today, James Brokenshire is what is called the Minister for Security and Immigration, with Sir Keir Starmer serving as Labour's shadow minister.

In short, there have been eleven different ministers and eight changes to the post's name in less than two decades. That's a change almost every other year in one of the biggest areas of public concern. About the same timeframe as the average lifespan of a mouse. Or less.

Such high turnover is a recipe for potential disaster. Too many people are given too little time to come to grips with this difficult and potentially volatile area. Nor has there been any recent minister who had been an immigrant himself, experiencing the system first-hand, to my knowledge. Migrants I spoke with who became British citizens found this last point obvious: anyone who had been a migrant would not be satisfied with the system in place, whose complexity and constant changes benefit neither British citizens nor anyone else.

The mixed messages are startling. First, there is every effort by current ministers to make clear their view that net migration must come down. Many migrants feel understandably unwelcome. If I had a pound for every speech that starts with a few words about the benefits immigration brings to Britain followed by a string of remarks about how their number can be reduced, I'd be a millionaire many times over.

But there is also another, very different, message from government. After I was approved for British citizenship, in 2011, I received an invitation to attend a citizenship ceremony – mine was in Gateshead, though more than half of citizenship ceremonies take place in London or the south-east.

You only become British on swearing an oath to the Queen and reciting a pledge that reads: 'I will give my loyalty to the United Kingdom and respect its rights and freedoms. I will uphold its democratic values. I will observe its laws faithfully and fulfil my duties and obligations as a British citizen.' The pledge is really an unnecessary restatement of the oath, more than anything else. Since I declared my loyalty to both the Queen (in the oath) and democracy (in the pledge), I continue to hope they don't start moving in different directions. God save the Queen and Her Majesty's democracy.

The ceremony lasted about an hour. New citizens were surrounded by friends and family while children from a nearby primary school sang us 'local music'. I will never forget their choice of songs. They started off with 'The Candy Man' from the movie *Willy Wonka and the Chocolate Factory*, and then followed it up with 'The Bare Necessities' from *The Jungle Book*, a choice that seemed especially far from appropriate. After all, many of us might have only the bare necessities left after paying the hefty fees to reach citizenship! To hear children sing, 'It's just the … bare necessities' after paying a few thousand pounds in fees was bewildering at best. But, then again, what do you sing at an occasion like that beyond 'God Save the Queen'?

The fresh pizza waiting to be devoured after our ceremony turned out to be for the schoolchildren – only the tea and biscuits were for the newly sanctified citizens.

The actual process of conferring naturalisation certificates and a commemorative gift – in my case a medal with Gateshead stamped on one side and 'British citizenship' on the other – following a signing of a register took all of five minutes. For all of us in the room. It was even timetabled in our booklets as lasting from 3.10 to 3.15 p.m. One naturalised UK citizen summed up her ceremony in one word for me: 'weird.' Not a ringing endorsement.

At the event, I received a greetings card with a message from the then leader of Gateshead Council, reading: 'On behalf of the people of Gateshead, welcome to British citizenship' and proclaiming: 'We welcome the energy that new citizens bring to our borough.' Now those are words of welcome you'll not see strung atop any tabloid or billboard. Yet, this is the message that we who become British are given when our fellow British citizens aren't paying close attention.

A letter in my citizenship ceremony pack from Theresa May, the Home Secretary, took me by surprise:

> Her Majesty the Queen asked me to welcome you on behalf of Herself, the British Government and your fellow citizens into our national community. I hope that in the years to come you will look back with pride on your decision to become a British citizen. The talents, background and experiences you

are bringing are very important to us. As a full and equal citizen I know that you will help make the United Kingdom a
more prosperous, generous and open society.

What a contrast from May's government and its narrow focus
on reducing net migration. Now I am someone to be welcomed
– by order of the Queen, no less! That's right, *me*! It's enough to
genuinely bring a tear to one's eye. I am someone of value who
is 'very important' to my new country.

Compare these words with a speech by May just over a year
later, in December 2012, when she talked of the need to 'bring
down the numbers'. Reducing immigration, she suggested, is 'in
the national interest', with benefits including improving social
cohesion and stemming the negative impact of immigration on
public services and jobs.

One minute migrants becoming British are praised and even
celebrated by Queen and country, the next we are to be rounded
up and stopped at the border. No immigrants allowed. The
UK public are told one thing, but new British citizens are told
another – in what many may see as confused messages if not
rank hypocrisy.

It doesn't help that the welcoming letter is written awkwardly:
sometimes it refers to 'you' in the singular and other times in the
plural, such as its talk of 'your local communities', as if migrants
live in more than one at the same time. Not exactly a warm welcome with a personal touch – there is nothing personalised at all

in this 'Message from the Home Secretary', and it at times reads like a press release written by some boorish committee. It turns out, as one former Home Secretary told me, that was probably exactly how it was written. At least the secret is now out.

And we migrants can see through all of this.

The most common motivation for becoming British reported to me was pragmatism. Let that sink in. Most migrants I interviewed simply wanted to end yet another round of increasingly expensive visas and surcharges to stop the uncertainty that has come with frequent changes to the immigration rules. One migrant told me: 'They're charging you for the privilege of being British' – when all she wanted was permanent residency without the need for further visas. As the novelist Kamila Shamsie, a Pakistani national who became British, put it, immigration laws seem designed to keep migrants 'perpetually insecure'.

The rising costs of applying for citizenship is the biggest sore point for people coming through the creaking immigration system. A three-year temporary work visa can cost £1,151 per person and another £1,328 or more to extend for up to another five years – as long as your total stay in the UK is not more than six years. These may be needed to fulfil minimum residency requirements of at least five years for most applicants. Prior to citizenship, migrants must obtain permanent settlement – the right to abode and the right to settle permanently. The application fee is currently £1,236 per person if submitted by post or another £500 if applying in person at a premium service centre.

The cost of becoming British for a family of four, after factoring in annual health surcharges of £200 (£150 for students) and the fifty-quid fee to take the citizenship test, can be as high as £15,000, and possibly even more depending on individual circumstances. According to official records, it costs the Home Office about £2.80 to process each passenger at the border and £166 to decide each permanent and temporary migration application, whether made in the UK or overseas. The fees paid by migrants working or naturalising in Britain are far higher and disproportionate to the costs of processing their forms.

Several migrants I spoke with believed the increasingly high fees were designed to soak migrants as much as possible. This is perhaps the worst-kept secret in Westminster concerning immigration policy. Harley, an Australian hoping to become a British citizen, told me people like her were viewed as 'money-making cash cows – it's so blatant now'. Ed, an American who became British, agreed: 'They keep milking us for cash.' Another woman I spoke with whose citizenship application is currently under review told me the process seemed mostly like 'a fee-grabbing exercise'. People like Harley and Ed are the migrants who could afford to enter the process. Many others cannot. Kwame, a Ghanaian living in London, told me, 'If you can't pay, then you go.' He's right.

The general consensus of professionals working in the field is that the system is a mess. They are not alone. Elena, who was Russian and became British, told me her British relatives were at first amazed and then angry at seeing all she had to do in order to earn citizenship and remain in the UK. Similar experiences were reported by most people I spoke with who had naturalised, too. For once, the lawyers are not to blame for it – so no need to recite Shakespeare's comment about 'the first thing we do, let's kill all the lawyers'. Sorry, but it's really not our fault.

We have a constantly expanding and changing system that few understand, at rising costs. A former immigration minister offers useful insights into how we got to where we are. Phil Woolas was a minister from 2008 to 2010. He told me that the UK seems a long way off managing the borders. Phil said that 'you can't get a grip on numbers until immigration is better managed', a view he said Prime Minister Tony Blair had come around to by about 2005. But Phil stressed an important point: '*Managing* immigration is not the same as necessarily *cutting* immigration.' While he admitted New Labour were 'probably guilty of coming to this too late', there was too much focus on the benefits to Britain overall and not enough to its effects on local communities, where there were growing concerns. Controls like e-Border entry and exit checks and biometric visas have been seen as 'get-tough' policies whereas, in fact, the real motivation behind them was to simply start managing a highly complex system – but which has evolved into a complicated machine few know how to operate effectively.

Britain's continuing struggle with immigration and citizenship says as much about the challenges faced by the United Kingdom as a declining world power as it does about its difficulties with

British identity. These twin struggles with Britain's understanding of itself now, and its relation to its past, help explain many of the problems that British citizenship faces today. In the shift from subject to citizen, 'British' citizenship went from global coverage to a return to the British Isles, with lasting consequences. Perhaps the most significant dilemma is identifying what Britishness is. We turn to this now.

CHAPTER 3

WHAT IS BRITISHNESS?

' Trying to pin down "Britishness"', said Chelsea, a native Briton living in the south-west, 'is like trying to grasp a will-o'-the-wisp.' She is right. Britishness is an identity that many claim, but few fully understand. I found that just about everyone has a different view about what Britishness is. So what explains the confusion?

The unique history of British citizenship discussed in the previous chapter provides some insights. Traditional views about citizenship based on parentage or a particular territory were more applicable when the United Kingdom was born in 1707 than during the later British Empire.

The unifying connection since the eighteenth century was an allegiance to the British monarch, which lay at the heart of British citizenship as a political and legal identity from its earliest inception. Since then, the law has defined, redefined and redefined again who should be recognised as a citizen. Less than 100 years ago, individuals could become British without knowing English and without ever having been to Britain once in their lives. 'Britishness' was about more than being from Britain. Britain was even greater than we might normally think.

Now things have gone swiftly into reverse with booster rockets. But this history of expansion of who was recognised as British in a global empire is impossible to ignore. The time when citizens of British colonies and dominions could claim British citizenship is well within living memory. This may be history, but its legacy continues.

Britain's imperial past is crucial when considering different ideas about what Britishness is. Public opinion is deeply divided. Should someone's parentage or ethnicity matter for someone to be British? Does having a non-Christian belief count against someone being British? Is Britishness about accepting certain 'British values' and, if so, what might they be? Or is being British little different from other kinds of citizenship – is being a good British citizen just the same as being a good citizen of any other state?

Contemporary Britain is a diverse country of so many ethnicities, religious beliefs and ways of life that it can be challenging to locate the 'it' that brings us all together as 'British'.

Jonathan, a British citizen in his thirties from Scotland, said being British has changed so much over time that it is best understood as an 'administrative' category that marks out a formal relationship in law, but otherwise lies empty.

As a legal form of identity, British citizenship is little different from many other types of citizenship elsewhere. Each has its rules on who should be formally recognised as citizens and what someone must do in order to naturalise. The big issue, then, is what makes being British, well, *British*? Is Britishness different from other kinds of citizenship elsewhere?

But let us start by addressing what Britishness is *not* head-first. Britishness has had a troubled relationship to race since its beginnings. As we have seen, British citizens were defined from the beginning by their allegiance to the monarchy. The importance of having a British father was that a British subject would beget British subjects. What mattered was not his ethnicity, but his allegiance. Things have changed with the emergence of British citizenship. Since 1983, British citizens can beget British citizens, whether through a British father or a British mother.

The situation has changed for migrants seeking to become naturalised British citizens, too. There are now formal requirements that demand non-citizens acquire a visa first and then live in the UK continually for at least five years in most cases. Anyone wanting to become British must satisfy additional obligations sufficient for obtaining 'indefinite leave to remain' to live and work permanently. If successful, they must wait at least one year and a day before applying to become a British citizen: permanent residency is needed before you can obtain citizenship. Curiously, permanent residency is also needed before you 'create' British citizens: these residents might not be sufficiently British to be a citizen, but they are British enough that their children are British from birth. Thus, what all British citizens have in common – whether they are born British or naturalised – is a direct connection to the United Kingdom under the Crown; not the colour of their skin nor religious background. God Save the Queen.

Britishness is a constructed identity. It was created by legal magic in 1707. Now, people were no longer only English, Scots or Welsh. Abracadabra! They now also became British. Like all European countries, Britain has been a place of migration for centuries, not least post-invasion by the Romans, the Normans, the Vikings and many others. Britishness is not a race and there was probably never a time that any part of today's United Kingdom lacked migrants, however few their number. The simple facts are that Britishness has never been tied to any one ethnic view, and people from a variety of different heritages have been recognised as British since Britain began. This is not least true because people from different backgrounds can and do become British, too.

Britain's history as a constructed identity bringing together England, Wales and Scotland (and, soon afterwards, Northern Ireland) does not prevent some from claiming that what should make us British is our blood connection to being English, Scots or Welsh. Such views harbour back to a particular view of a nation state where to be a nation's citizen is to have some blood tie to some national group. England for the English or Scotland for the Scots. Or so it is said.

This is a minority perspective, but it is not too difficult to find someone who holds these views if you look. I heard from Richard, a native British pensioner from the Midlands. He told me:

> The reality is that the term 'British' 300 years ago identi-
> fied people who were white, Christian, spoke English and
> who, together with their guns and flags, brought civilisa-
> tion to the colonies to form the British Empire. Sadly, this
> is no longer the case and the term is now so widely applied
> as to be meaningless and confusing.

Richard is not alone in finding Britishness confusing. The political scientists Andrew Gamble and Tony Wright have said: 'The British have long been distinguished by having no clear idea about who they are, where they are, or what they are. Most of them have routinely described England as Britain. Only business people talk about a place called the United Kingdom ... It is all a terrible muddle.'

Richard's positive view of colonialism will not be shared by all, but what is interesting about his comments is that he associates Britishness with what Britain created: namely, a global empire. Britain's imperial creation may have extended widely, but for Richard it included land and not people. This means that not everyone born and bred in the same British Empire is British. Being British is not about being part of Britain's empire, which might seem an odd view. But Richard is not ultimately interested in Britishness.

Richard views himself as 'English' rather than British, and this says a lot. His claim that to be British is to speak English, as things were in the UK three centuries ago, is a mistake no one from Wales would make: they would know Welsh was spoken at that time, too. Richard said he prefers 'English' to 'British' because only English is 'a clear and unequivocal definition, which is "white and born in England"'. But that's hardly true. Not every white person born in England will speak English. Not every English-speaking person born in England is white. Yet these mistaken representations live on in the minds of many.

England is more diverse than Richard considers. Speaking with England-born British citizens makes clear that many would think of themselves very differently – as a Londoner, Geordie, Scouse or Yorkshireman for example. Each has shares in a cultural narrative of England, but have their own traditions and words that are unique – my time in Newcastle has led me to appreciate that the Geordie dialect can look and even sound like a different language altogether. So the idea that being English trumps all other identities for British citizens born and bred in England does not reflect how many from England would see themselves.

To be clear, only a small minority would agree with Richard

that citizenship should be tied to an ethnic background. But he's not alone. A short survey I conducted on British citizenship saw some favourable to the idea that white Europeans should be able to gain additional points when applying for an entry visa. Most reject this view, but there is some support and it is important to understand why it should be rejected.

The British National Party (BNP) is a far-right political party formerly led by Nick Griffin. Richard is in no way a supporter of them, but the BNP does appear to share his concerns about Britain as a land for the 'indigenous' population. Their website runs an appeal for money. That is not unique for a political party, but their pitch is. It shows a young white girl with the Union Jack behind her and says: 'Rebecca will be an ethnic minority in her British ancestral home when she grows up *unless you take action today*.' A BNP leaflet carrying this same image adds: 'She'll be lost in an overcrowded melting pot.' Their policy on immigration is 'Britain's full and it's time to shut the door!'

The message is clear: being British is a white-only club. Paradoxically, this view of what it means to be British rejects much of what the nation has achieved during its imperial history – which such groups typically celebrate with pride. Defending a purely racial view of Britishness denies Britishness itself, which became a constructed identity of fellow members in a British Empire that covered much of the world far beyond Britain's shores. It's as if three centuries or more of history never happened and can be forgotten. But they did and they can't. This view of Britain isn't about closing borders, but closing minds – while turning back the cuckoo clock to never-never land.

The BNP website carries an image of the former Conservative MP Enoch Powell with the words 'It's never too late to save your country.' Powell was already a controversial figure before he delivered his famous 'Rivers of Blood' speech on 20 April 1968 – and soon became a more divisive figure whose words have left their mark on British politics ever since. Any mention of Powell today immediately conjures up his best-known remarks.

Addressing a Conservative Association meeting, he talked about a conversation he had had with a 'quite ordinary working man' in his constituency who wanted to leave the UK with his family. The reason for the move was allegedly because whites were becoming outnumbered, making his country not worth living in any more. The problem for Powell was 'Commonwealth immigrants with their descendants' who came to the UK as 'full citizens'. The fact that this group would also include white individuals is conveniently overlooked. He remarked that the white British citizens were 'made strangers in their own country'. Powell foresaw increasing civil disharmony leading to violence as the white population became less dominant. Britain, he said, would somehow become less British and so risk falling apart.

Most British citizens do not share these views about race. But some do and will agree that they feel like 'strangers', as Powell predicted. Britain has undoubtedly changed a lot over the past few decades, becoming a more culturally and ethnically diverse country. Rising immigration is a cause of this increased diversity of peoples and cultures – and so support from some British citizens for curbing or ending immigration is built on a concern about how being British – i.e. being white British – may have changed with it. The name 'Welsh' comes from the Germanic *Walhaz* meaning 'foreigner' or 'stranger', but the Welsh are strangers no more and Wales has been long integrated into the United Kingdom. Britain has changed over time and so too Britishness with it.

These views on citizenship and race might explain a split in public opinion. People who are white British citizens since birth are more likely to identify themselves as English, Scottish or Welsh first and British second. I asked people up and down the country a simple question: what does it mean to be British for you? In fact, most white British citizens I have spoken to would describe themselves regionally – as from London, Manchester, Scottish Highlands, north Wales, Cornwall and others. Part of the reason for not saying they are English, Welsh or other identities is because they think this will be obvious from their accents when they speak.

The opposite is true for everybody else: most British-born citizens from black and ethnic minority (BME) communities identify more strongly as British. This is also true for most people who become British through naturalisation, like me. Of course, there are plenty of exceptions, and identities can change over time. But this research seems to suggest that Britishness is perceived as being more inclusive and open to differences, whereas other identities are less open to diversity.

This may sound abstract, but it is not for many people – including me. This is no philosophical thought experiment. It's real life. I have many ties to England. After a few years in Dublin, I have lived continually in England since 2001. I am a native English speaker. My wife is English. I am a direct descendant of an English blacksmith from Nantwich in Cheshire – and I have the English surname of Brooks (originally 'Brooke'; changed shortly after my first ancestors to America settled in New Haven colony around 1680).

My family also includes relations from Scotland, and I would count myself one of the eight in every ten naturalised citizens that identifies as British and not English. Partly, this is because my UK passport identifies me as a 'British' citizen and not English; this is true for all British citizens. But probably the main reason is that I can justifiably claim to be British, and other British citizens are more accepting of that self-identification than if I claimed to be English or, worse, a Geordie, based on my several years living and working in Newcastle upon Tyne.

Part of who we are is shaped by how others see us. Identities are not forged in isolation. I cannot choose to become an Australian or a South African by snapping my fingers and wishing it were so. I might never be considered English. I lack the right accent. Mine is a product of someone on the move for many years – a foundation of Connecticut Yankee blended with bits of New Jersey, Arizona, Dublin, Yorkshire, some London and north-east infusions. Few guess that I am originally from New Haven, but they can usually hear a clear American accent whenever I speak. And this plainly marks me out as different, as a migrant.

A Durham University colleague put it to me this way: 'Even though you might have lived in Britain longer than they've been alive, many of your students will always see you as American and not British – how strange that is.' Being British for more years than others might not make me British enough for some.

My situation might be strange to some people, but others face a far more worrying problem. It is not uncommon for BME individuals to tell me they regularly face questions about what their 'true' heritage is. One woman who has an Indian mother told me that 'people often seem disappointed when I say I'm British'. Her experience is not unique.

Another woman named Pooja, who was also born British, said: 'Being a "citizen" doesn't really capture the sense of belonging people desire. I think the notion of being a citizen can often pave the way for nationalist sentiment, which I completely detest.' From the conversations I have had with BME citizens and people like me who became British through naturalising, 'being British' is seen as much more inclusive and is preferred to claiming other national identities like being English or Irish.

Whenever concerns are expressed about the swift changes in Britain relating to immigration, they are usually expressed in terms of culture rather than race. These concerns focus on a worry that British culture is under threat and requires preservation and protection. This was captured well by Rebecca, a model living in London who was born British to a Sri Lankan mother. She explained that being British is 'about how you see yourself'. Rebecca agreed that for many people there was 'a difference between being "British" and being a "British citizen"'. We might all be equally British citizens, but some are viewed as more British than others – especially anyone from a background not thought to 'respect' British culture.

My interviews with British citizens made clear a moral panic about one thing in particular: Islamic culture. There are some people concerned that immigration has allowed too many Muslims to come to Britain and now the country is at risk of becoming dominated by them. Such fears are misplaced – Muslims are only about 5 per cent of the total UK population today.

But these worries remain nonetheless. Joining ISIL or becoming a member of the Taliban were seen as actions that would justify stripping someone of their British citizenship. This is hardly surprising given recent terrorist events perpetrated by these organisations. Yet, membership of groups like the Real IRA was mentioned by no one. What Samuel Huntington once called 'the clash of civilisations' between East and West speaks to what some people feel about Islam and the West.

The broadcast journalist Anila Athar recounted speaking with an elderly woman named Tasnim Bibi who had made Britain her home nearly forty years ago. Tasnim laid bare what Anila coined 'the quintessential Muslim dilemma', saying:

> We are a community that thinks we are the best, because our
> religion is the best of all. Everyone else is second to us there-
> fore it's futile to expect us to adopt British values as we see
> them as inferior to our values by virtue of [our] being the fol-
> lowers of the best book given to humankind. Why would we
> leave our superior values to take on something that is inferior?

The British values objected to are usually related to sex, such as
the acceptance of same-sex marriages, pre-marital sex and cohab-
iting couples.

Anila concluded that 'multiculturalism as a policy of diversity
management has failed' – and it's easy to see why. The Muslim
dilemma, for Anila, is that Britain is a place that so many, like
Tasnim, want to make their home and yet they see themselves in
conflict with its values, creating an ever-present tension. For many
people, there is a choice: either keep the values you have already
or reject them in favour of others.

But no such choice need be made. There are two confusions.
The first is thinking that a specific set of values is incompatible
with other values. There is no contradiction in accepting the right
of others to make choices that you would not choose for yourself.
British values like democracy, respect for the rule of law, and individual liberty are not inconsistent with the values of any major religion.
They can serve as what the Harvard philosopher John Rawls called
'an overlapping consensus' that helps connect us to each other.

The second confusion concerns multiculturalism. Critics seem to think support for multiculturalism is an endorsement of 'anything goes'. But multiculturalism is not anarchism. It is a respect for cultural differences that matter to the individuals that have them. Respect for diversity is not a rejection of our sharing in a community. If we appreciate that Britishness is not a monoculture set in stone but a set of values that can be endorsed by citizens from a wide variety of cultural, philosophical and religious backgrounds, then we can see that multiculturalism is not the problem it is often made out to be.

While these concerns about ethnicity and religion were raised by some of the people I met, the overall picture is more complicated. The overwhelming majority of people I spoke with did not think race or religious beliefs essential or even important for becoming British. A much deeper issue, which I suspect is at the root of these concerns, is not about how people look or worship, but about how people feel socially and politically alienated from one another.

In 1979, then Prime Minister Margaret Thatcher said: 'We are a British nation with British characteristics. Every country can take some small minorities and in many ways they add to the richness and variety of this country. The moment the minority threatens to become a big one, people get frightened.' And it need not take much to get some people worried. We hear much about the importance of so-called 'stakeholders' these days, but the plain truth is that many people don't feel like they have much of a stake in society. They feel powerless and voiceless.

Globalisation and its disorienting effects on how we work and communicate have no doubt brought benefits, but these benefits have not been felt by all, especially those struggling at the bottom of the socio-economic ladder. Some feel greater disconnection from society as they fall behind financially, and begin to suffer all the problems this can bring. Migrants become an easy scapegoat, especially when there is a squeeze on living standards and people look for someone or something to blame. They are accused of taking what is not theirs to have, like public housing and benefits paid for by British taxpayers.

One person told me: 'The news I read, and I read many news sources, gives me the opinion that Britain just lets anyone move in, get on the dole and receive free housing without having a job or permission to come.' I have little doubt he believes this. And he has some reason to. After all, such headlines are not difficult to find. Never mind the compelling evidence that migrant workers offer more of an economic boom than bust or that anyone in the UK illegally is unable to receive any benefits. But to reject this view for its false reasoning would be to miss a crucial point. The arguments might not hold up, but they do not invalidate a sincerely held sense of alienation that affects what people think about modern Britain and Britishness.

Enoch Powell's 'Rivers of Blood' speech made him a controversial and divisive figure, and led to him being sacked from the Tory shadow Cabinet by Edward Heath. But this speech is important because it also identifies this sense of feeling alienated, losing out and falling behind that resonates with some today:

> They found their wives unable to obtain hospital beds in
> childbirth, their children unable to obtain school places,
> their homes and neighbourhoods changed beyond recog-
> nition, their plans and prospects for the future defeated ...
> they began to hear, as time went by, more and more voices
> which told them that they were now the unwanted.

In an age when we are interconnected in so many new ways made possible by technology, we remain increasingly apart from one another, as we rely much less on face-to-face interaction. Powell's words will resonate fifty years later with those who feel alienated today, whose alienation is only accentuated by austerity policies that have left some public services struggling to cope. When people don't see themselves as having a stake in how society functions, solidarity breaks down – and anti-immigration sentiment starts to grow.

This raises an important issue about diversity and solidarity that the former universities minister David Willetts calls the 'progressive dilemma'. The political left welcomes greater diversity, but it also supports welfare programmes of social democracy. The dilemma is that more of one can lead to less of the other. Willetts claims social welfare programmes can only survive in their current form in a culturally homogenous society – and this is threatened by rising immigration, which increases diversity. The problem of high immigration is that it can undermine the solidarity required to support social democracy: citizens need to see themselves as all in it together, but this sense of togetherness takes time and effort to work.

Willetts may be a former Tory MP, but this is not a view confined only to Conservatives or to those on the political right. David Goodhart, the director of Demos and former founding editor of *Prospect* magazine, agrees. He quotes a letter to Clement Attlee sent by a group of Labour MPs in 1948: 'An influx of coloured people domiciled here is likely to impair the harmony, strength and cohesion of our public and social life and to cause discord and unhappiness among all concerned.' Goodhart goes on to defend the view that Britain 'has had too much ... too quickly' of immigration. The problem is that relatively big changes in demographics can break down the collective sense of everyone being committed to a shared project worth investing in. The more people become strangers to each other, the less committed they may become to supporting such a project and the more they may come to reject the social democracy they built together.

The views of Willetts and Goodhart are supported by controversial research that high levels of ethnic diversity are associated with low social capital. Harvard political scientist Robert D. Putnam claims that as a society becomes increasingly diverse, community members 'tend to withdraw from collective life, to distrust their neighbours' as they 'hunker down'. Or, in the words of Goodhart: 'To put it bluntly – most of us prefer our own kind.'

Not all studies reach the same conclusions, so there is

disagreement to be found. Some, like Jonathan Portes, the former chief economist at the Cabinet Office, claimed Goodhart was engaged in 'an exercise of scapegoating' that should be rejected. Others, like James Laurence at the University of Manchester, looked at the evidence from a different angle. He conducted a study in the UK to see if we really did 'hunker down' in the face of growing diversity. Laurence found that people who lived in more diverse communities did exhibit lower trust in their neighbours and have fewer close friends. So community diversity does seem to undermine social capital in a given locality. But Laurence's point is that this effect is often offset by social networks elsewhere. Local social capital might be lower than expected, but residents often travelled to maintain strong links with others outside their neighbourhood. They don't hunker down – they hunker away. And so increased diversity may not undermine social democracy after all.

Even if diversity need not undermine social democracy, a community requires some connection to bring its members together. Goodhart places his faith in the promise of our shared citizenship, saying: 'Citizenship is not just an abstract idea.' British citizenship may be a legal status, but it is also meant to capture something of importance: our common bond of Britishness. The issue is uncovering precisely what this is, and how it can serve as a basis for keeping us connected.

Former Home Secretary David Blunkett has said that 'strengthening our identity is one way of reinforcing people's confidence and sense of citizenship and well-being'. Our identity as citizens has value for people. An informal survey I ran found 80 per cent agreed or strongly agreed with the statement 'citizenship is important'. The question then is how it should be cultivated. What is it about British citizenship that can form a shared bond among citizens in a multicultural society?

One observation I picked up frequently is that many British citizens don't think much about themselves as being British. Judith, who lives in the south-west, said that being a British citizen is 'something you don't think about unless you have to'. Another respondent I spoke to said: 'To be honest, I don't give any thought to how being British affects the decisions I make or the way I feel about things – it's simply what I am.'

Sarah, a graduate student from London, told me she only feels British 'when travelling abroad'. It is only when plunged into a different country that she becomes conscious of herself as a British citizen. This can be triggered by simple, everyday things like different senses of humour, how people naturally stand on an escalator, or whether she is acknowledged on entering a shop.

Many UK citizens only feel British when they see certain differences. To be British is to be distinctive, and to do things differently from the Americans or the Chinese; it is to follow a specifically British winding path to our shared future. Or, stated differently, to be British is do British things in a British way.

There are many things that could be picked out as distinctively British. Afternoon tea, bulldogs, Mini Coopers, James Bond movies and laughing at *Monty Python's Flying Circus* fit the bill. There are distinctive foods, from Cornish pasties and haggis to Marmite and Yorkshire puddings – preferably washed down with a pint of bitter in a Victorian-era pub.

And then there is the queue. Before moving to the UK, I didn't know what a queue was. The very first time I saw a sign saying 'Queue Here' at a sandwich shop, I made sure I stood somewhere else, away from the sign. I didn't know what a queue was and I only wanted a coffee. But I learned fast – and so do other migrants. Queuing was literally not a part of my vocabulary until coming to live in Britain. It is now.

A vice-chancellor at another British university remarked to me his amazement at how queueing works. He had come to the UK from South Africa and his big mistake was to get on a bus as it collected everyone from his stop without letting others on first who had waited for it longer. He soon realised that while no one spoke to each other as they waited for the bus, everyone knew their place in the queue – who was before them and definitely who came after – and this unstated order was enforced through icy stares if anyone dared break with it. We could have benefited from the Channel 4 programme *Very British Problems* and its advice: 'If you're not in the queue, don't stand near the queue.' We know what to look for now.

Another well-known British practice concerns the pub. As the cognoscenti will be well aware, individuals in a group would never buy only a drink for themselves. Instead, drinks are purchased in what is called 'a round', where one person gets drinks for everyone, taking it turns as the evening progresses, in successive rounds. It does not always work out perfectly – some rounds can cost more than others as people choose different drinks and whoever starts the rounds may find himself paying for a round more than others. But if anyone were to refuse or complain, it would be a – pardon my French – *faux pas* of a tall order. And definitely not 'on'.

Understanding Britishness in terms of what makes us different from non-British cultures does not work. The clearer we get on what these differences might be, the more we find that they are not only dividing lines between the British and non-British, but that they may actually divide British citizens too. Haggis may be seen as a British food, but its identity is with Scotland – to call it a national dish would not be accepted by other parts of the United Kingdom. Another example is the Welsh language. It is virtually unspoken outside of the UK, with the exception of Patagonia, and it is not a unifying characteristic of everyone who is British, as only a small minority would speak it. The conclusion is simple: identifying what makes Britain different does not pick out what all British citizens share in common.

So is Britishness nothing more than a loose umbrella of cultural characteristics from its member nations? In her book *Watching the English*, Kate Fox finds that Britishness seems to be 'a rather meaningless term', often used synonymously with Englishness. Britain is 'a purely political construct, composed of several nations with their own distinctive cultures' and so lacking in real content.

Fox argues that if we are looking for the glue that binds us together, we should abandon trying to locate any particular set of British values and instead focus on English values and those of the other home nations. A *Times* newspaper readers' poll conducted in 2007 lends some support for this view. The poll asked readers what should be a new motto for Britain – and what they got was the winning entry 'No motto, please, we're British.' The anti-motto motto. How very British indeed.

To paraphrase Shakespeare (badly), to articulate or not to articulate our Britishness – that is the question. Some say it is about being white and speaking English, but this fails to include everyone who is British and the many who speak Scots, Welsh or other languages. Others claim it is what makes the British different from other cultures. But this is unconvincing too because often these differences between the British and non-British are also differences between the English and the Welsh and so on. Yet there is still something unsatisfactory about saying that there's nothing there to articulate and that Britishness is about as full as an empty glass. The literary critic David Gervais said: 'Not only do the English resist articulating their "Englishness", they feel truer to themselves by not articulating it.' Maybe it's as ethereal as a will-o'-the-wisp after all.

But there is another view. An important report was published in 2000 by the Commission on the Future of Multi-Ethnic

Britain. The commission was chaired by Lord Parekh, an Indian-born scholar who is one of the most respected political theorists in Britain today. The Parekh Report, as it was known, rejected the view that Britain was 'a' single community. Instead, it insisted that Britain is a 'community of communities' where Britishness should be defined not by what makes a nation or region different, but by what they share in common.

Parekh made his name promoting multiculturalism. In his more recent work, he argues that the state cannot be 'morally and culturally neutral', as it must make choices from within a sea of difference. It is crucial that bridges are built on common interests and mutual trust centred on a shared political structure – 'and not the widely shared personal characteristics of its individual members' that divide them, such as a majority ethnicity or religion.

If this shared political culture is not affirmed, the community's national identity will prioritise some groups of citizens over others. This would make it difficult, if not impossible, for all citizens to identify with it. A Britishness for some is not a Britishness for all British citizens. Something important would be missing. Parekh correctly recognises – as perhaps only someone who is acutely aware of the first-hand experience of becoming British can – that once someone becomes a citizen they are not to be given a second-class status.

Yet this is the risk we take in claiming that Britishness is captured by personal characteristics: it will leave those citizens that do not fit this mould feeling second class and second best. This is not a recipe for a healthy democracy of equal citizens. Britishness must be something everyone British can relate to.

Integration is important, but too often it is viewed as a one-way street as minorities become absorbed into a homogenous majority. Parekh argues this is incorrect. Integration is not only about one group coming to identify with others, as if the hard graft is only to be done by new members. Existing group members should play their part too. Integration requires an openness to acceptance and shared belonging. We should be aware that cultural identities are never fixed, and change over time.

As Parekh says in his report, 'Britishness is an idea in transition.' We are neither at its beginning nor at its end. What it means to be British is not set in stone. So we should avoid any conception that is inflexible and fails to include everyone who is British. Our community is an achievement and every citizen should be able to identify with it.

Multiculturalism is no longer in favour. In 2011, David Cameron claimed that it had 'failed'. Britain needed to redouble its efforts at integration, but through a commitment to 'British values'. These values are the new black and back in fashion. But they're also very much retro, having been aired before.

'British values' hit the political agenda in 2001. The 9/11 terrorist attacks in that year had a profound effect on much of the world, and Britain's citizenship rules were changed in the aftermath. But the roots of the British values debate lay not in trying to combat the influence of Al-Qaeda, but in trying to address rioting that took place in northern cities like Bradford, Burnley and Oldham. 'Parallel communities' were found divided along racial lines, with relatively little interaction between them. As then immigration minister and MP for Oldham East Phil Woolas told me, this division, combined with fast-rising migration from Eastern Europe, 'created a toxic impression' of a country under siege. They certainly did – and both happened during my first months in the UK as a student.

The consequences of this 'toxic' mix were profound. Born from them was a greater – and more active – interest from government in promoting integration. The only genuine surprise is that it took so long, but it developed quickly. Key to this strategy were changes to the requirements for British citizenship. Attention soon turned to considering which approach to follow. The idea at the time was that there was merit in migrants becoming citizens because – as citizens – they should see their voices heard. But it was also recognised that existing requirements should be reformed to modernise how British citizenship was granted.

Shortly after 9/11, the Denham Report – named for its chair, John Denham MP – highlighted the idea of Britishness as a set of shared principles; a notion heavily influenced by Parekh's commission. Similarly, Denham stressed the challenges of locating commonalities inclusive of all current British citizens in light of their great diversity of cultural and regional backgrounds.

The Parekh and Denham reports also set the scene for the

only major review of citizenship to date. This was the Life in the United Kingdom Advisory Group, launched by then Home Secretary David Blunkett and led by his former university tutor Sir Bernard Crick. The group was set the task of advising Tony Blair's government on the form and content of Parliament's newly approved citizenship test and citizenship ceremonies. Crick's group led a national conversation – that we have not had since – about what Britishness meant to people.

Crick's group concluded in 2003 that Britishness was best understood as a shared set of principles and experiences of everyday British life held by British citizens. Being British is about being able to function in British society. This is explicit in a White Paper published by Prime Minister Tony Blair's government in 2005 setting out a five-year plan on managing immigration and asylum. The government confirmed it would 'strongly encourage' all permanent residents to become British citizens. But there was no interest in creating 'a monoculture' because 'British nationality has never been associated with membership of a particular ethnic group. For centuries we have been a multi-ethnic nation. This diversity is a source of pride.'

Charles Clarke, who was Home Secretary at that time, told me in 2015 that this White Paper is 'key' because its five-year plan has been effectively rolled out and largely only tweaked by later governments, which he thought 'spoke volumes' for how much comparative progress was achieved – and one part of this progress is the view that Britishness is not an ethnicity, but a set of values in a multi-ethnic society. The government swiftly published a new citizenship test – which we will look at in the next chapter – that prioritised knowledge about British institutions and everyday life rather than British history and culture. First launched in 2005, the British citizenship test remains a requirement for applications for citizenship.

Thus, Britishness consisted in having certain values. But which values or principles make someone British? To even ask the question can make people hesitant, such is the association of Britishness with some form of prejudice. There is a feeling that when we talk about 'British' people there is a particular caricature in mind, such as someone white. Rachel, a British citizen who lived in Zambia before moving to Cambridgeshire, told me she was very concerned that 'Britishness' conveys some sense of snobbery, making unfounded assumptions about its superiority. Rachel agrees that 'citizenship means something', but not Britishness. Britishness is an emperor without clothes: 'There are no distinctive British values.'

She's not alone. BBC reporter Mark Easton has said that defining Britishness was 'like painting wind'. It may appear that in order to cover every British citizen, Britishness must be so open and indistinct that it is nothing at all. Yet it is something – when we speak about British values there seems widespread agreement that they exist, but not what they are.

The key to unlocking this puzzle is offered by Bhikhu Parekh. He found that 'our' shared norms of citizenship are also norms for others too. So, to be a good *British* citizen is to be a good

citizen. What is 'British' about them is how these norms are realised. For example, democracy and fairness are British values
that exist in other countries as well. But a part of what makes
these British values ours is the distinctive ways they are realised.
Not every democracy adopts the Westminster model of Parliament and there are different ways of ensuring fairness – not only a
single procedure is acceptable. It's not the values that make being
British different, but how they are realised.

That British values are global values is a view that many in the
public share. A British citizen from the east of England thought
it important that new citizens accept British values, but realised
that they are 'similar to the values of other countries, too'. This
made these values no less important.

We can find some further guidance when looking to the
Department of Education's current view that schools promote
'fundamental British values'. These are listed as democracy, the
rule of law, individual liberty, mutual respect and tolerance of
those with different faiths and beliefs. These values are to be promoted in the classroom in part by 'challenging' anyone in school
expressing 'opinions or behaviours' contrary to British values.

Schools from across the country plan activities around having students reflect on their own identities and beliefs, becoming
more sensitive to stereotypes and the diversity in Britain. The
goals are to improve their self-knowledge as well as their self-
esteem as students grasp not only their differences but their
commonalities, and take responsibility for their behaviour.

While the list of British values above is by no means complete, all of these would likely make any such comprehensive
list. Democracy is about a respect for the public's right to
choose their representatives and speak out on political issues.
Our Parliament is the mother of all parliaments and the heart
of modern democracies worldwide. The rule of law is a hugely
important value that says none of us is above the law. Individual
liberty concerns our right to live autonomously and to respect
the autonomy of others, which comes with mutual respect and
tolerance. Values like democracy or the rule of law are not unique
to Britain – similar values can be found in the United States or
Australia. But they are realised in different ways that help make
our values British. Democratic politics is very different in Britain
than in America. So too is the way tolerance is practiced. These
values matter intrinsically.

But they are also vague. Daniel Finkelstein, a *Times* columnist and Tory peer who advises David Cameron, said recently that
British values amount to being 'willing to accept the same basic
laws, a common attachment to Western democracy and a shared
responsibility for the nation's security'. These values may be universal and realised in different ways in different states. The values
are nonetheless abstract, and making the important emotional
connection to most people – to win over hearts and not only
minds – is not obvious.

Bernard Crick has argued that Britishness 'refers to a narrow if
strong and important political and legal culture: the Union itself,

the rule of law, the Crown and Parliament, perhaps the practice of a common political citizenship'. These are institutional connections we all share. Crick cites a speech by Gordon Brown about Britishness:

> The values and qualities I describe are of course to be found in many other cultures and countries. But when taken together, and as they shape the institutions of our country, these values and qualities – being creative, adaptable and outward looking, our belief in liberty, duty and fair play – add up to a distinctive Britishness that has been manifest throughout our history, and shaped it.

But even if these comments help us think about what any British values might be, it remains unclear how we should make our list.

Perhaps the most striking thing about these British values is how they were decided. There was no public debate or consultation. No army of social scientists trekked across the country to speak to people near and far. No, probably a small group of special advisors sat in their London offices and scribbled down what they had brainstormed on their smartboard.

It does not help that current and former government ministers rarely discuss these issues beyond making press releases. I contacted James Brokenshire, the current immigration minister, to discuss these issues. He did not reply, but the Direct Communications Unit in the Home Office did – making clear his refusal to meet with me. I was asked to send any questions to the national policy team inbox.

I then reached out to former immigration minister Damian Green, who served in this role within the coalition government. His office sent me a polite reply that he 'no longer gives detailed interviews on immigration'. When so few are willing to speak and only communicate when forced to, it does nothing to improve confidence in how the government makes crucial decisions concerning becoming British.

The irony of the government's approach to British values is simple. These values are seen as fundamental and in the public interest to protect. Yet the public is somehow not worth consulting about something so important. British values exist in our society and they are something to be celebrated, even cherished. But they do not live by some decree from Whitehall. It is only by understanding what they mean to the public that they can be transformed into something meaningful.

Professor Martin Ruhs, a former Migration Advisory Committee member, told me his personal view that, whatever else citizenship is, 'it should mean something' and 'not be purely theoretical'. Having British values is about recognising them and internalising them. Elaine, a Scot living in Brussels, said that, for her, being British was about accepting 'unwritten values' such as 'a certain openness of mind to others and cultures'.

This view was shared by Don Flynn, the director of the Migrants' Rights Network in London. He said that becoming

British was not about memorising some catechism, but about 'a way of thinking' and 'an instinctive grasp – this is the point that you become British'. One respondent told me citizenship should be for 'someone happy to espouse British values like tolerance and humour over the advantages of a British passport'. Julian, a Welsh son of an Italian father, said being British requires some kind of an emotional 'buy-in' – it is more than obeying the law; it is an acceptance of common values. Yet, we may still wonder what it is that we are to buy into. Abstract values drawn up by a civil servant or special advisor in a London boardroom? Or is there more to it than meets the eye?

Britishness consists in a knowledge of British life lived through interacting with others in the community. Britishness is also composed of values and principles like democracy, personal freedom and tolerance that should be somehow inculcated. But this only raises more questions. If this is all that Britishness is about, how do we know someone has it? If we only have vague principles, how could any test be designed to verify if people have them? This raises the specific issue of testing Britishness through the use of the British citizenship test. And it is as difficult as it sounds.

CHAPTER 4

TESTING CITIZENSHIP

It was Thursday 22 October 2009. This was the night that the BBC decided to invite Nick Griffin, the leader of the British National Party, to join its *Question Time* panel. It was the first time anything like this had happened – and the decision drew a public outcry as well as an appeal by Peter Hain to block it. All to no avail.

Controversy can attract a crowd – and this one did. The full panel of Griffin alongside Jack Straw, Baroness Warsi, Chris Huhne and Bonnie Greer, chaired by David Dimbleby, was viewed by over eight million people – more than twice the show's previous record high. Everyone was expecting a verbal fight and the audience was not left disappointed. There was a tension in the air so thick

you could see it from your sofa. From start to finish, each panel-
list denounced Griffin's views on immigration and being British.

The BNP might have enjoyed little support that night, but
there were serious concerns expressed about Britain's borders
being out of control. For every welcome denunciation of the
far right, the *Question Time* audience was equally clear that not
enough was done to keep immigration in check.

I sat cold listening to the hostile crowd, wondering if they were
talking about some other place. Surely it was not the Britain I
knew. And was about to join.

That afternoon I had carefully looked over my application
form for what the government calls 'indefinite leave to remain';
permanent residency in the plain English conspicuously absent
in the countless immigration documents spread across my desk.
I had printed off a copy several months earlier and kept it to one
side until that day. I had received a message out of the blue from
Human Resources at my then employer Newcastle University,
informing me of something important: if I did not extend my
work visa, such as through permanent residency, I would be
fired when my current visa expired. Not the kind of email anyone wants to see. A lovely start to a long day. OK, so I can do
sarcasm. Isn't that enough to become British? Turns out it is a
lot more complicated than most people think.

The application form was long and confusing. The accompanying guidance was little better. Its careful prose the masterpiece
of a committee that probably never once spoke to anyone

who had to complete their paperwork. Like doing a tax self-assessment form, but duller.

The form wanted to know everything about me worth knowing – or, at least, worth knowing to a bureaucrat – covering the previous five years, including home addresses, where I had worked and my bank account details. Oh, and it asked me if I had ever 'glorified' terrorism – presumably suicide bombers would come clean and answer that honestly. There were the sections I expected, such as questions asking about my non-existent criminal record. But there were others I didn't care for, like having to list each and every day I had spent outside the United Kingdom since I moved from America.

But then I discovered it, catching me by surprise. Buried in the middle was a section I had overlooked when I first scanned the form months earlier – and I began to panic. The section clearly stated that I should bring proof of having passed the Life in the UK test. *Huh?* No one had ever said a peep about this – and not the surprise I wanted with only two months left before my temporary work visa expired.

A quick search on Google revealed this test was none other than the Life in the United Kingdom *citizenship* test. Confession time: I did not want to become a British citizen.

I enjoyed my job lecturing university students. Academic positions are hard to find and I was not looking for a change after only five years in my role. I was not looking for handouts – after all, I was an American and as a non-EU citizen I was forbidden from claiming public benefits. That could change if I had citizenship, but that was not part of my plans at that time. Besides, becoming a permanent resident wouldn't change that anyway. Once upon a time US patriots fought a battle for independence with the motto 'no taxation without representation' – and yet here I was happy to pay my tax with no vote to show for it. Feel the earth move? That is my American forefathers spinning in their graves. They've been doing that a lot ever since.

Still shocked I had to pass a citizenship test simply to keep working in the same job, I did what anyone in my position would do: I found an online practice test – and I failed it big time. Like, only a couple correct and almost every one categorically wrong. I remember thinking to myself, 'Oh no. This was a test I had to actually *study* for!' I ordered the official handbook and a sample test guide that would be delivered in the post by the end of the week. Twenty pounds not so well spent.

I then went home hoping to forget about the test until morning. The number and scale of requirements for permanent residency were quickly doing my head in. But that was simply not to be as soon I switched on my telly to find the Nick Griffin Show courtesy of *Question Time*, capping off an awful day.

There is a serious gulf – maybe the size of an ocean – between what the public says it wants on immigration and how governments respond to it. A generally popular perception exists – and many readers will share it – that Britain's borders are uncontrolled. 'How can they be controlled if net migration is rising?'

some might ask. Certainly newspaper headlines readily give the impression that the UK's borders are as watertight as a damp sponge.

The reality would shock most people. New immigration rules are changed all the time. Virtually every day I receive messages from the Home Office alerting me to that day's changes to what the rules are and how they are to be applied. This makes it very difficult to keep up. Welcome to the not-so-glamorous coal face of British immigration policy.

There is no better illustration of how good intentions can turn out so very badly than the British citizenship test. It fundamentally changed how becoming British works. Previously, people learned they had citizenship when it was confirmed through the post. The test now meant there was more to it than simply living in the country for a few years and then filling in an application form.

The Life in the UK citizenship test is essentially a short exam. There are twenty-four multiple-choice questions to answer in forty-five minutes. Eighteen or more must be answered correctly to pass. Over 1.5 million tests have been sat since it was introduced in 2005.

In 2009, the test cost £32.24 in exact change payable only immediately before sitting the test. I used to think having the correct coinage was a secret extra question meant to trip applicants up and see if they knew their pounds from their pence. Times have changed since. Now the test costs fifty quid and payable online when booking. The golden rule of immigration is the costs keep going up and the bills keep coming earlier.

If you fail the test, you can retake it until you pass. The current record is held by an unknown and unfortunate soul who sat the citizenship test sixty-four times before passing. At the current price of £50 a sitting, this would cost £3,200. The test can be sat no more than once per week. This may not sound like a problem, but it can be difficult to book a time at a local test centre. The earliest I could book was one month later.

Failing the test costs not just the fees, but also precious time you might not know is needed before a visa expires. If I had failed my test, I would be unable to book a second before my visa ran out and I would be forced to sell off everything I had in a fortnight before returning back to my former home town of New Haven, Connecticut. Quite simply, if I didn't pass my test, I would be sent packing. No pressure then.

The aim of the citizenship test is a popular one. It is meant to confirm that someone shares the same basic values as others in society and has sufficient general knowledge about the country. Former immigration minister Phil Woolas told me that backing for a citizenship test by Tony Blair's government was 'given a boost' by a combination of factors, including rising immigration from Eastern Europe, riots in cities like Oldham and Burnley, and 9/11.

In short, passing the test is supposed to show a person has integrated into the community and is not about, as Woolas told me, 'what plays Shakespeare wrote'. Just about everybody I have spoken to who was born in the UK believes it is crucial that anyone wanting to become British is willing and able to integrate into and contribute to British society. The citizenship test is a certification that someone makes the grade.

The British citizenship test is best known as the test few British citizens can pass. The irony that foreigners must know more about their new country's institutions and cultural history than native Britons in order to share equal citizenship is lost on no one. An American lawyer from the south-west told me that fellow solicitors at her UK firm barely knew a correct answer to any of the questions. An Australian currently applying for British citizenship told me it is like the government is trying 'to trip people up' with inessential facts that would require effort to memorise. Laura, who was born British, told me, 'I think the current citizenship test is ridiculous – I would fail it and I've lived here all my life!' It's hard to disagree with the view that any test of Britishness for migrants should be a test most British citizens could pass too.

We immigrants do rather well in spite of the abstruse questions. Most pass on the first attempt. Of the 737,559 tests sat between January 2011 and June 2015, there were 539,958 passes – 73 per cent. This pass rate is declining in recent years, dropping from 77 per cent or higher to about 62 per cent over the past two years. The cause is that more people are required to take the test in order to have permanent residency or citizenship. Pass rates can vary widely by nationality. The Americans and Australians pass 98 per cent of tests sat – coincidentally, they also use citizenship tests – while Bangladesh and Turkey nationals pass only 45 per cent of the time. There are no statistics for pass rates by gender or age.

This does not mean it is easy. The Australian singer Natalie Imbruglia has said becoming British was a very emotional experience after living in Britain for over twenty years. She admitted that, despite her long acquaintance with the country, passing the Life in the UK test was no simple matter. 'None of my friends knew any of the answers,' she said, so 'I had to study – I got a tutor!'

The citizenship test has been through several editions. Each has had its share of problems. The first test handbook appeared in 2004 ahead of the test launch in 2005. The text was immortalised in the *London Review of Books* as 'the funniest book currently available in the English language'. Perhaps the most famous of questions reported from the test was about what to do if you accidentally knock over someone's drink in a pub. Answer: apologise and offer to buy them another. Once the giggling subsided, a lot of people I spoke with thought that was probably an acceptable query about British etiquette – almost as crucial as knowing how to queue! But any trace has since been removed from subsequent tests. Such is the high price to be paid when any hint of public ridicule sets in.

There were errors galore. These ranged from mistakes about which country Charles II was exiled in to misquoting Sir Winston Churchill. The most glaring mistake the first test made was the total number of MPs in the UK. The citizenship test claimed there were 645. This was one off – there were actually 646 at the time. A simple mistake to make for probably most citizens, but it makes you wonder when even ministers and distinguished authorities don't know the answers to a test migrants must pass to become British.

Bernard Crick had led the advisory group that recommended to the Blair government how the test should be structured. He and several group members then wrote the test handbook. When asked about the many avoidable factual problems in the test handbook, Crick told *The Guardian* that 'there are errors in it because it was done fairly quickly'. If only that excuse would suffice these days for anybody else. To be fair, his group was under intense time pressure because relevant immigration applications had been put on hold until its release.

Unsurprisingly, Blair's government swiftly produced a revised, polished and more readable second edition two years later, during the last weeks of John Reid's short stint as Home Secretary. If the first edition read like a poorly written textbook, the new edition was more like a boring handbook more effective at inducing sleep than any medication. Confusingly, not all chapters in the test handbook were included in any test questions, such as information about British history, like the Magna Carta or World War II, and some basic law, like what rights someone has under arrest. This gave space for key questions about the technicalities of government departments and their programmes. Not the kinds of things someone might expect from a test aiming to ensure integration into British society unless you were in the Home Office.

But, what everyone really wants to know is what is actually *in* the test. What does the government consider to be a good test for Britishness?

I know this edition of the test very well: I sat and passed it. The questions can be divided into three groups: the good, the bad and the very ugly.

The 'good' questions are the kinds of things most people would expect to find on the test. These include whether 'the Geordie dialect is spoken in Tyneside' – getting that wrong is near-certain automatic rejection in Newcastle, where I took the test. Another is knowing which 'government department is responsible for collecting taxes'. This is also fairly easy, with HMRC flanked by incorrect answers like the Home Office and 'the Central Office of Information'.

Some of the good questions are intentionally tricky. I know that GCSE stands for 'General Certificate of Secondary Education', but others might be thrown off guard by alternative answers like 'Graduate Certificate of Secondary Education' or 'Grade Certificate of School Education'. So far, so OK.

Then there are the 'bad' questions. These are a problem largely because they became quickly outdated: there was a gap of six years between the second and third editions of the test, during which much changed. For example, the second edition corrected the number of MPs from 645 to 646.

The only problem was that Parliament changed it to 650 for the 2010 general election. But still the question remained on the test: 'How many parliamentary constituencies are there?' The options were 464, 564, 646 and 664. The correct answer – 646 – was factually untrue. The test also failed to identify the number of British Members of the European Parliament, claiming it was seventy-eight when it had changed to seventy-two.

We all have our favourites and for me these are the ugly questions. A question I actually had on my test was 'Which two places can you go to if you need a National Insurance number?' To get this right, both correct options must be selected. The options were Department for Education and Skills, Home Office, Job-centre Plus and Social Security Office. The 'correct' answers were the last two, but there is a big twist. One of the correct answers – the Social Security Office – no longer existed while the test was run. People had to select it as a place you could go even though there were none to be found any more. The Department for Education and Skills had also been rebranded while this was a live question.

But the fact that two departments no longer existed, including one of the correct answers, is not why this question was my favourite. The reason is that I went to none of them to get my National Insurance number. While living in Sheffield, I phoned the local Home Office number and they arranged for me to be interviewed in city centre at an office in the Department of Work and Pensions. So to actually acquire my number I went via one

of the 'incorrect' answers – and yet had to say something different to pass a test so I could confirm I had sufficient institutional
knowledge warranting my becoming a permanent resident.
The mind boggles – and it makes you seriously question if anyone really knows what is on the test beyond the people like me
who have to pass it.

It is easy to wonder what any of this has to do with British
values and integration. One clue to what the revised test makers thought important is a question that really stands out: what
is a quango? Yes, *a quango*. I genuinely wonder – I really do, or
at least when I am restlessly bored – about how many British-
born citizens believe the fact that this acronym stands for
'quasi-autonomous non-governmental organisation' is crucial
information. These are not the values of British citizens, but the
bureaucrats who assess their paperwork – and maybe even enjoy it.

To be clear, I have no problem with bureaucrats. Some are my
proverbial best friends. But there is a problem when the values
of a professional class become substituted for those of everyone
else. And worst of all, no one seems to notice.

It would be fair to say that the problems with the test were
obvious from the start. I taught political philosophy to university
students and had little idea how many MPs there were –
I could not vote, after all, as an American – and I had not heard
of half the government departments listed. This was a test I did
not want to take for citizenship because at the time I had given
virtually no thought to it.

Want to liven up a dinner party? Whip out the citizenship test handbook and see how many answers no one in the room knows. It's a laugh. The test became a part of my life. I clearly live on the edge. When I went out to see friends, people would inevitably ask what I was up to and the answer was simple: I had a few weeks only to ace the British citizenship test. Cue surprised faces, and the sound of audible gasps followed by begging to hear some of the questions. If it hadn't been such a serious matter, it might have even been a bit enjoyable.

It was in running sample questions past interested friends and students that I gradually came to discover how much of what the test claimed was correct was actually factually untrue. Yes, this did increase my insecurity about how well I would perform. As an academic, I always did very well on tests. But those were exams based on correct facts. Until the UK citizenship test, I had not sat a test based on incorrect and outdated information before. I was in a brave new world.

Admittedly, I did not shout out to all who would listen that the test was becoming a farce. My successfully applying for permanent residency was too important to wake sleeping beasts in Whitehall. I made a vow to myself at the time that when this matter was finished I was going to make a difference in improving the system for others coming through after me. Sitting the citizenship test changed me – literally – for ever. I'm still talking about it. The experience affected others too, but the normal reaction is to forget about it and move on. But I could not – and cannot – do that.

Citizenship can be so easily taken for granted until you find yourself fighting – and at substantial financial costs – to earn it.

An immigration officer told me that the British citizenship test 'creates a large degree of anxiety in applicants that seems unjustified' and avoidable. That is an understatement. Preparing for and taking the test is a lonely business. Of course, there is no reminder in the post or by email, pointing out that the test must be passed and offering advice on how to succeed. Everyone is left on their own to figure this out and then pass or fail.

Test centres I have visited tend to be in the worst parts of town. One person I spoke with described them as places where 'you should not walk to by yourself'. My test was in a building site directly opposite the local hospital. This was convenient in case my day went wrong – I might need to be admitted to A&E if I failed, to help me recover from the shock.

To be fair, the test was over in a few minutes. I had studied my test handbook until I knew it cold and spent most of the forty-five minutes allowed for the test waiting for others to finish. This is not unique among those who have passed. Carol, a South African, completed the test alongside her son in six minutes and passed. Similar stories are reported to me all the time. There was no truth or falsity, only what was correct or incorrect for the test. Lauren, a researcher in the Midlands, said the test was 'the worst I've ever taken in my life – and I am a PhD student'. Quite.

Our 'test authoriser' for the UK citizenship test was a Polish national named Ryszard. He logged us each into a separate computer and the test was taken online through a secure website. When finished, the results were submitted and we left the room to sit in a waiting area until the full time for the test had passed. Not all were able to complete the test on time in my group. We were each called individually to be told the good or bad news.

Failed tests can be resat and another must be booked online. If you pass, the good news is it is over, although the bad news is no one who has not taken the test understands what passing it means. One of the first things you do when the citizenship test is passed is tell the world on social media. Maybe two hundred people congratulated me on becoming British – only to have me inform them that the *citizenship* test is a test required for permanent *residency*: it is after you have residency for a year that citizenship can be applied for. Not only has the government failed to make a British citizenship test most Britons can pass, but even fewer know its purpose. This is through no fault of the public. Ministers can and should have done much more. They have dropped the ball.

On guessing the test questions correctly, I received a 'Pass Notification Letter', which is as soulless and anticlimactic as it sounds. A computer print-off in black and white on standard paper with a splotchy red stamp bearing the crucial words 'Life in the UK Test Pass'. Not the kind of thing you put on the wall to brighten up a room. Dated November 2009, my letter states up top in prose that will only stir the most unfeeling bureaucrat from a deep fog:

Following your test today in knowledge of life in the United Kingdom this is to certify that you have reached the level required for the purposes of obtaining indefinite leave to remain under the Immigration Rules or for naturalisation as a British citizen under Section 6 of the British National Act 1981.

No need for Byron or Shelley when you have these deep words to ponder.

Now that I had passed, I could book an appointment to submit my permanent residency application in person and have it approved that day. This cannot be done until the citizenship test is passed. It was a good thing I phoned immediately because there was only one slot left in the UK. It was in Liverpool early on a Saturday morning – this meant booking return trains and accommodation for the Friday night so I could make the appointment.

The journey was unforgettable. I sat scrunched in a seat that seemed built for young adults – I did not seem to fit comfortably in my Transpennine Express coach. It did not help that I spent the full journey clinging to my luggage and briefcase. I was required to show original documents, including at least five years of bank statements and payslips. Nothing was left to chance.

The Friday evening wait was awful. I was consumed by stress. I have always sailed through every interview I have had with anyone in the immigration business, but the stakes were so very high: success, and life continues as normal; failure, and it's time to start all over again in the US. I do not think I have ever known such anxiety.

I arrived early for my appointment. After clearing security, I was led to a room upstairs where the first thing they did was take my money. At least I knew what the priorities were. About £1,100 disappeared before my eyes in the time it took to punch my four-digit code in the card machine. No cheques accepted.

Once I had paid, I could join the queue. The atmosphere was uncomfortably tense. I sat in an open, square-shaped room along-side the other hapless souls gathered that morning. The wet drizzle outside mimicked the soft tears on the faces of many of us inside. There were four people ahead of me to speak to border agents. All their conversations took place in the same open space while the border agents sat behind thick glass. Each of the four before me were rejected. I could hear why – as we all could. Privacy was kept outside the waiting area. We were in the jungle now.

The biggest hurdles were not accepting British values or making a contribution to society, but satisfying box-ticking tech-nicalities designed to exclude – and that is what they did. The first couple I noticed being considered were rejected for submit-ting the wrong form. If they had selected differently, things might have turned out very differently. A second person came with the correct form, but lacked some supporting documents – I came fully prepared yet these were not requested from me. If only he had been so lucky. Getting permanent residency should not be like a crap shoot.

A particularly awkward moment was sitting on a stool next to a Spanish citizen. He and I were both applying for permanent residency, sitting opposite our own border agents carefully flipping through our applications. As my application was being checked to ensure I had not been out of the country beyond a set number of days that would make me ineligible, I heard the other agent tell the Spaniard that she had counted his time out of the country and 'I am afraid your application will be unsuccessful'. He had visited his young children living in Spain with his ex-partner more often than the Home Office allowed.

I will never forget her using the future tense as if dangling it in front of him like it was conjured from a crystal ball. The man just wept. He had spent much more than I had, as he had to pay additional charges for dependents. My border agent swiftly confirmed everything with my application was in order and I was successful. But I can still visualise the man who sat next to me. For an hour or so we sat side by side, only to have different fates.

Being a permanent resident without citizenship is an odd status to have. As your official letter explains, you have the right to work wherever you like in the UK, but you have no entitlement to vote or take public benefit. Despite not being British citizens, permanent residents can make British citizens: any child born in the UK would be a British citizen regardless of parentage. Most people find that surprising.

After a year and a day of being a permanent resident, you can apply for British citizenship. This can be done through a local council – for a fee, of course – and it is largely a quick box-ticking exercise. Most migrants who have permanent residency in the UK and apply for British citizenship are successful: 91 per cent were accepted in 2015. This is because both have the same requirements: so long as there is no change in status, all tests – including the citizenship test – are fulfilled.

When I became a British citizen at a local ceremony in 2011, I made a vow to myself to make some contribution to improving how citizenship is done. Later that same afternoon I was contacted by a producer at BBC Radio 4. His wife worked for local station BBC Newcastle and had phoned me earlier to talk on air about being from the greater New York City area on the ten-year anniversary of 11 September. She had naturally asked just where I was from when she heard my accent and I happened to mention how much I wanted to change the citizenship test run by the then coalition government. She sensed this was more a national story that could go big, and had her husband ring me as soon as I finally had my citizenship – I was not doing anything until I had that in hand.

We agreed I would be interviewed on air. But first he wanted to get the Home Secretary Theresa May on air with me. As it turned out, this was the first rebuff of many. To this day, May has never agreed once to go live with me on immigration. I can only ponder the reasons why. So I recorded the interview for Radio 4 on a Thursday. And then I waited.

In my interview, I highlighted the many problems that existed in the system. Primarily, my concern was that much of the test had become outdated and even obsolete. I explained that I wanted an updated test for British citizenship, but I also said something I have come to regret. I called on the government to act and in particular to include information about British history and culture. I ended by offering my help to improve the test, as someone who had taken it, an immigrant on the front line. Someone was listening.

The programme finally aired the following Monday – and immediately before a new speech on immigration from none other than the Prime Minister, David Cameron. Snuggled in his comments were words that rang out loud and clear to me. I was right. It was time for a substantively updated test – and it was to include British history and culture questions for the first time. I was delighted. So much progress with my first effort! Little did I know how difficult further progress would be.

I first wrote to Damian Green, the Minister of State for Immigration, that week. I highlighted errors I had found in the citizenship test handbook and offered my assistance to help fix the test. The following month I heard back from Ann Robertson, the Migration Policy Leader at the Home Office. She wrote to say her team had 'recently commenced a full review' and 'we will take on board your helpful comments' with possible opportunities for further involvement 'at a later stage'. I never heard from Green or Robertson about this again and felt like I might give up.

A full year went by without hearing another word. I later spoke on a panel at a migration conference alongside Newcastle MP Chi Onwurah at the Tyneside Irish Centre. My talk about the problems with the citizenship test went over well and Chi wrote to the government to find out what was being done about false answers counting as correct on the test. She forwarded to me the reply from Damian Green in September 2012 that the new test handbook planned for that year would remedy 'some out of date information'. Invalid questions were removed in the meantime.

And then it happened. Later than promised, the government finally produced its new, glossy Life in the UK test handbook. A bright red, white and blue cover with full-colour photographs throughout, in a far more readable layout. The book's appearance gave the impression the government might actually want more migrants to come into the UK and become citizens.

The current citizenship test is a missed opportunity that deserves all the criticism it receives. It's difficult to know where to start. The handbook appeared in January 2013 for use on all tests from late March. However, the Home Office was publishing two different test handbooks – the second edition and the third edition – at the same time. Both stated on their covers that they were the one and only 'official' handbook for the test. But one was for tests until the last week of March and the other for those afterwards. Neither book said which test it was for. This was important because they tested very different things and studying for one would not help in passing the other. It is fairly certain that people used the wrong books for the wrong exams.

That was not all. The new handbook said there were twenty-four questions on the test. But it said nothing about how many must be answered correctly to pass or what format the questions would take. Any school or university that tried to pull off a similar assessment stunt for their qualifications would be shut down as incompetent. But not a single Tory or Liberal Democrat minister in the coalition government seemed to notice. Why would they?

The only way to find out what to expect on the test is to buy more books from the Home Office. The handbook itself is £12.99. There is also a companion practice test book costing £7.99 and a very curious 'Official Study Guide' also worth £7.99. The official study guide is bizarre because, like the handbook, it lists the number and types of test questions, but not how many need to be answered correctly. It is as if the government does not want anyone to know.

Stranger still, the official study guide – which is cheaper and more compact than the official handbook – is no official study guide. It can help someone study for parts of the test, but it is openly selective in the material it includes, and only the official handbook – it can get dizzying how many of these texts remind you how 'official' they are and yet seem so badly put together – actually has everything one needs to know. Only the Home Office would produce a study guide that is an incomplete resource for its official tests.

The closer I looked into the new test, the more I found that had been badly bungled. Inspecting the practice test booklet, I discovered that studying only two or three of the five chapters should be enough to pass any test – the chapters were weighted very differently and skewed. This meant that to become British you need not know much of what the government thought important.

In 2013, I published the only comprehensive report on the UK citizenship test, concluding it was 'unfit for purpose', and my press release stating it was like 'a bad pub quiz' went down a real treat. My report was covered in over 300 media outlets worldwide and even got a mention on BBC2's *Mock the Week*.

I uncovered several serious problems with the current citizenship test. The first was that it is impractical. The test handbook exclaims it is 'a compendium of useful information' to help migrants 'integrate into society and play a full role in your local community' – so this key idea motivating the creation of the citizenship test remains rock solid. The Home Secretary Theresa May claimed the new test would enable migrants 'to participate fully in our society' and her then immigration minister Mark Harper said only 'mundane' information had been 'stripped out'.

But what was actually removed from earlier editions was information everyone must know. This included how to contact emergency services, report a crime, register with a GP and use the NHS – all of this was cut out. In its place, May and Harper wanted migrants to know the approximate age of Big Ben's clock (apparently 150 years) and the height of the London Eye in both feet (443) and metres (135). The test handbook is clear that 'questions are based on ALL parts of the handbook' and nothing, save the glossary, was off limits. The citizenship test had a new focus – out with the practical trivia, in with the purely trivial.

The government did not like it one bit when I started doing national and local press interviews highlighting how impractical their new test was – and it caught them off guard. After all, why would anyone know about this stuff? They certainly did not know much of what they were talking about. Their best response came from Lord Taylor of Holbeach, who said, 'The majority of those applying will have been in the UK for at least five years and should therefore be aware of practical matters, such as emergency services.' That's all right then.

In fact, the handbook does require people to know a full range of 'practical matters' someone resident for several years would know, such as: London and Edinburgh are UK cities; London is the UK's biggest city; British currency includes the £1 coin and £5 note; Christmas Day is 25 December; the Queen is the head of state; refuse bags should only be out when due for collection; social networking – according to the citizenship test handbook – is 'a popular way for people to stay in touch'; and – my favourite – everyone must be reminded that, yes, the United States of America is an independent country. Facts like how to contact emergency services are precisely the kinds of things most people would expect a test about 'Life in the UK' to include. After all, immigration minister James Brokenshire said in a written statement in spring 2016 that the test is meant to reinforce a shared 'expectation' that new citizens will abide by the law, engage in our society and respect 'our shared values'. But the evidence for the test meeting these expectations is difficult to find. The test migrants sit can seem very distant from the claims ministers make to defend its continued use.

Inconsistencies were another problem. As noted previously, earlier editions of the test handbook got wrong the number of MPs. I have heard many people say that getting this right did not seem all that important to becoming British – although hugely embarrassing for governments to have left it uncorrected for so long. The new test avoids getting it wrong by cutting it out. So no one need know how many MPs are in Parliament. But you still must still know the number of elected representatives in the regional Welsh Assembly, Scottish Parliament and Northern Ireland Assembly. It is difficult at best to see why knowing the number of MPs is unimportant, but these other bodies are crucial.

There are other examples. You need not know there is a UK Supreme Court, but you are required to know about the lesser courts. The strangest inconsistency is that the test handbook includes five telephone numbers. These include the national domestic helpline and HMRC self-assessment hotline. But there are also the phone numbers for the House of Commons, Scottish Parliament and Welsh Assembly so that 'you can get information, book tickets or arrange tours through visitor services'. I have never met anyone who did not work for these bodies that knew the contact numbers or thought it important in the slightest. But, incredibly, the test handbook neglects to include the Northern Ireland Assembly. Another rushed – and botched – job?

The current citizenship test is chock full of spurious information that serves little purpose in testing Britishness. The test handbook catalogues nearly 3,000 facts, including 278 historical dates covering seventy-seven people. None of these dates includes either of the Queen's birthdays – and it might be obvious that this quirky British fact would merit inclusion if any birthday did. But it does not.

Instead, the handbook lists four dates and several key events for the only non-royal in the book deemed so important he is the only one over 280 pages whose spouse is named – and must be memorised. I am not talking about Sir Winston Churchill, Admiral Nelson or William the Conqueror. No, I refer to Sake Dean Mahomed.

The citizenship test handbook requires everyone to know that Mahomed was born in 1759 and raised in 'the Bengal region' of India, later serving in the Bengal Army. Everyone is to know he moved to Ireland to elope with 'an Irish girl called Jane Daly' in 1786. But it is what we learn next that might explain why a Tory-led coalition government included him at all: 'In 1810 he opened the Hindoostane Coffee House in George Street, London.' The significance? 'It was the first curry house to open in Britain' – at least it is an insight into the minds of whatever committee rushed this through to print.

We can delve further into the government's thinking behind the test when we look carefully for specific changes made for the third edition. The previous version had a lengthy glossary running to more than thirty pages. This was now reduced by two-thirds. Look at the terms cut out and see if any pattern emerges: ante-natal care, asylum, bursary, disability, discrimination, emergency services, free press, harassment, higher education, immigration, legal aid, maternity and paternity leave, racially motivated crime, sick pay, torture, victim and welfare benefits. Only a few terms were added, like 'House (history, for example, House of York)', rural and sonnet. Out with the new and in with the old in an antiquated vision of Little Britain by committee. We can only speculate why it is that the government no longer thinks being British includes knowing about education, health care and pro-tection from discrimination.

Unsurprisingly, the test handbook forgets that many British citizens are women. The historical chapter lists the dates of birth for twenty-nine men and just four women. Only male musicians get a mention. In the Home Office's triumphant press release announcing the new test handbook's launch and noting the 'people that have shaped Britain', nine men are noted but no women. How interesting it would be to learn if any women were in the group that wrote the handbook – I suspect not.

And then there are the new questions. Would-be citizens need to know that people spoke Celtic during the Iron Age. My favour-ite true-or-false question is 'Catherine Howard was the sixth wife of Henry VIII' – the answer is false because she was not the sixth, but the fifth. Being one off on who married Henry VIII in which order can see someone barred from becoming British. I doubt most people know that Inigo Jones designed both the Banqueting House in Whitehall and the Queen's House at Greenwich.

But there are some other treats. One question asks, 'When walking your dog in a public place, what must you ensure?' My first guess would be to keep the dog on a lead, especially around other people. However, this is a multiple-choice test and that is not an option. Instead, we have options like: ensure the dog wears a special coat, keep the dog no more than three metres away, make sure there is no contact with other dogs – all of these are incorrect – and then the right answer: the dog must wear a collar with its name. That is what being British means to people writing the test: knowing where to find the name of someone else's dog. I admit this never came up remotely in any discussion I've had with anybody on what Britishness is and what should be tested, across hundreds of conversations.

Another question asks about what responsibility someone might have as 'a citizen or permanent resident' of the UK. The first option is 'using your car as much as possible'. That might be the kind of answer that former *Top Gear* presenter Jeremy Clarkson might give, but it is false. A second is to visit local pubs regularly. Many pubs are struggling at the moment and this might sound plausible, but it is also not right. The third choice is to keep an allotment – a very British pastime and you need not ask Alan Titchmarsh to know that. Still not correct. The true answer is 'looking after the environment'. Surprised? Welcome to the new politics.

If any of this sounds confusing, it is because the test *is* confusing. The House of Lords held a short debate not long after my report was published and peers from the Labour, Liberal Democrat and Tory benches made reference to it, including Angela Smith, Baroness Smith of Basildon, now shadow Leader of the House of Lords, and Roger Roberts.

When asked about whether information in the test handbook like the age of Big Ben's clock and height of the London Eye was actually on the test, Lord Taylor again spoke for the government and announced that no one need memorise these facts because – take his word for it – neither appears on any test. This confirms the test handbook has more information than necessary – perhaps intended to ensure more people fail. It is shocking that some facts presented are actually omitted from every test – but this information avoided discovery until months after its release, when the government was asked more than once to respond to the criticisms in my critical report about the test. There is still no note in the handbook confirming this. So memorise everything in the book except the stuff not on the test, which is only knowable if you ask the right questions in the House of Lords.

Despite its many flaws, I remain in favour of the citizenship test – just not the one we have. Several countries introduced similar tests in the wake of 9/11. But often the information is easy to locate, more transparent and freely available. The Australian test includes information about what being a citizen of Australia means, listing such things as a duty to vote, to work in the

Australian defence force or public service, and to serve on a jury. Australian values include a respect for equal worth, freedoms of speech and religion, support for democracy and the rule of law, and tolerance. There is also information on demographics and general history.

Not everything in the Australian test handbook is commendable. Some of the descriptions read awkwardly. For example, consider: 'Sir Donald Bradman was the greatest cricket batsman of all time. He was small and slight but amazingly quick on his feet, playing his shots almost like a machine.' Perhaps knowing about Sir Donald's cricket acumen is an important part of Australia's cultural history. I am much less sure that 'so who was small and slight, but like a machine' is the best way to test that point.

The American test – first launched in 1986 – is more straightforward. It includes historical and political facts, but these are much less contentious in the form and content. Questions range from knowing the US Constitution is the supreme law of the land to identifying the name of the sitting US President. Someone might be asked to name one of the many Native American tribes or one of the two longest rivers, the Mississippi and the Missouri.

My report into the UK citizenship test did not simply expose problems, but also highlighted recommendations – twelve in all. I still think the current test handbook is presented well and should retain its full-colour, reader-friendly format. The test should keep its broad coverage of subjects. There are minor, but not unimportant, points made: for instance, each new edition should state clearly its start date, to avoid confusion. All information included should be consistent and gender balanced, and should correct for errors or omissions in the current test handbook.

But the main recommendation is that a full public consultation is now long overdue. We need to ask what new citizens should be expected to know and gather some evidence in support. It should be shocking that more than a decade has passed since Bernard Crick led a group to write the citizenship test, which came into being long before net migration rose sharply and immigration became a top public concern. Over 1.5 million tests have been sat and I am now one of many who have become British through the new, post-2001 rules.

Surprisingly, there has never been any consultation with either the general public or the naturalised British citizens who have sat the test. This is a failure of policy management. If the test is meant to help ensure new citizens are integrated, they must be asked about their experiences. This is not about giving migrants or new citizens a veto, but about drawing attention to the importance of hearing their voices: they do not have a monopoly on assessing how well they have integrated, but similarly any feelings of alienation or estrangement ought to become known.

Yet it is doubtful the government wants to listen. When I sent a copy of my report to 10 Downing Street, it received a frosty reception. Thanks, but no thanks, more like.

If ministers bother to ask, what they hear may alarm them. The feedback I received from people who have sat the test is damning. 'Silly and patronising', 'an utter waste of time', 'I don't understand why we have a citizenship test that most citizens would fail', 'a relief to get it over with' and 'an experience to forget'. These are the words not of people who failed and are bitter but of those who passed. The view of the many who take the test is not a feeling of belonging and solidarity, but of alienation. This should be alarming.

After speaking with so many applicants, I have come to the conclusion that the current test is counterproductive. More see it as a barrier than a bridge. One person who became British said it was 'another hurdle meant to make immigration policy look legitimate' to native Britons. A former immigration tribunal presenting officer called it 'pure drivel'. The problem here is legitimacy – neither citizen nor prospective citizen has much confidence that the test as currently designed is fit for purpose.

It does not help that what everyone knows as the citizenship test is not the last step to citizenship. A more accurate description is the Life in the UK test *for residency*, because passing it is necessary for permanent residency, whereas applying for citizenship must wait for at least another year. This is now reflected in an unreported change to the test handbook's subtitle, from 'A Journey to Citizenship' to 'A Guide for New Residents'.

There are also more deep-rooted problems. Education experts I spoke with have expressed serious concerns about the 'quite poor design' that raises questions about the validity of the citizenship test. Dr Simon Child is a senior researcher at OCR, a leading awarding body for A-levels and GCSEs. It was unclear what systems were in place to ensure that each test examined the same kinds of things with equal difficulty when the types of questions were so varied and wordings vague.

An expert who attended meetings with Crick when the test was first launched – and asked not be identified – said it was nothing short of a 'reputational car crash' because it was 'testing completely the wrong things'. This person agreed that the test was neither valid nor reliable.

Both highlighted to me how the test has evolved to become a very different type of qualification but this has yet to be acknowledged. Their point is that the current test is a decisive break away from earlier versions. In essence, it is simply 'not testing the same things'. This is emphasised by the fact that from 2005 to 2013, the test had been a confirmation that the taker had not only sufficient knowledge of life in the UK, but also sufficient knowledge of English. This latter requirement has changed and is no longer a part of the citizenship test; this is discussed in the next chapter.

The result is that we have had fundamentally different tests over the past ten years, all resulting in the same qualification. Not only is this an appalling failure of quality control, but it raises serious questions about the exercise as a proper test, whatever one's views on British values and wider immigration policy.

So what is the purpose of the test? If it is to be a barrier to residency and citizenship, it should be modelled very differently. Research by Oxford University's Migration Observatory found that the test has not appeared to have had much of an effect on the number of people becoming British. Their report says it is 'possible that there would have been more' new British citizens had we not introduced the test – but then again it is possible that there would have been fewer.

The Office for National Statistics shows there were notable increases in applications for citizenship from 211,911 in 2005 to 232,262 in 2013. This probably reflects the launch of the citizenship test in November 2005 and the requirement that all naturalisation applicants take the test from October 2013. Of the 125,653 grants of citizenship in 2014, most were to nationals from India (22,425) and Pakistan (13,000), followed by Nigeria (8,076), South Africa (5,289) and Bangladesh (3,892). All these countries are part of the Commonwealth – and their citizens were once British nationals as citizens of the United Kingdom and Colonies. The UK's imperial history continues to have relevance for immigration to Britain.

David Blunkett was the Home Secretary who led the introduction of the test. He wrote to me thanking me for the work I had done examining the citizenship test's development. Blunkett said the government had made 'a complete dog's dinner' of the test and he was pleased to see the publicity I had drawn to it. He added: 'I hope the front bench start using this and making a monkey out of the Home Office ministers,' while admitting,

'We didn't get the first test entirely right, but this one is a complete mess.'

A similar view was expressed by another former Home Secretary, Jacqui Smith. She told me that 'the principle is right' regarding the citizenship test. It's useful to have such an exercise. Like so many things, though, the devil is in the detail, and she admits it is difficult to construct a multiple-choice exam that can demonstrate whether or not someone should become a British citizen. No test can be a guarantee of loyalty or acceptance of values. In the aftermath of the 2013 Boston Marathon bombing, it emerged that Tamerlan Tsarnaev, the eldest of two brothers behind the deadly attack, had passed his US citizenship only three months before. The test can serve a useful purpose, but we should not expect or demand too much for what it can deliver.

Blunkett and Smith are right: the test is worth keeping, if we are up for the challenge of reforming it. What is needed is a review that asks current citizens about their views on Britishness and British values and what this means to them today. Crucially, any such review must engage with people who have sat the test. They might listen to one naturalised citizen who told me the test should be improved to 'make information useful – I can't remember any of it now'. This is not good enough. If the test is to remain a key requirement for permanent residency and citizenship, it should include information worth knowing.

The citizenship test should be relevant. Elena, originally from Russia and living in the north-east, told me she just had 'to pass, not to learn'. Ideally, we should work towards a hurdle worth jumping. For the moment, the test is more like a necessary procedure to be merely endured for no greater purpose than sticking a cross in a box on a long application form.

But, what is also needed is public confidence. Arizona, where I used to live, now requires high school students to pass a citizenship test in order to graduate. Other states have also followed suit, including Idaho, Louisiana, North Dakota, South Carolina, Tennessee, Utah and Wisconsin. This is an excellent idea championed by Labour MP Tristram Hunt for the UK. This is not about creating barriers that keep people apart, but about building a bridge that brings people together.

If the test is only meant to help keep people out, there are more efficient and fair ways of doing it. The residency requirements can be lengthened or the income threshold raised. But if this is not the citizenship test's purpose, we must ensure that passing it is a worthwhile achievement and not only a way to collect further fees. The test and its reputation are broken. It is often mocked with little concern for the tens of thousands of people who take it each year. Ministers can be quicker to say they share public concerns about immigration than to act to resolve them. A national conversation is waiting to be had. Testing citizenship may not be easy, but we can do much better than the dog's dinner we have at present. The test should be either reformed or binned – skipping along singing, 'It's all right, Jack' is as defeatist as it is counterproductive. British citizens deserve better.

CHAPTER 5

THE ENGLISH QUESTION

The main concern that current British citizens have about accepting future citizens is that they should integrate into and contribute to society. This is true for people across the political spectrum and every region of the country. While there is disagreement about Britishness and what should be on citizenship tests, a solid consensus favours integration and contribution.

This is summed up well by one person I spoke to, who said that 'being a British citizen is about being a part of a community'. The key is that the path to becoming British should focus on new citizens coming together with existing citizens. This can be difficult with migrants who come with their own cultural attitudes – they may not choose to adapt or relate them to the attitudes in their new British community.

Integration and contribution can be promoted through a shared language – and successive governments have pursued integration in this way. It is widely popular with the public. Judith from the south-west told me that 'if you're going to live here, you should have some basic language skills'. A Russian citizen wanting to become British named Ekaterina went further, saying that a working knowledge of the English language should be the main requirement to be a UK citizen.

Similarly, when Joshua – a student from the south-east – told me that new citizens 'must be able to integrate', he made a point of saying that this meant they 'should be able to communicate in English'. If they could not speak English, Joshua said, this is not good for either them or the community. This was echoed by Sarah, a student living in London, who said that being incapable of speaking English was a problem because it 'can be isolating for people to be unable to integrate'.

The public are more united about the need for new citizens to integrate into their new society than they are about whether immigration is a problem. This also chimes well with the government's position. Former communities secretary Eric Pickles said: 'Speaking English is crucial for everyone to get on, integrate in their communities, interact with their neighbours and gain employment, and our society is weaker when people cannot speak the language.' For once, we all seem to be in agreement on an immigration policy.

The public's understanding of integration is based not merely on an acceptance of British values – however ethereal and contested these may be – but on an ability to share in conversations. For most people I spoke to, the level of English they thought mandatory was a basic understanding sufficient to engage with others in everyday British life. New citizens should be able to listen and respond, but also have some written skills.

Some people went further and told me – like John, a British-born citizen from the north-west – that 'we should develop an oral exam in which we assess the values of the applicant focused on tolerance, humility and togetherness'. An oral exam would help guarantee that new citizens could communicate effectively – whereas an online multiple-choice test could be passed through luck. This is a minority view, but it illustrates the kind of importance most people give to knowing English.

Knowing English has been a central requirement for new citizens for over 100 years. Long a part of the common law, it was incorporated into statute through the British Nationality and Status of Aliens Act in 1914. This is one area where the law seems to have got things right.

But there is also a twist. The Act permitted certain exceptions, which also had deep roots. New citizens were required to satisfy the Home Office they had sufficient knowledge of English – or a language with 'equality'. This has included Scots Gaelic and

Welsh, but not Ulster Scots or Irish Gaelic. As a consequence, a Welsh speaker from Patagonia migrating to the UK would be exempt from demonstrating any knowledge of English.

The legal equality of English, Scots and Welsh continued with the introduction of the Life in the UK citizenship test. While the test handbook has only ever been published in English, it used to be possible to sit the test in Scots or Welsh. This has happened only once: it was sat in Scots in 2010, and was never taken in Welsh since the test was launched in 2005. These facts came to light thanks to a Parliamentary Question asked by native Welsh speaker Roger Roberts, a Liberal Democrat peer from Llandudno, who is the vice-chair of the All Party Parliamentary Group on Migration and a leading champion of migration issues in Parliament.

Perhaps surprisingly, many people recognise that exceptions to knowing English should be permissible. What seems essential for them is that migrants can effectively communicate in everyday life with people in their local communities. If this is an area in Scotland where many speak Scots Gaelic, then this language would be a fitting substitute for English. Jonathan, a Brit born in Scotland, said that 'you can be a productive member of society without knowing English'. He made clear that 'not everyone can learn English anyway – personal circumstances must be taken into account'. Many would agree with him – and not only people living in Scotland, either.

This brings us to what I call *the English question*: how important is knowing English to becoming British?

It might first appear that it only matters insofar as it promotes integration. The great majority of the UK speaks English as a first language, and the importance of English flows from its being the dominant form of communication across most parts of the country. Making exceptions, as in the Scots Gaelic example above, also then makes good sense. This has been a part of the British legal system for a long time and perhaps rightly so.

However, my interviews with British citizens revealed something. No matter which part of the country I surveyed, every region – England, Scotland, Wales and Northern Ireland – put knowing English at the top of the list for what we should expect from new citizens. The Welsh in Wales or the Scots in Scotland did not rank Welsh or Scots Gaelic equal in importance to knowing English.

This finding surprised me somewhat. I expected to find at least a nominal commitment to language equality that was not there. I also expected a greater appreciation for giving other languages equality with English outside England, but this is not the feedback I received. On the whole, nation by nation, English rules.

This may sound like a minor discovery, but it helps explain a massive symbolic change by the coalition government that seems to have avoided any notice.

The equality of Welsh and Scots Gaelic with English, which has existed for decades, if not centuries, is under threat. In 2013, the government changed the rules. Anyone applying for permanent residency or citizenship was now required to know English

– without an exception for Welsh or Scots Gaelic. Almost overnight, a longstanding legal right was torn up and no one – not even the Scottish National Party – seems aware of it.

An immediate consequence is that the right to sit the citizenship test in Welsh or Scots Gaelic came to an end. I have spoken to more than one parliamentarian who only discovered this when I told them.

To be fair, the government did make an announcement about the change. But the statement is perhaps more interesting for what it omits than for what it says. On behalf of the government, Lord Bates said:

> The ability to speak to and understand the wider community is key to integration. As English is the language spoken throughout the UK, an ability to speak English enables interaction wherever an individual chooses to live. Therefore, a person can only meet this part of the knowledge of language and life requirement by demonstrating speaking and listening proficiency in English.

English should be promoted to best enable integration – perhaps more a government mantra than a fact, but undoubtedly widely accepted. But what this announcement glosses over is the removal of age-old exemptions for Welsh and Scots Gaelic speakers – exemptions which recognised that, for some communities, knowing English may not be enough to foster integration.

It might be said that English is sufficiently embedded into the lifeblood of the UK that any Welsh or Scots Gaelic speaker will surely possess fluency in English as well.

This is probably correct. It is certainly true that part of the reason only one person has sat the citizenship test in a language other than English is because the test handbooks are only available in English. (Unfortunately, there is no public information about whether the person who took the test in Scots Gaelic passed.) This might be seen as evidence that the equality of English with Welsh and Scots Gaelic has lived on only in theory and not in practice since the test's launch in 2005.

But, to be fair, there is some confusion about whether the government knows what it is doing. In the first pages of the current citizenship test handbook, there is a howler: 'The Life in the UK test is usually taken in English, although special arrangements can be made if you wish to take it in Welsh or Scottish Gaelic' – yes, arrangements the government chose to scrap one month after the new test was launched. It makes one wonder how much of this was planned or well known by ministers and their advisors overseeing immigration matters. (Not to mention, of course, that phrase about the test being 'usually taken in English' – a slight understatement, given that only one of over 1.5 million tests was in any other language.)

There is perhaps further confusion in that the oath or affirmation of allegiance and the pledge to the Queen and the United Kingdom required from newly fledged Brits at their citizenship ceremonies can be affirmed in either English or Welsh (if in Wales). But it cannot be said in Scots Gaelic.

Besides this, there is another anomaly. Newly elected MPs are required by law to take an oath of allegiance to the Crown on taking their seats. The wording is prescribed in the Promissory Oaths Act of 1868, which permits the oath to be said in English, Welsh, Scots Gaelic or Cornish. This raises questions about why Parliament allows some oaths of allegiance to the Crown in English only, but in multiple British languages for others. Then again, Britain's ancient customs are sometimes best grasped by not asking why it is, but for how long has it been that way – although this is still unsatisfactory.

The language requirement was not subject to any formal certification by a test until the New Labour years. Previously, sufficient language ability was assumed unless there was evidence to the contrary. This changed with the Nationality, Immigration and Asylum Act 2002, which required new citizens to take one of two routes to prove satisfactory knowledge of English.

The first was to pass the Life in the UK citizenship test, which was designed not only to confirm the applicant's knowledge of everyday British life and values, but also to guarantee they had satisfactory English – so that people with poorer English will fail. As a consequence, it was written in a terrible style. An Australian who sat the test told me she was surprised to find that a paper that 'lacked plain English clarity' was supposed to somehow confirm English fluency. Others said the test was a model in how not to write sentences or ask questions – the awkward formulations were thought to be designed to mislead even native speakers and encourage them to make mistakes.

The second route was via the ESOL with Citizenship course. ESOL – an acronym pronounced 'Ee-sol', which stands for 'English for Speakers of Other Languages' – is a course of study with many benefits and costs. There is no equivalent in Welsh or Scots Gaelic acceptable as an alternative. ESOL with Citizenship was designed for people whose English is generally poor, opening up a path to citizenship for many people that might otherwise be closed.

Unsurprisingly, this pathway was popular. From 2005 to 2013, more people took this option than the citizenship test. However, solid figures are difficult to come by. This may be explained by the diversity of ESOL provision across multiple providers delivering a suite of different programmes.

An estimated two million people have sat ESOL programmes to date. From what is known from available data, approximately 1.07 million people passed the programme between 2005 and 2012 for a pass rate of 75 per cent, comparable to the citizenship test results. But these figures must be treated with some caution as all are suspiciously rounded up to numbers ending in 00.

There are several downsides – and the ESOL with Citizenship pathway to citizenship has been closed since 2013. It assessed listening and speaking, but not writing. What's more, people learned about British citizenship as they were being introduced to English; language classes were taught using information found in the citizenship test handbook. This led to some odd-looking assessments, such as the first sample quiz I read, in which people without any prior knowledge of English were asked about the Houses of Parliament. This was probably not what most citizens regard as the first priority for learning a new language. It was certainly a far cry from my first German lessons, where we began with greetings and progressed to reading menus or learning to ask for directions. If learning English is important for integration purposes, something may be missing in ESOL's approach.

A bigger worry was finding the right class. While the citizenship test was managed by a single organisation, there were a multitude of ESOL and ESOL with Citizenship providers. This means that, unlike the set fee charged to sit the citizenship test anywhere in the country, the costs could vary considerably depending on where it was taken and what baseline level of English the student was starting from. A cursory glance at prices reveals a range from at least £200 to as much as £800 – all a lot more than the £50 citizenship test.

It can be difficult to get a place in an ESOL or ESOL with Citizenship class. Waiting lists vary as widely as their costs. Some places can take on new students on short notice, but many have waiting lists that can stretch for several months. It can take people with little English living in areas of high ESOL demand like London or Birmingham a year or more to achieve, from what I have heard from ESOL teachers. A postcode lottery appears to exist.

This might be a significant issue when it may take someone several weeks to a few months to pass and so continue with an application to the Home Office. It can easily take six months from contacting a college or educational institution for a place to completing a programme of study. If they leave it too late, an applicant may be at risk of overstaying on their visa and facing deportation. It goes without saying that the Home Office does not send emails warning prospective citizens in advance that it may take extra time to get past their red tape. If they can fail an applicant, they often do.

ESOL with Citizenship was a unique programme that some might find a weird way to learn English, but it was wonderful too. An educational manager who taught the course in Leeds told me it 'can build solidarity for students to help welcome and integrate them while they study'. The classes gave people a reason to come together. They were not just learning about English skills or British values, but learning from each other as migrants in Britain. Building lasting relationships and real friendships with others were some of the most positive aspects of the programme, and were treasured by participants – a perhaps unintended, but highly prized result.

What this indicates is that if English language is important as a means to integrating, we should consider not only the skills or words migrants learn but how they learn them. Working together in a group of people in a similar position can have clear benefits. The advisory group led by Bernard Crick that set out how the citizenship test should work had also recommended that everyone making an application to become British should sit citizenship classes together. One reason was to ensure information was learned and not retained purely for the test. But a second reason was that it was seen as important to bring migrants together so they could share experiences and help support each other's integration into society. These early plans for a programme sat by all prospective citizens eventually became a course for only those taking ESOL with Citizenship. Better some than none.

Now that this pathway to citizenship has been closed, all applicants have to both pass the citizenship test and provide evidence that they possess sufficient English skills, unless exempted. ESOL courses remain – and the good news is their focus is on English, not on exploring parliamentary democracy while trying to learn how to ask for a cup of tea at the same time.

The programme's closure was not about making it easier to pass this requirement – it made it much more difficult for people to pass. The reason behind this change is simple. The citizenship test is cheaper and takes less time to do, but it required people have an intermediate level of English ability. That is not a problem for anyone able to read this book (I hope!), but it is for someone illiterate in their first and maybe second languages before trying to learn English as a third.

The ESOL with Citizenship was a helpful alternative. People

would be checked to see what level of English they had. To gain a pass certificate, they would have to improve by one level. This meant that someone coming to study English with virtually no knowledge of the language must improve their skills – but need not reach anything like a GCSE level to pass.

Now, the ESOL with Citizenship is no longer an alternative to the citizenship test for those seeking naturalisation, as the test must be sat by everyone – and ESOL courses have become even more popular. They can often include some of the content from the earlier programme incorporating citizenship. I was told that the examples that were discussed as part of ESOL with Citizenship have been useful in ESOL programmes since, to get students talking, in English, about their experiences as migrants and so develop their speaking and listening skills.

Everyone is required to reach an 'intermediate level' – which is conversational English. This is easier for some to achieve than others, depending on overall literacy skills generally and baseline level of English specifically. It is obvious that the less English someone knows at the start, the more ground they must cover before they qualify – requiring far more time at far greater cost.

At a workshop run by the National Institute of Adult Continuing Education (NIACE), some found that it could take a beginner up to three years to reach the current standard. A private survey of ESOL providers found waiting lists at up to 80 per cent of the reported institutions. The numbers of people waiting ranged from ten to 1,000, but were typically between 200 and 400.

The main problem identified was insufficient provision for low-level learners, especially those with basic needs.

The majority of people taking ESOL courses are migrants on valid visas, including successful asylum seekers. Many classes are chronically underfunded. Despite the government's belief that such courses help promote much-needed integration – a position endorsed by David Cameron himself in July 2015, when he said that we must 'ensure people learn English' as part of his government's counterterrorism policy to tackle extremism -- there were further cuts planned of up to £45 million. This is on top of a steady decline: ESOL funding already dropped from £212 million in 2008/09 to £128 million in 2012/13, so investment is only slipping further.

This is a serious concern for providers of English language provisions, where – according to Dr Melanie Cooke, a leading expert in migrant language education based at King's College London – 'everything is driven by funding' and 'funding cuts are a major problem'. Not only is it becoming more expensive to teach migrants English, but as funding shrinks, the costs rise even more because more students need to progress much further than before.

In addition, an often overlooked problem is a lack of computer literacy, which further complicates learning English, particularly given how digitally driven much of the delivery can be. Many may run into problems when sitting the citizenship test on a computer if lacking familiarity with how these machines work.

Matthew Henderson, an ESOL teacher in West Yorkshire, told me there can be little support for people with learning difficulties or physical disabilities affecting their vision or hearing, raising concerns about equality. Philippa Scutt, an ESOL programme manager based in the Midlands, said there were additional challenges in teaching women from some cultural groups who were unable to use public transport and would only be taught by other women. This required going to them – which she and many others like her do – thus making teaching even more costly.

Cuts to state funding of ESOL programmes have been coupled with a reduction of approved English test providers to only two from 2015. James Brokenshire, the immigration minister, said this is part of their effort at putting in place 'new, strengthened arrangements' to end 'significant abuses' that have been uncovered.

Saiqa Bibi and Saffana Abdulla Mohammed Ali challenged the Home Office's requirement that they produce a certificate confirming satisfactory knowledge of English prior to entering the UK in the courts in 2014. This was another effort at raising the standards of English that migrants needed to come to Britain. Each woman was the spouse of a British citizen. Their cases were unsuccessful in the courts. Lord Justice Maurice Kay ruled the government's test was relatively simple and achievable within a short time frame. Given its purpose was to help facilitate integration of non-English-speaking spouses, the policy was proportionate, if only because the standard required was deemed 'rudimentary'. This might still be a significant challenge for another who is illiterate in their native tongue.

ESOL is not required for everyone. While tightening the regulations, the Tory-led coalition government also introduced a wide range of exemptions – nearly a dozen in total. Some of these are sensibly based on age, and include exemptions for children and persons over sixty-five years old.

Others are based on nationality. These are a problem because they expose a major loophole in the policy. Several countries listed for exemptions are those we might expect. Citizens of Australia, Canada, New Zealand and the United States need not demonstrate they know a single word of English – they satisfy the criteria by having the right passport. But some other countries that are similarly exempted may be surprising, such as Belize and the Dominican Republic.

The nationality exemptions lack a clear rationale for how countries are selected for inclusion on the list. Countries where English is the official *de jure* language are sometimes included and sometimes not; those where English is the unofficial *de facto* language are treated equally erratically. Countries with very high English fluency rates like Singapore – to choose just one example – fail to make the list without rhyme or reason. No guidance has been made readily available to explain why over a dozen countries made the list but others did not.

Additionally, the exemptions confirm an expectation that every national from a listed country will have satisfactory English language skills. This is clearly misguided. There are about 45 million people in the United States for whom English is neither a first nor a second language. Many more Americans lack the intermediate standard of English that the British government wrongly assumes they possess.

Exemptions are also made for anyone with a degree taught in English – even if it is not from an English-speaking country. To qualify, a person must have an academic qualification recognised by UK NARIC as equivalent to at least a UK bachelor degree. NARIC – the UK's National Recognition Information Centre – is a government agency that recognises and compares international qualifications and skills. This comes with a fee of about £50. Kwame, a Ghanaian whose naturalisation application is currently being processed, holds a degree taught in English, and paid NARIC for a certificate. He told me it took two weeks before it arrived in the post. Frustratingly, he was never asked for it when interviewed for his permanent residency. Kwame said that if he had not had a certificate, 'the Home Office would not know'. This is evidence that exemptions to the English language requirements are not being enforced as they should.

If qualifications are not checked when applications are processed, it only reinforces the view of most migrants becoming British that many of the requirements serve little purpose other than soaking migrants for as much of their cash as possible – a view that can harden over time and undermine the integration that many of these policies are intended to promote.

So, what records are kept? It would appear none at all. Lord Roberts of Llandudno asked the government to confirm how many people had been exempted from the English language requirement on the grounds that they held a UK NARIC certificate. He discovered that the government is not counting and there are no statistics being collected. They have no idea how many people may be using this route to slip through the net and 'prove' a fluency in English they do not possess.

Many might think that requiring a degree such as a BA, an LLB, an MBA or a PhD that is undertaken in English will mean that the English language skills of the graduate will be satisfactory. While this may be true in many cases, it will not be true for all. In 2015, I was asked to review applications from several senior academics for a national funding agency in Kazakhstan, where English is spoken by only a very small group of people. The applications were in English and came from people in charge of awarding degrees taught in English. Take my word for it – their English was appalling. Missing words, spelling errors – you name it, they did it.

Just because English language instruction may be on the menu at a university or college somewhere in the world does not mean its students will all be OK. It is very possible that many lacking adequate skills will slip through the net. Degrees are no doubt beneficial for finding work, but they are no guarantee the student's English is up to scratch.

This is an important issue, as government ministers may not

know exactly how good the quality is of English certificates from non-British universities. The immigration minister James Brokenshire even admitted, in response to a Parliamentary Question from his Conservative Party colleague Graham Brady MP, that the Home Office lacks data on the number of cases of fraud or abuse in English language testing centres abroad. This answer should satisfy no one.

So is this really about integration or economics? Phil Woolas, a former immigration minister, told me that government is always looking at the issue of 'does it benefit Britain?' He said that this view is short-sighted because we must account for how local Britons perceive social change and the impact British immigration policy may have on the countries of origin for the people who come to the UK. Phil is right.

Providing more accessible ESOL training for migrants, boosting their employability skills, helps them better compete against native Brits – potentially stoking misgivings about the value of immigration for the UK. Those struggling to secure employment may feel even more left behind. We need to think more carefully about the consequences, both intended and unintended.

It is clear that much more work needs to be done. According to the last census, over 850,000 migrants reported that they could not speak English well or at all. *The Times* revealed in 2014 that a quarter of councils in England and Wales have areas where little English is spoken. They found from the last census in 2011 that 138,000 people in these areas could not speak any English while nearly

750,000 could not speak it well. If being able to converse in English is so important for integration and making a contribution, there are too many people left out who need to be brought in.

One ESOL teacher told me that often his students would be in the country for several years and only come to him when they realised they had to fulfil this requirement. The longer they waited, the more difficult learning became, as the deadline for their expiring visa could be heard virtually ticking in the background. Studies also suggest that the longer someone waits before starting English classes, the slower their progress. A welcome change would be to help encourage people to get started much earlier. But this is easier said than done.

There are diverse ways of learning English and no set national curriculum for getting from zero to hero. This flexibility to best suit the particular needs of individual learners is welcome and should remain. But many teaching on ESOL programmes complained that the quality of study materials for the citizenship test was much better than the quality of those for the English language tests.

This shortfall should be addressed and government must look into making it easier and more rewarding to learn English. It is in the national interest and also in the interests of every one of us living in Britain. Making ESOL compulsory for more people while providing less funding does not help. The government must consider whether it is a price worth paying to make it more difficult to learn adequate English skills, given its importance for integration and social cohesion and given their efforts at countering extremism.

The government should take the importance of English more seriously. It can begin by ending unnecessary loopholes. Exemptions for the very young and for pensioners should remain, but exemptions based on nationality should go. A recommendation I made to Ed Miliband's home affairs team in regular meetings prior to the 2015 general election manifesto – but which was not taken up – is that there should be an expectation that everyone pass an English test. No exemptions based on nationality or holding a degree. Perhaps it will be very easy for some to pass. But that is not the point. It is in the public interest that new citizens can converse in English, and tightening the requirements much more than the current government is doing would be a welcome step in the right direction. Keeping exemptions to a minimum would help streamline the process and shrink the associated unnecessary bureaucracy.

There might be a fee of £50 to take the listening and speaking English test. This new fee could reduce expenses for applicants and cost less than UK NARIC certificates for degree-holders. People I spoke with who deliver ESOL programmes thought the influx of additional revenue would help make their programmes more sustainable by creating a new source of income. This would come from migrants and not burden the taxpayer. The extra funding created could go to improving provision for the lower-ability learners where it is needed most. And this would not increase the costs for those who might otherwise be exempt through paying UK NARIC for a certificate – everybody wins.

Lara, an Italian national in London trying to become British, told me, 'What has to be done to prove English language ability was silly' – especially when anyone could simply speak with her and see she is fluent. There should be a simple test for her and everyone else that holds all to the same standard. Fluent speakers like Lara could directly sit the required brief test, saving time and money. More importantly, we can become more certain than we are now that new citizens really are suitably fluent in English.

There are English language test providers that conduct assessments for the UK Visas and Immigration department of the Home Office, valid for citizenship applications already in place. The assessment consists of a ten-minute speaking and listening test, with results normally available that day and a certificate received in the post within seven days. The costs can be as high as £150. This could be reduced if more took it as a standalone assessment with a standard test and fee – as there is with the citizenship test. Migrants like Lara do not need a several-week language course and should not be required to take one. But a fair test that all are expected to pass would better ensure standards are maintained, produce much-needed income for ESOL providers and best secure policy aims.

Taking English provision seriously should include a wider approach. The United States runs their test provision very differently. It covers writing in addition to speaking and listening, but it also provides a wide array of free materials to help prospective new citizens learn English. This includes vocabulary flash cards, self-tests and downloadable videos. Likewise, the British government should adopt a similar high standard and provide more materials for free online. This would better promote raising the bar on literacy for all – it is not only *migrants* who should have good English, but *everyone*.

Literacy is not a problem for migrants alone. Illiteracy rates in the UK are surprisingly high. While only 1 per cent of the UK is fully illiterate, there are roughly 16 per cent who are 'functionally illiterate' and have the literacy levels of an eleven-year-old or worse. That's over five million people.

If the government is so committed to fluency in English to boost social cohesion and employability, then requiring literacy from immigrants addresses only one part of the problem. If literacy is good for all, it should not be required from only some. There is a case for providing free English instruction for all. Let migrants pay a fee like £50 for certification if planning to apply for citizenship, but the availability of English support should not be aimed primarily at migrants alone when so many native Britons remain functionally illiterate too.

The government recently changed part of its strategy. In January 2016, David Cameron made a statement that improving English standards was central to ending segregation in the UK and tackling extremism. He promised £20 million to support ESOL providers to deliver English training to women-only groups, as women lacking English fluency were deemed to have greater needs than men. Cameron also announced new English language checks for everyone on spousal visas after two and a half years – or halfway to the five years of residency in the UK required for permanent settlement – to ensure progress is being made.

These measures are not as helpful as they might look. The £20 million is presented as 'new' funding, but it is much less than the £45 million slashed from ESOL funding in 2011 and 2015, during Cameron's time in 10 Downing Street. While funding was available to support men and women before, less than half has been restored to help women alone. Although English training for women in single-sex groups is crucial for engaging with some communities, and delivering more of it is a welcome development, this support has already been provided for some time by many existing ESOL programmes.

Cameron's plan to introduce mid-visa English progress checks sounds like a tougher standard, but that is an illusion. Under New Labour, spouses had been able to apply for permanent residency, ahead of a citizenship application, after two years. This meant that anyone wanting to continue living permanently in the UK needed to meet the required English standard in two years. But Cameron lengthened the residency requirement for spouses from two to five years. This meant that spouses had more time to reach sufficient English fluency and they could delay their learning. It is doubtful that any mid-visa review is practical or the consequences of failing it would be lawful. There would need to be clarity on what qualifies as 'mid-visa', which could become unnecessarily complex – and it is difficult to see the legality of rejecting settlement by a fluent English speaker who started learning more slowly but had reached the required standard by the time they applied. In short, the government's changing strategy is more a bag of gimmicks that steady progress.

Other European countries take a harder line on language and integration that we might learn from. Germany offers integration classes (*Integrationskurse*). These teach migrants German language, history, culture and basics about its legal system. Failure to attend can lead to cuts in eligible benefits. France has a similar system based around 'integration and welcome contracts' (*contracts d'accueil et d'integration*), where attendance at classes is required and monitored. These programmes are more to the spirit of Bernard Crick's recommendations a decade ago, which have yet to be put in place, where migrants are to come together to learn, share and transition to citizenship.

The German and French models are not perfect. I understand that migrants do not receive much support in learning about and joining integration programmes. Applications for citizenship in France are more likely to be rejected than accepted than in the UK. This suggests that either such integration programmes should do a better job at supporting prospective citizens to become naturalised or, if the programmes are well run, that more should have access to them. My point is that if integration has crucial significance and language ability is a key means to integration, then we should look to establish more opportunities for future long-term residents and citizens to benefit from integration programmes. They exist elsewhere and should be here, too.

Perverse incentives exist in the UK system that undermine the way it works. For example, someone on Jobseeker's Allowance can receive funding to help cover the costs of completing an ESOL programme – financial support that might be lost if he or she obtained work while taking ESOL. The problem is not only the disincentive to choose work where possible, but the priority of obtaining the certification over acquiring skills.

If it were about improving skills, more focus would be placed on improving English over the long term and not merely until it is good enough for immigration purposes. For example, Home Office guidance states that some English language qualifications on its approval list expire as qualifications after two years. However, they 'will still be accepted as proof if you're applying for citizenship, even if it has expired'. It does not matter how many years ago the qualification was earned or expired – if you have it, you are OK. But this reduces the importance of knowing English to a mere box-ticking exercise for little clear public benefit.

Finally, ESOL teachers made clear to me that what they wanted most of all was for English language teaching to become depoliticised and centred on an effective, long-term strategy. In a report for Demos, Ally Paget and Neil Stevenson diagnosed problems with current ESOL policy very well. They said it 'suffers from fragmentation, a lack of clarity about the aims and intended outcomes of learning, disagreement over the analysis and description of English language levels and abilities, and a general tendency to take a short-term view'. While funding has moved to a one-size-fits-all model, the range of learners becomes more diverse as standards are raised and many more must pass to stay. Such a situation can only stoke frustration and anguish for those who engage with the system – and may do little to help promote the integration that is supposed to drive the policy in the first place.

Producing a long-term strategy might also help to tackle the many blurred lines of accountability. For example, the Welsh government is responsible for managing the provision of ESOL as a part of Lifelong Learning. However, it is the British government that has responsibility for immigration and citizenship policy for everyone, and this can affect the provision available in Wales. There are additional challenges in learning English in Wales, not least recognising and understanding Welsh place names and signs 'when English is "alien" as well', as the Welsh government acknowledges. Requiring English can mean supporting different approaches in different parts of the UK.

There is an eye-wateringly long list of bodies that inform ESOL training and delivery, including the Home Office; the Department for Business, Innovation and Skills; Ofqual; the Skills Funding Agency; the Department for Communities and Local Government; and the Department for Work and Pensions (through Jobcentre Plus), each of which feeds into ESOL policy

or provision one way or another. A streamlined, joined-up structure could bring clarity and improved accountability.

No government can guarantee every citizen knows English.
There will be children born abroad to British parents who may
never hear a word of it, but can still earn a British passport – this
is not a problem. But the government can do much more than
it currently does to ensure more British citizens are literate –
whether they are born British or become British. The question
is not whether the necessary reforms are beyond our reach –
they are not – but rather whether any government will show the
commitment to complete the modernisation project launched
under Blair and New Labour and win the war against illiteracy
and functional illiteracy.

CHAPTER 6

THE FREE MOVEMENT MYTH

After most significant historical events, the question people ask is – so, where were you? What were you doing when you heard? I doubt many people think about 1 May 2004 this way. But maybe they should.

On this day Britain made what then Home Secretary Jack Straw now calls a 'spectacular mistake'. The EU was to see its biggest ever expansion, with eight new member states, including Poland and Hungary. The government at the time decided against transition restrictions that would limit the numbers of people able to live and work in the UK for a period of time. Instead, they agreed to be one of only three EU countries to grant them all 'free movement'.

The expansion represented progress for many European leaders – and an opportunity to bring countries out from behind their rusted Iron Curtain into the heart of Europe. As Vladimir Putin's Russia continued to press for growing influence on Europe's borders, the addition of Eastern European states was seen as nothing short of a victory in uniting Europe.

The cost of the politically symbolic expansion was believed a price well worth paying. Straw's government predicted only 5,000 to 13,000 would actually come from Eastern Europe, in what he now describes as a 'well-intentioned policy we messed up'. The path to hell might be said to be paved with such intentions.

But for many – especially Eurosceptics – this was one 1 May when 'May Day!' had a different meaning. Communities across Britain saw unprecedented change. In 2001, Boston in Lincolnshire had a foreign-born population of about 3 per cent. Ten years later, it had grown to 15 per cent – a five-fold increase. Over two million Europeans have come, leaving 'lots of red faces', Straw says, 'mine included'. He is not alone. Former Home Secretary Jacqui Smith agreed and told me that there should have been transition checks in place. If only we all knew then what was to happen next.

In 2015, there was a net migration of 172,000 EU citizens to the UK: of these, about 96,000 came with a job and 69,000 came looking for work. There are two million EU citizens currently employed in the UK – almost double the 1.2 million non-EU citizens in work.

Today, the Polish have quickly established themselves as one of the larger national groups in Britain, numbering about 800,000

– and in the top ten nationals to become British citizens, a group growing from 458 in 2009 to over 6,000 by 2012. This has been described by Lord Green, chairman of Migration Watch, as 'an encouraging sign of the developing integration of the Polish community' – and for once I agree with him. There are plenty of Poles reluctant to take this step because of cost or lack of necessity. One Polish woman from Liverpool told me, 'This is my home and so it would be natural to have citizenship to be protected,' but she was only likely to apply if Britain left the EU: 'I'm an EU citizen so I'm fine now; if the UK leaves then it'll be mayhem.' This fairly represents how many EU nationals in Britain feel.

Other EU nationals are increasingly applying to become British too. Interestingly, the Germans win hands down, with no penalty shoot-out required: more German nationals are becoming British citizens than any other Europeans – and I know of several first-hand. This is mostly motivated by concerns that the UK could vote to exit the European Union. British citizenship for EU nationals works in much the same way as it does for everyone else, with residency and English language required in addition to passing the UK citizenship test.

At the time of writing, Britain faces a choice about whether to remain a part of the EU, and European migration is an issue that may determine the referendum vote. I have little confidence in the government's handling of it – and for good reason.

When the Electoral Commission launched a public consultation on the referendum question, I submitted evidence identifying two problems. The first was that the original question – 'Should the United Kingdom remain a member of the European Union?' – was not neutral and should be changed to avoid any hint that the dice were being loaded. Secondly, I argued that if the referendum was to have a yes or no answer, it would be one out of sync with recent referendums (for example, the referendum on Scotland's independence followed the convention of 'yes' is for change and 'no' is for the status quo), which some voters may find confusing. The Electoral Commission agreed with both points, forcing the government to not only change the question, but also its possible answers – and that left the government with its tail firmly between its legs. Not a good sign that careful scrutiny and sound judgement are at work.

But there is also a very serious problem lurking in the background: there is a central myth about migration so big that all sides believe it to be true, and it could push the UK into Brexit by mistake. If ever there was a need to help set the record straight, the time is now. Before it's too late.

Crossing borders has never been easier. Modern travel has transformed what was once unimaginable into what is now all too common. For many British citizens, a holiday means travelling abroad somewhere, maybe anywhere. So much of the world is now readily within reach it is easy to take it for granted and forget what a significant change this truly is. British residents made a total of 62.6 million visits abroad in the year leading up to June 2015 – a rise of 6 per cent on the year before – spending an estimated £36.5 billion.

But our ability to travel abroad so easily – at least across much of Europe – is due to much more than cheap oil and a competitive tourist market. European history has been an unfolding of great advancements coupled with unspeakable horrors that too often pitted states against each other, leading to truly global wars.

From the blood-soaked ashes of these horrific conflicts arose a determination that never again would such destruction and murder be seen in Europe. A new peace – a *Pax Europea* – dawned and the European Union was born. And, with it, the myth of free movement between Britain and Europe.

This is the myth that Britain can do nothing at all about EU citizens who want to live in the UK. It is a mantra continually repeated by our Prime Minister and our Home Secretary, among others, but let me quote a representative statement of this myth by Migration Watch: 'The government has no means of controlling the number of EU citizens who come to the UK to live, work or study because they have the right to free movement throughout the EU.' Thus, the myth goes, Britain is powerless to fully control its borders so long as it remains a part of the EU. The UK can only choose who can enter if it takes power back from Brussels.

This is not the view from only one side of the political spectrum: the free movement myth is defended by Europhiles and Eurosceptics alike. Their disagreement is not about whether there is free movement, but whether its consequences are beneficial and should be continued or whether it should be stopped dead in its tracks as soon as possible. Migration Watch and pro-EU campaigners agree on little else, but they share a common ground in accepting this myth. Even progressives like David Goodhart speak of European movement 'which cannot be controlled'. This myth needs to be put to rest.

In a 2014 speech on immigration, David Cameron said of free movement that it has 'evolved significantly over the years from applying to job-holders to job-seekers too, from job-seekers to their non-European family members, and from a right to work to a right to claim a range of benefits'.

If we believed him – and many will because he is the Prime Minister – free movement is a free-for-all in which EU citizens have a right to become British benefit scroungers, sponging off British-born taxpayers. Free movement may leave a divided Britain if it does not leave it broke first. This is one EU founding principle that has become unfit for purpose. Or so we are told.

Imaginary legends can often spring from some real event. Out of a truth emerges a powerful falsehood. It infects our thinking and contaminates the debate. When I surveyed citizens about what being British meant to them, more than one said, 'Free movement through the EU.' People don't just believe it – they even identify with it.

The myth of free movement has not appeared out of nothing. Those who believe are not fools, even if they have been fooled. So let us start with the rules found in a text I doubt many people have on their bedside tables: the Treaty on the Functioning of the

European Union. This is more interesting than it sounds, and is a must if you want to get to the bottom of the free movement myth.

The Treaty sets out several important rights for citizens of any country within the EU and wider European Economic Area, which includes Iceland, Liechtenstein and Norway – free movement concerns them all. Every citizen in each EU member state is automatically an EU citizen too. By being British, I am also a European citizen. So too are the Germans and the Italians. EU citizenship is held in addition to, and subject to, citizenship of any EU country.

This fact leads most to speak of European *migration* instead of immigration: this is because people are moving internally within a shared European political space rather than coming from outside. They don't immigrate, they migrate. There is therefore an equal status between British citizens and all other EU citizens. However, if someone were to lose his or her British citizenship, they would at that same time no longer be a citizen of the EU. The two are linked.

All EU citizens have 'the right to move and reside freely' within any EU member state or, more specifically, any country within the European Economic Area. Language like this certainly gives the clear impression that European citizens possess free movement. How deceptive it can be.

But, let me share an insight easily overlooked – treaties and other legal documents are rarely as clear-cut as they might seem. They certainly keep my fellow academics teaching law at schools like Durham University and Yale University, where I have written this book, very busy indeed. The quip that if you put two lawyers – or sometimes even two law professors – in a room, you may get three (or more!) views is not too far off the reality.

The devil is so often in the detail, and European law is no exception. The 'right to move and reside freely' comes with strings attached. It is 'subject to the limitations and conditions' laid down in European law – otherwise known in everyday English as the fine print.

Speaking on the BBC's *Question Time* programme in 2014, Chuka Umunna raised more than a few eyebrows when he argued that free movement should be limited to those already in employment, claiming, 'The founders of the EU had in mind free movement of workers, not free movement of jobseekers.' The Labour MP and former shadow Business Secretary knows a thing or two about the law relating to workers – he was an employment lawyer for many years in the City of London before entering politics.

At the time, these words were viewed with suspicion. So many believe the free movement myth that Umunna's call for a stop to the free movement of jobseekers was seen as Labour's starting to 'toughen up' on immigration in calling for 'the end' of free movement. Umunna received criticism as some accused him of trying to push some shift in the party's immigration policies.

The truth? Umunna, the svelte former City lawyer, was simply telling it like it is. The genius was that this was a Labour-led migration policy that would be easy to get EU states to agree – it was, in fact, already the law. So the problem here isn't the EU – it is that existing EU law is not being enforced.

There is no absolute right of free movement for EU citizens – and there never has been. Not all have the same rights to enter and remain in any EU country. British citizens have more of these rights than French or German citizens, as it is possible to exclude the others from entering Britain. This is not to argue – yet – that this is good or bad, but simply to set a much ignored record straight. Former European Commission President Jacques Delors once said that 'one should speak at the same time of national citizenship and wider European citizenship', but the two are not – and should not – be one and the same. What you often hear is not what we actually get.

Instead of 'free movement', we should think of migration by EU citizens in Europe as controlled movement regarding the economically productive and self-sufficient.

In practice, this means that any citizen of an EU or EEA state can work or study on the same terms as nationals of those states. Polish students can attend British universities subject to the same hurdles that face UK citizens – and *vice versa*. This has helped open up Europe's higher education in exciting new ways, creating research networks that benefit students, industry and scholarship immensely. But EU or EEA students must meet academic entry requirements, enter the country with comprehensive sickness insurance and provide a declaration that they have sufficient resources to not be a burden on the UK's social assistance system during their studies if they want to be eligible to claim certain means-tested benefits like British citizens, such as housing benefit or universal credit. There are conditions on movement from one EU state to another.

This is a crucial point. In summer 2015, there were serious concerns raised that EU citizens could obtain European health insurance cards. The worry was that they could be used to get free treatment from the National Health Service, opening the door for so-called 'health tourism', covering trivial, but expensive, treatment.

Such fears are misplaced. These insurance cards are only for use in emergencies – there is no cover provided for planned treatments, non-emergency surgeries or over-the-counter medicines. In short, they are no substitute for travel insurance – and anyone wanting to exercise their treaty rights and enter Britain for work or study as an EU citizen is required to have comprehensive sickness insurance.

If there is a problem, it is only that the existing requirements are not properly enforced. This is apparent from a report on health tourism produced by Health Secretary Jeremy Hunt's department. It offered a cost–benefit analysis – that was a model of how *not* to do it. Rough estimates were given for everything, from how many foreign nationals might use the NHS to how expensive each national group might be – and this guesswork was used to drive policy.

But the numbers are purely conjured up, as if by Harry Potter's wand. When asked how much the NHS had spent on non-UK citizens over the last five years, the government admitted that 'it is not possible to provide the cost to the National Health Service of providing treatment to non-United Kingdom nationals'. This was because its statistics lack information about 'nationality or migration status'. In early 2016, the government also admitted that it lacked any factual evidence that in-work and out-of-work benefits are a factor in encouraging migration to the UK from the EU. If health tourism exists, the government has not found it.

This should not be a surprise. Until 2011, I was a foreign national. While I had been asked in Ireland for my passport and required to pay a fee to see a doctor, I have never been asked for my nationality at any time when registering at or visiting a GP or hospital in Britain until very recently. The government simply did not keep accurate records – and to its credit there is an effort underway now. However, again we see that so often fears emerge about what migrants might be doing where there is little available evidence and plenty of rich imaginations.

Europe's *controlled* movement has allowed British employers to hire staff from a wider workforce than UK nationals alone – and exposed the deep concern that Europeans take jobs on the cheap by their being more eager for work and more willing to accept lower wages. In theory, opening the door to a wider talent pool can make Europe a more competitive trade area, but at the cost of removing barriers that can protect employees from a greater exposure to a free market. The reality is that the movement of labour across Europe has seen an influx of highly skilled talent that has supported one end of the economy, but there has also been a similar influx of people in low-skilled work, at the other end of the spectrum, where many Britons have felt they have lost out. Competition comes at a price some find too high to pay.

We should not think there is a perfectly level playing field, because the same terms do not apply for every worker. EU law permits 'limitations [on free movement] justified on grounds of public policy, public security or public health'. This crucial condition allows countries like the UK to ensure that its governmental and intelligence agencies are run by British nationals and not migrants. It is possible to make some jobs for British nationals only – although there is a high bar to pass. This condition also allows EU member states to bar EU nationals found to have some infectious or contagious parasitic disease.

The key is that any restrictions must be 'justified' – a higher standard of permissibility than 'because we said so', as any justification must be defended in Europe courts. This brings us to another myth: the view that the EU is a threat to Britain's sovereignty. After all – some will tell us with self-righteous delight – must not Britain follow whatever Brussels says? The answer is a firm no. When it comes to much of the European law the critics object to, for the regulations apply to the UK not because Brussels says so, but rather because Parliament consents to

European law as incorporated in the European Communities Act 1972. These European laws have the force they do because Britain's Parliament gave them that authority – and Parliament's sovereignty is preserved.

Dispelling the free movement myth exposes the elephant in the room: there are several lawful limitations on EU movement; the issue is that these are rarely enforced. Anyone with a passport from an EU country might enter the United Kingdom. Each has a right of admission – and this includes the right of non-Europeans to enter the UK as family members travelling with an EU national. This category is surprisingly small. Looking at the number of dependents claiming a permanent residency card after living for five years in the UK, we find a small increase over the past three years – from 6,703 in 2012 to 9,962 in 2013.

Rights come with responsibilities – and restrictions – that are often overlooked. If I have learned anything about immigration law and policy, it is this: just about nobody knows what it is or how it works beyond people working in the field or who have experienced it first-hand. There is more fiction and hyperbole to be found than can fit in any large public library.

Let's start with workers. Most migrants are working. The UK has done especially well on this measure, as the only EU country that has a lower unemployment rate for migrants (7.5 per cent) than nationals (7.9 per cent). Migrants are net contributors to the economy and are only rarely on qualifying benefits – less than 5 per cent claim Jobseeker's Allowance.

A citizen of an EU or EEA country can come to the UK for work. They have a right to enter the country and pursue earning a living. But there are conditions. Part-time work can be acceptable – unless it is purely marginal and supplementary. Being temporarily out of work because of illness or an accident still renders someone a 'worker' in the eyes of European law – but there are limits on how long job-seeking is allowed.

If an EU citizen wants to work and plans to look for a job after moving to the UK, this can be permitted if he or she can provide evidence they are seeking employment with a genuine chance of securing it. You read that correctly. The right to enter for work applies only to those who can and want to work. 'Free' EU movement comes with clear strings attached.

If that sounds like the UK can lawfully boot out of the country someone who has failed to find work – it is because *it can* and *it does*. While there is no set time limit, the European Court of Justice has lent some support to what I call 'the six-month rule' – unless someone can provide evidence that they are continuing to seek a job with 'genuine chances' of success, they can be removed from a member state after six months. Official guidance from the Home Office is clear that EU or EEA citizens have an initial right of residence for only three months after arriving in Britain. And they can be removed during this time if engaged in fraud – so even this initial period is subject to conditions.

The free movement of workers and students is also extended to what are called 'self-sufficient persons'. These are people who have sufficient resources that they will not burden the social welfare system while in the UK, and they are required to have comprehensive sickness insurance cover during their stay. In other words, they must be able to support themselves.

While there is no set amount of money that someone must earn, the law simply could not be clearer – EU 'free movement' does not allow anyone to hop over to the UK, claim benefits on arrival and kick up their feet doing nothing while handing the tab to British taxpayers. If people are slipping through the net, this is no fault of the EU – it is a failure of the UK government to put in place adequate safeguards to ensure the controlled movement of economically productive or self-sufficient persons who fit the legal requirements. Blaming Europe only deflects responsibility from the current government for its failure to do more.

Only a small number of European nationals are removed from Britain each year. There were 2,731 enforced removals in the year ending June 2014 and an increase of 25 per cent to 3,407 twelve months later. These were mostly people who had been criminals or had not been self-sufficient or looking for work or in study – and represented a mere fraction of the numbers living in the UK. EU or EEA citizens removed must wait at least twelve months before applying for re-entry – and they must provide evidence that they will lawfully exercise their rights of movement. Of 1,109 forcibly removed in 2014, there were 163 applying for re-entry, but only nineteen requests were granted.

There is a hardening attitude across Europe as other member states take steps to enforce the rules already in place. Mrs Dano, a Romanian citizen, moved to Germany and soon applied for job-seeker benefits. However, she had not worked in Germany – nor was she looking to find work.

Germany refused to provide Dano with benefits. She was not coming to work or with a realistic prospect of work. Dano had failed to exercise her treaty rights and so Germany could deny her claim for benefits. The case went all the way to the European Court of Justice. The court rightly supported Germany, holding that the current requirement is important because it 'seeks to pre-vent economically inactive Union citizens from using the host member state's welfare system to fund their means of subsistence'.

The case is clear: Dano might be entitled to benefits in her native Romania as a Romanian citizen, but she does not have the same rights in Germany as a European citizen. The court does not say she has no right to some level of support – but it did say she cannot move to wherever she pleases and let their taxpayers pick up the tab. There is no right of European citizens to become benefit scroungers in other EU countries. Full stop. End of.

In another case that was considered by the UK Supreme Court in 2016, Roksana Mirga was a Polish citizen who came to the UK and worked from April to November 2005. After becoming pregnant in February 2006, Mirga applied for income support. She claimed that denying her income support would be a breach of her right to be in the UK, as it was essentially constructive expulsion; she would be forced back to Poland. The Supreme Court was unconvinced and ruled she could be denied a right of continued residence in Britain. Again, European citizens have no right to benefits without important strings attached – and the courts back this up.

There is no reason why cases like this should be surprising – they only have this effect because so many believe the myth of free movement is real. But it isn't. Commenting on the Dano case, the distinguished professor of EU and human rights law Steve Peers said, 'Some people have the impression that all EU citizens can move and reside in any other member state without restrictions', but the truth is, 'there are limits'. The main issue is that they are not enforced as strictly as they could be.

These limits also include what is called a 'habitual residence test' of at least three months before an EU national can make any application for benefits. It can be longer, but it is for each member state to decide and impose fairly without discrimination between its nationals and citizens of other member states.

And this can have consequences for British citizens. If there is a residency test of six months to a year, it would have to apply to all European nationals – including Brits. This would mean a British citizen who had been living outside the UK would have to satisfy the same requirements that might apply to an Italian or Spanish national before qualifying for support. UK rules on residency can impose restrictions on British citizens living abroad too, not only on foreign nationals.

No doubt these facts – which may be a revelation given so many headlines repeating the mantra that there can be no controls on EU migrants – will not satisfy everybody. The aim of Eurosceptics is withdrawal from the EU while retaining access to the EU single market – the idea being that Britain can trade more on its own terms.

But this is a load of stinking bokum. As Jonathan Portes has wisely pointed out, the rule on European movement 'actually applies to EEA [nationals] on pretty much the same basis' – as with Iceland and Norway. If we want access to the European market, there is a price to be paid whether or not Britain is in the EU. Brexit won't fix it.

Some might think, then, that free movement might not exist for the EU or EEA, but in fact it does for countries signed up to the Schengen Agreement. All EU countries are part of this agreement (with the exception of four that have applied and are pending final approval: Bulgaria, Croatia, Cyprus and Romania), covering a population of 400 million people. Only two have opted out – the Republic of Ireland and the United Kingdom. Any country that wishes to become an EU member is required to sign up to the agreement.

Not everyone thinks Britain's being outside the Schengen Agreement a welcome policy. Former Home Secretary Charles Clarke told me, 'It might be unpopular to say it, but free movement of workers in Europe is a good thing.' In a pamphlet, Clarke makes a strong case for the UK improving its border security by joining Schengen countries. While Clarke is vociferous in his support, it is probably safe to say it is an idea that has a long way to go before it becomes even a remote possibility.

The Schengen Agreement is often talked about like a free movement zone, and it did for the most part create an internally borderless Europe. Passport checks remained, but fixed checkpoints along the borders were often removed. Europe's refugee crisis has forced a rethink from some member states – some, like Austria, have brought back some border controls, and Germany's Interior Minister Thomas de Maizière has hinted that participation in the agreement could be suspended – but it remains a firm policy throughout most of the EU.

But, for all the talk of Schengen as a free movement zone, it is not. The rights of entry are similar terms to EU 'free movement' controls. What the Schengen Agreement did was help create harmonisation of visa policies, bringing the varied rules for each member state into a common arrangement.

There is, however, one country that has enjoyed more genuine free movement than most others: the United Kingdom. As we saw in Chapter 2, in 1948, Parliament passed the British Nationality Act. This created a new type of British citizen: the citizen of the United Kingdom and Colonies (CUKC). This transformed millions of people living in the UK and its shrinking global empire into British citizens with the right of – here it comes – free travel throughout the empire. An exception was made in excluding countries that were semi-independent, like

Australia, Canada, India and Pakistan. This still meant that people around the globe could all be British citizens – without needing to travel to Britain or even know any English.

The CUKC did not last long and there were significant changes to British citizenship law in the 1960s and '70s that put an end to this form of free movement. But it is important to note that Britain once led the way in promoting free movement of people without many of the restrictions now in place not all that long ago.

But for those really, *really* worried about the free movement of Europeans, the biggest shock is how few even notice one area of borderless travel directly under their noses.

Before moving to the United Kingdom in 2001, I lived in Dublin and enjoyed life in a vibrant capital city. I spent two very happy years first as a graduate student at University College Dublin, studying philosophy, and then as administrative assistant, working in the philosophy department, when I was not gigging with my jazz trio in Temple Bar. Things were grand, as they say in that place across the Irish Sea.

But I ran into an unexpected problem. I had a short interview with Ireland's Department of Enterprise, Trade and Employment so that I could become certified to work as a non-EEA national at my university. Most of my brief time was spent confirming what dates I had left and returned to the country. No more than half an hour later I was on my way with a permit in hand.

After I moved to the UK, I had to take a similar interview, this time with the Department for Work and Pensions in the steel city of Sheffield. Everything looked similar and I expected roughly the same experience, but nothing of the sort happened.

Like in Dublin, most of the time I spent in the interview was simply going through my passport to confirm dates I had left the UK and then returned. But there was definitely a puzzle I never saw coming: missing dates of entry into Britain. The dates when I had arrived into Ireland had been easy to find – large green stamps littered my American passport with each flight back from New York or London. The problem – or I should say *my* problem – was that I had evidence of every time I went to the US, Ireland or abroad. I just didn't have any proof that I had returned to Britain. And I had no clue why.

This was a conundrum that needed a cunning plan. Thankfully, I persuaded the interviewer about my trips abroad – I received my National Insurance card soon afterwards and I started working for the first time in the UK the following week. But I racked my brain – why were some border entry stamps missing in my passport? Was someone tampering with it without my knowing? What was I missing?

It wasn't until I was flying back to the UK from the Republic of Ireland that it hit me. Not everyone looks forward to entering border controls. It is rarely exciting, but this time crossing borders was an education. I was ready to take notes.

Walking through Dublin's international airport was so very normal. I've done it frequently, especially when I called Ireland's capital my home. There were the queues dividing the Europeans from foreigners like me – each of us required to move through passport control. Just like you would expect when flying from one country to another.

The realisation did not hit me until disembarking my return flight to Newcastle. My Eureka moment. Down the steps off the plane, across a short jog into the terminal and following signs for the baggage control. You spot what happened? That's right: baggage control – not passport control. And then there it was – the luggage carousel spectacular of various treadmills full of other people's stuff. (Do airports know which luggage is mine? More than once I have had the last bag taken off the plane. Maybe that is one mystery I can't solve.)

But no passport control. *No passport control – at all!* This is why I did not have the dates stamped in my passport when I returned from Ireland – there are only checks going out, but not coming in. As rappers Cypress Hill might say, this was 'insane in the membrane' – or, as my students might quip, 'mental'.

This was no mistake by the British government, although it may come as a surprise to ministers. Theresa May, the Home Secretary, confirmed in February 2016 that there are '100 per cent checks on all arriving passengers' to the UK. James Brokenshire, the immigration minister, claimed there are 'full checks on all arriving passengers' in reply to a question about immigration controls from a Northern Irish MP. These statements are wrong.

There are two reasons that help explain it. The first is that while Britain and Ireland are not part of the Schengen Agreement, they are part of a different arrangement called the Common Travel Area. This is a similar idea, where there is generally unencumbered travel from one area to the next.

But there is also a catch. As with controlled movement in the EU, the same restrictions are supposed to apply in the Common Travel Area. Not anyone or everyone can simply board a plane or ferry in Dublin with a right to enter Holyhead or Edinburgh. Checks can still be made, but while British and Irish nationals have a right to enter, not everyone else does – everything depends on their nationality and any visa restrictions.

The point is the Common Travel Area is no unrestrained free movement zone, as some might claim. There can be checks at the border – and Ireland does more of them than the UK.

It is fascinating to me that for all the many, *many* worries some express about a free movement in Europe (which, in fact, is not nearly as 'free' as they believe), no one seems bothered about the Common Travel Area. Put bluntly, people seem much more concerned about anyone migrating from the Continent than they are from across the Irish Sea.

Someone recently put the case for Brexit to me like this: 'We need to make the UK an island again.' But this is a typically jaundiced view you only find on the largest British island. There is also a place called 'Northern Ireland' that is a constituent nation of the United Kingdom – and it just so happens to be on a different island.

Making Britain 'an island again' forgets that it includes Northern Ireland – not to mention the Isle of Man or Channel Islands.

This means it is not enough to be an island or two, because Northern Ireland shares a border with a separate, independent country: Ireland, sometimes called 'Southern Ireland' on mainland Britain. Yet no one – and I genuinely mean not a soul – today calls for border controls to return along the border between Ireland and Northern Ireland. This suggests that Ireland is not seen by many as a foreign country like other independent states are.

And this brings me to the second reason behind Ireland's exceptionalism for the British. This is about a law known to most Irish I have spoken to, but virtually no one British. If there was a citizenship test question about it, this would be another most would fail.

The law is the Ireland Act 1949 – and it is extraordinary. The Act acknowledged the Republic of Ireland and it ended its status as a British dominion. Ireland's independence was recognised. Well, sort of.

The Act states that Ireland 'is not a foreign country' for the purposes of any British law. This is more significant than it might first appear. It means that even if the UK left the EU, rejected membership in the EEA and wanted to end the Common Travel Area, it would require no less than an Act of Parliament before the UK could begin imposing restrictions on Irish nationals entering Britain.

And there is more. Because Ireland is not considered foreign, neither are its citizens. So I tested it. After I became a British citizen, I applied for a UK passport. The guidance had it all in black and white: applicants for a passport needed references – and they could be either British or Irish nationals. I couldn't believe it – can anyone imagine the United States accepting references for American passports from Mexicans or, worse, Canadians? I jest, but the point should be plain – this is unusual.

I tested the guidance by asking a former Irish colleague from Cork who did not and would never want a British passport for himself to provide a reference for me. I explained to him how curious I was to see if what I had read could actually be true, and it took no time to convince him to join my experiment. Perhaps only academics think about making the everyday act of a passport application into an experiment testing a law from 1949. But I had to. I wanted to know if this would really work.

I wrote his Irish passport number on my application, popped it in the post and waited to see what happened next. My former colleague was asked to confirm my application – which he did promptly – and after a few months I became the owner of a new British passport. All thanks to Britain's treating Irish nationals as if their country had never become independent all those years ago. This occurred in 2011, but it remains the case now too. Try it.

I suppose one day there will be front-page headlines aimed at frightening the public about the numbers of non-British migrants – Irish nationals – who have had a hand in the Home Office's granting passports to British citizens. They don't collect data on it, although this might change. It should surprise, maybe shock, and yet it does nothing more than raise a few eyebrows. And that's not because of some inherited stiff upper lips.

But from what I can tell, the reason there is no outcry is because the concerns about so-called free movement are not how people tell it. And here I can only conjecture, but so be it: the resistance to European migration is an opposition to others coming 'here' – e.g. the British Isles, including Ireland – and not 'our' going there. Over 14 million EU citizens live in a different member state – including an estimated 1.3 million Brits. In fact, the UK has a larger share of its citizens living abroad than any other European country. If movement across Europe is viewed as such a problem for Britain, perhaps it should consider the effects of Brits moving to other European states too. Should Brexit come, the UK could see over one million British citizens returning home. Oh, the irony: trying to leave Europe and lower net migration to under 100,000 could see many times this number cross the border instead.

British citizens living abroad in Europe have the most at stake in whether Britain remains a part of the EU and yet they will be denied a vote. If those who have a stake in outcomes should have a say in how they are decided, they are being woefully mistreated. The Prime Minister should hear the voices of all British citizens both in the UK and in Europe – and permit all of them to have a say in a referendum that might redefine the next generation.

Two weeks after winning the 2015 general election, David Cameron gave a speech calling for 'immigration to be properly controlled'. A central part of his plan was to create restrictions on EU migration 'by renegotiating in Europe'. But in doing so he peddles a falsehood – the myth of free movement for European citizens. When we look closely at the rules, we see the problem is not 'free' movement but the government's failure to enforce existing restrictions. This raises questions about why this failure has occurred.

A possible answer is that the government knows all this, but does not acknowledge it for fear that clamping down – as they can – on EU migration might deter highly skilled talent from coming to Britain and benefiting the economy. A cynical guess, but no more outlandish than the scare stories peddled by some Eurosceptics. I wonder if their children do not hear creepy tales about werewolves or the bogey man, but rather that European migrants might steal their Christmas.

For example, a key part of David Cameron's proposed reform of the EU is an 'emergency brake' on in-work benefits for EU migrants. This would restrict access to these benefits and is aimed at reducing EU migration by providing a disincentive. The problems this reform faces include not only the lack of evidence that benefits are a pull factor attracting EU migrants to Britain, but also the number of conditions that must be satisfied in order to apply the proposed measure. The UK would have to convince the EU Council, first, that it had 'objective' data that paying out in-work benefits to EU migrants is a problem and, second, that there were 'exceptional circumstances'. Instead of a full ban on claiming benefits for four years, at best the new brake would be up to four years and possibly much less in proportion to what the EU deemed necessary, with any restrictions graduated and lessened over time. Cameron's emergency brake turns out to be a lever pulled by another driver – and it may not bring our car to a stop.

An alternative answer to why the government has failed to do more to act on EU migration is the poverty of imagination about how progressive border controls can be implemented consistently with European law. One idea is to change how people can acquire a National Insurance number, required for employment in the UK. I interviewed in person for one, but a large number of eligible people living overseas do not, registering instead from abroad.

The government should strongly consider requiring anyone who wants a National Insurance number to start work to sit an interview – just like I did. While most people automatically receive their number, there is no right enshrined in law to receive one and it can be subjected to this requirement. It could ensure all successful applicants qualify and – while a National Insurance number card is not a source of identity – the interview could help preserve the integrity of this system, combating any identity abuses.

When he was Chief Economist at the Department for Work and Pensions, Jonathan Portes gave evidence to the Home Affairs Committee that these numbers 'are an internal reference number that lets us link an individual with their social security, or their child support, or their tax or their contribution record' – so having accurate information is important for monitoring these areas in the interests of public policy. There is already a precedent for using interviews for getting a National Insurance number – as I was required to do.

A useful model for how these interviews might work can be found in the new rules for getting a passport. Anyone seeking a new passport or replacing an expired one is now required to sit an interview. Questions asked test information on their application – and the applicant cannot use notes, forcing them to rely on memory alone. The process I underwent in Durham was short and fairly pleasant, and readily confirmed for the Home Office that, yes, I was who I said I was and their information about me was accurate and up to date. The process is relatively straightforward, but not all pass this test – 239 people failed in 2014.

The extra effort of requiring an interview for National Insurance cards need not prevent anyone from receiving it who would normally qualify. If required, it would add a cost in terms of time spent applying and then making preparations to appear for an interview. This can prove a disincentive for wanting to work in the UK, as it would make it more difficult without making the process less fair or denying work to anyone entitled to it.

The impact of European migration on British public services is routinely highlighted as a key concern. Because controlled migration permits entry to all qualifying EU citizens, there cannot be application fees or other tariffs levied on European citizens wanting to come to the UK. This is not true for non-EU citizens, and they are frequently the target of higher fees and new surcharges, which help defray costs relating to their being in the country, but also cover some of the costs relating to EU citizens. In effect, non-EU citizens are exploited to try to make up the balance.

But there is more that can be done. There used to be a European Integration Fund, an EU funding programme that supported the integration of third-party nationals into Europe. It ran from 2007 to 2013, spending €825 million, with over €110 million (£81.7 million) spent in the UK during this period. The funding supported projects conducted by colleges, local councils and charitable organisations like the Royal Association for Deaf People and the YMCA. Funding also was used to help support the UK Border Agency develop its points-based system. It was disappointing to see this programme close given the excellent work it did in supporting community cohesion and raising standards of English literacy.

In November 2014, then shadow Home Secretary Yvette Cooper called for the creation of an EU migration impacts fund, paid for from the existing EU budget. The fund would target those regions that have seen the most migration by EU or EEA citizens – helping with the costs for providing world-class public services, additional school places and extra medical staff, and supporting housing investment. Many worry about the impact that migration has, notwithstanding its many benefits. Britain is not alone in facing such pressures. A migration impacts fund is in the British interest – but also in the interest of its European partners. This is an idea whose time has surely come.

The key problem that emerges with EU restrictions is the

ability – and perhaps determination – to enforce them properly. One policy that could help – though it may prove unpopular – is to reintroduce the national identity cards first proposed by New Labour under Tony Blair. These were defended at the time as a means to combat security threats. But they were undermined by fears that they would violate individual liberty.

Identity cards could instead be seen as a way to better manage the conditional rights of EU migrants and others – as well as keeping much better records of their access to public services. A further benefit might also be to EU migrants. An Italian citizen I spoke to who is planning to become British claimed that there were 'clear problems for EU citizens', such as proving they were in the UK legitimately, exercising their treaty rights. Identity cards would be one way among others to make this case and help support their transition to British citizenship.

I am not the only one to have seen their usefulness for this reason. Lord Green, chairman of Migration Watch, has also called for the introduction of identity cards. I do not agree with his reasons for wanting their reintroduction – and I do not buy the claim that Britain is a soft touch – but the point here is that this is neither a left-wing nor a right-wing political issue.

Debates about European migration have too often shed more darkness than light, with otherwise sensible human beings declaring pure fantasy to be fact. I received an unsolicited email from one reader of my LabourList columns who told me – with no hint of irony – 'Do you honestly think your ancestors and mine fought and in some cases died for what Britain has become? No, they would mostly be horrified to see our beautiful land overrun. Europe would be better today if we had come to agreeable terms with Germany in 1940.' So there we have it – it is so important that Britain remove itself from Europe that we would be better off now if we were under Nazi control. The mind boggles.

This is an extreme case, for sure. But it signals the fanciful thinking that permeates public discourse about the myth of free movement for EU citizens. No such uncontrolled, unrestricted nightmare exists – so those who would find such a world worse than an anarchical *Lord of the Flies* dystopia can sleep easy.

The problem of free movement is a reluctance of government to act and to enforce the many restrictions already in place. More can and perhaps should be done in order to rebuild public confidence in Britain's ability to control its borders, thus putting to rest a myth that should never have been allowed to become an article of faith for so many.

CHAPTER 7

LOVE AND MARRIAGE

I t started with a kiss. Jasmine met Martin and they fell for each other from the start. Marriage followed soon after, and the birth of the first of their two children a short time later. Things could not be better between them, and their future together looked bright.

That is exactly as it should be. A couple so dedicated to each other and to their young family is a life that many people can only dream about. Some do not know how truly lucky they are that they have it.

Jasmine and Martin's problems began when they decided to move to the United Kingdom. This is not a story I asked or wanted to hear, but one they asked me to tell. Their names have been changed to protect their privacy.

Jasmine was Indonesian and they lived in Jakarta. Martin was British. They wanted to make a change because of the better schools in the south-east of England, where Martin was from. Jasmine told me that they thought 'it would be good for the children to be in the UK for their education'. This was no slow boat to Kent but, in her words, 'the start of a very long nightmare'.

Things went wrong as soon as they arrived at the UK border. They had taken advice from the British consulate that Martin could give up his job in Jakarta and they could part with their possessions and uproot with easy entry to Britain as a married couple. But the advice they had was wrong.

When they landed in London Heathrow airport and made their way to passport control, Jasmine and Martin faced some unexpectedly hostile questions. Martin was asked about how he might financially support his young family. But the truth was they had sold up and had just landed. Martin explained he was a British citizen returning with his wife and children to his native country. He did not have a job as he had only just arrived home. But he would find one and had never been on benefits, so he had every reason to think a swift job offer was around the corner.

But Martin did not have a job on arrival. So their new life in Britain could only be temporary. He was allowed to stay and so could his children, but his wife could only be on a visitor's visa for a few months and then she would have to leave. British immigration rules meant a happy, young, self-sufficient family without any history of financial or legal troubles had to be split up – and this bombshell hit them only a few minutes after disembarking from a near round-the-world flight, having been assured by the British consulate that all would be well. They felt badly let down, but nothing would break their spirits.

Jasmine soon took the lonely, painful journey back to Jakarta, leaving her family behind in England. It was heart-wrenching. Martin found work quickly, as expected, but only on zero-hours contracts. This did not allow him to earn enough to sponsor his wife so she could join their family in Britain as their children were preparing to start school. Martin was desperate. Leaving the children with his mother, he landed a new job in Saudi Arabia that did pay him the right amount. He started renting a house in the UK that Jasmine could move into. The family would remain split, but he was willing to live apart so she could be with their children.

But their problem continued. He was not only required to earn above a certain threshold, but – crucially – he had to be earning in the UK to sponsor Jasmine coming over. This part about the job having to be in Britain had not been explained to them. Now the family was spread across three continents, trying everything they could to be together, but their lives were kept on hold by British immigration rules that few officials seemed to know or be able to explain to them.

Today, Jasmine and Martin have remained faithfully married to each other for almost twenty-five years. This was no sham marriage, but two people meant to be together. Their children are grown up and the youngest has nearly finished college. Jasmine is now on a two-year visitor's visa that does not allow her to work and is almost expired. They have understandably had enough of living on separate continents and 'don't feel the same any more' about Britain. They are likely to leave when their children's education is completed.

Jasmine and Martin's experience of British immigration is not unique – nor their feeling of incomprehensibility at how British citizens can receive a raw deal from a government claiming to have their interests at heart. Another person I spoke to said that 'being British means being let down by your country because of falling in love with a non-EU citizen and having your rights stripped away! I used to be proud to be British.' Not so any more.

This is a Britain so keen to show it is asserting controls on its borders that it will readily sacrifice the happiness of one British citizen to make a point – despite the fact that most people will never hear about it unless they too find themselves facing the immigration services. This is a side of immigration and citizenship policy you only come across when you speak with people on the front line.

Many other people are similarly affected. The government is advised by the Migration Advisory Committee on migration policy. This committee is an independent body of five economists and one of their tasks is to advise on reducing net migration by using an income threshold, a key government target. The coalition government under David Cameron supported a £35,000 salary minimum for migrants wanting to settle permanently, based on the committee's advice. This change was predicted to cut applications by 16 per cent, with exceptions made only for jobs on a shortage list. But this was not all.

In July 2012, the coalition government also introduced a minimum income threshold of £18,600 for a British citizen to sponsor a partner – and this is raised to £22,400 for a partner and a child, with an additional £2,400 for each further child. Sponsoring a wife and three children would require a minimum income of £24,800. The problem with using these income thresholds is that they will break up legitimate, loving families – even those with British citizens.

And this can work both ways. Under the current rules, a British citizen who earns less than £18,600 but is married to someone who earns much more is forbidden from being able to bring his or her spouse to Britain. So this is not about ensuring non-British citizens will avoid being a burden on the state – if it was, then it would look to household income of the couple, not unlike a joint tax return by a married couple. Instead, the policy seems purely – and explicitly – about keeping people out to reduce numbers, however it might be done and without regard for the consequences for British citizens. People are reduced to a crude numbers game.

The minimum income threshold has been challenged in the courts. Initially, there was some hope for campaigners when

Justice Blake ruled in the High Court that the threshold dis-proportionately interfered with the right to family life under the European Convention on Human Rights. This, however, was promptly overturned by the Court of Appeal. The Court of Appeal argued that the income threshold did interfere with family life so it must be necessary and proportionate in pursuit of a legitimate aim in order to be lawful. The Court of Appeal ruled that the Home Secretary was entitled to make a political judgement about this policy's aim in improving social integration – and without the need of a particular standard of empirical evidence.

But now it is back under review at the UK Supreme Court. Advocate Manjit Singh Gill claims that nearly half of Britain's working population could be barred from living with a non-EU spouse in the UK. The minimum threshold can also have unexpected consequences. According to Gill, 'An applicant earning £250,000 with a £3 million property, where the partner is a British woman who is a full-time mother to children, would not be allowed.'

And the government may not always be enforcing its threshold consistently. In April 2016, the Home Office agreed to reconsider a visa for Katy James, an American mother. She faced deportation because her British husband, a self-employed bike dealer (like my father for many years), earns less than the necessary amount. Although they had married in 2006, six years before the rule change, they were forced to fight even for the right to challenge her removal. After the story made national headlines, the Home Office reversed its decision, permitting James to remain in the UK. The government does not have data on how many people with British spouses or partners have been removed in recent years – or the number of times they decided against enforcing the minimal income threshold.

Most new British citizens naturalise, like I did – they satisfy the residency requirement. Only a minority of people I surveyed became British through marriage. There were 118,152 grants of citizenship in 2015. About half – 60,812 – were made on the basis of residency. Applications made on the basis of marriage were less than half that, at 24,451.

While many I spoke to said that having family in the UK was a reason for wanting to become British, many more responded that their reasons were that they work in the UK, they pay taxes to the British government and – top of the list – they live in the UK. Interestingly, becoming British because of earning a salary above the national average salary attracted very little support. I suspect the rules on income thresholds are, as Professor Martin Ruhs says, designed to reduce net migration. The way it is done may not be popular, but the government may be banking on the ends justifying the means. Unfortunately for them, it is has been a dog's dinner.

I asked a few hundred British-born people about requirements for British citizenship and found something interesting. They were no more favourable to becoming British through marriage than through having a British parent – and being born in a

Commonwealth country bears almost no weight at all. It is like the days of the Citizen of the UK and Colonies never happened.

Many today expect that marriage provides a sure path to citizenship in Britain and most other countries around the globe. But such a history is relatively recent. Marriage did not traditionally have any effect on nationality status under British common law until a change in statute in 1844. The Naturalisation Act gave a foreign woman married to a British subject automatic British subject status. If the British subject was a woman and she married a citizen of another country, she did not lose her status – but he would not become British.

There were no provisions for the naturalisation of children until the Naturalisation Act of 1870. This made children under twenty-one of a naturalised father – or a widowed mother – British subjects if resident in the UK with the father or widowed mother. But almost in return, British women who married non-British husbands lost their British subject status on marriage. So while the children of naturalised fathers benefited, the British wives to migrants lost out. It only became possible from 1914 for these women to become British subjects again if widowed or divorced.

The immigration rules also account for a wide variety of cases – and in some areas have continued to become more progressive. The minimum age for being lawfully sponsored as a spouse for immigration purposes is now eighteen years old, thanks to a UK Supreme Court ruling in 2011 that brought it down from twenty-one. In 2015, the coalition government introduced a new registration route for illegitimate children of fathers born before 2006.

In 2014, the Court of Justice of the European Union found that a woman who gives up work because of the physical demands from the later stages of pregnancy or childbirth retains the status of 'worker', provided she returns to work or finds a new job within a reasonable time after the child's birth. Being considered a worker at such a time is important because it would permit receipt of income support and potentially other benefits.

One surprise I had when becoming a permanent resident by gaining indefinite leave to remain in 2009 concerned offspring. Permanent residents are not British citizens, but are allowed to live in the UK without restrictions. Any child born to a permanent resident automatically becomes a British citizen – even though the permanent resident isn't British themselves. However, this only applies if the parents are married. If unmarried, then any children only become British if one of the parents is British. So, while permanent residents are not British, they could bestow Britishness on their children.

But much else has become increasingly restrictive – including keeping British citizens from living with their partners in their own country. This contributes to the government's efforts at satisfying a net migration target that is missed by larger margins each year – making British citizens pay the price for the current government's lack of fair play and good judgement.

Spouses of British nationals used to be on a fast-track to citizenship following a two-year probationary period while resident in the UK. Now they are treated like everybody else and must wait for a period of five years. There used to be immediate settlement for migrant partners living together for at least four years while overseas. This has now been abolished. No doubt it will be expected that the abolition will deter sham marriages, but this is wrongheaded. While there is no question that standards must be in place that are clearly communicated and which command public confidence – neither of which currently seem true – there is likewise equal good sense in encouraging those who are committed to a long-term future in Britain to become British citizens.

In December 2015, I discovered another Home Office plan to tackle sham marriages. The Home Office published a new form on its website. Its purpose was for individuals to report their ex-partners after their relationship had ended. Spousal visas are only valid where a relationship is subsisting and can therefore terminate before their normal expiration date when a couple break up. Someone at the Home Office thought it a good idea to produce a form to make it easier for former lovers to tell on each other and expose relationships that had ended – but the way the form was designed can only be described as a shambles.

Naturally, it asked for names – of the person making the 'public statement' that the relationship was over and of the ex-partner. The problem was what it did not ask. Nowhere did the form request contact details for the person sending in the form, in order to verify their claims. It did not ask how to contact ex-partners, either – or what their nationality might be. Moreover, it forgot to mention where to send the form, and the Home Office never got around to issuing a press release to inform the public about this new border control tool that could only work with their help. The government wanted us to rat out those we once loved, but then forgot to tell us how. Troublingly, there was no evidence of any impact assessment to gauge the risk that the form could be used as a threat by one partner, contributing to domestic abuse.

There can be an uneasy balance between the proper assessment and waiting period of prospective citizens and the granting of full rights. But it is a balance that must be struck. If managed well, becoming British can foster integration through a sense of shared collective connections with others on equal terms.

Much of this history of the evolution of British citizenship finds women lagging behind men. It was men whose Britishness counted for the most – through marriage, they created British wives and children. But women would not catch up until only a few decades ago.

The historical lack of gender equality – and the importance of being the legitimate child of a married couple – in British citizenship is not old news.

Reyna was born in Bolton to a British father and Danish mother. Reyna is now twenty-four years old and has only ever lived in the UK. But she is not British.

The problem was what her mother did – or rather, what she did not do – before she died in 2009. Her Danish mother is the only parent registered on Reyna's birth certificate. Reyna was able to acquire a Danish passport to travel abroad, but has been unable to renew it since turning twenty-two, thanks to Denmark's citizenship laws. Reyna can only acquire a new Danish passport if she is able to speak the language or take up residence in Denmark. But she has only visited the country twice. Reyna was born in Britain, but being born in the United Kingdom is not enough to become British. She must prove her dad is British – which she cannot do because his name is not on her birth certificate.

But it gets worse. Reyna is engaged to be married. Yet she cannot marry her fiancé because she lacks proper documentation and she fears her marriage could be treated as a sham. That missing signature on her birth certificate has come at a huge personal and financial cost years later. Unable to travel abroad, she could not attend the weddings of her sisters in Turkey and Tuscany. Despite living her whole life in Britain, born in Britain and with a British dad, she must navigate the permanent residency and citizenship regulations like me – someone originally from the United States who did not set foot in Britain until I was older than Reyna is now. She is currently studying for her citizenship test with large fees of nearly £2,000 ahead – all so she can become the British citizen she already would be if only her father had been named on her birth certificate before her mother died. This is yet another face of current immigration and citizenship policy few members of the British public see.

Married spouses – often wives – face other problems. An EU national can enter Britain and stay permanently without needing a work visa or marriage to a British citizen. The situation is very different for non-EU nationals.

If a citizen of a country outside the EU marries a British citizen, he or she can apply for a spousal visa, which would be required before attempting to enter the UK. If granted, a spouse can build up their residency time towards applying for British citizenship after five years. But if the couple should divorce, his or (more commonly) her years are wiped clean – it is like she never was in the UK. This is why many non-EU citizens who marry a British national choose to apply to become British based on their residency in work. The only time that counts for the spousal route is while the marriage is subsisting – and any marital breakdown sets the years in residency clock back to zero.

This can raise real problems. Harley was an Australian who married an Italian. They came to the UK – allowed under the EU's 'free' movement rules as both were working. Harley found work and swiftly became very successful, going on to carve out a decade-long career in Britain at the time – precisely the kind of immigrant the public supports. Hard-working, talented, in a high-skilled role working in the healthcare sector.

After seven years living and working in Britain, their marriage unfortunately broke down. Harley wrote to the UK Border Agency to ask if she could continue working until her spousal visa expired – and they wrote back to confirm this was OK.

Harley worked until the end of her visa three years later and duly sent in her application for discretionary leave to remain. And that is where something went very wrong.

It took the Home Office an unforgivable *two years* to get back in touch with Harley. By that point, she had been in the UK for nearly a dozen years. The Home Office wrote to say she should never have stayed on her spousal visa given the marriage was over – and so she had to go. In effect, she was in the country illegally. From pillar of society and model immigrant to an illegal over-stayer. They gave her twenty-eight days' notice to pack her bags and exit the country. It made no difference to the Home Office that its own officers had advised her wrongly and in writing. She had to leave. Game over.

Except this story has a twist. The immigration rules constrain the discretion that the Home Office can exercise, but there is flexibility if political will can be found. Harley won the attention of *The Independent*, which championed her case. Her grassroots campaign saw thousands – including me – signing a petition for her to stay.

The story ends somewhat happily. The judge took her side and ruled it was 'palpably evident' her removal would be detrimental to British taxpayers. Harley received a temporary visa and could continue working.

But she told me that going public – which appeared to have turned the tide and made a real difference – was very much a 'double-edged sword'. It was an understandably emotionally draining and costly experience. The endless comments in the media about her and her case were often very painful to read. She remains unsure about whether to continue living in the UK – and found it hurtful to see what lengths the government was willing to go to in order to see her removed. It left a feeling that the immigration system was little more than 'a revenue-making thing', taking advantage of people who are vulnerable and lack a voice. A far cry from the lofty ambitions of the 'British values' championed by the same government.

Other women report different problems. Lauren has lived in the UK for seven years, five of them with her British husband. She passed the citizenship test, but her marriage broke down before applying for citizenship. Her residency clock had to restart – as if she had never been here. Ironically, if she had been more single-minded in seeking UK citizenship, she would have been entitled to it a few years ago. This is a case of someone who could have become British but did not apply quickly enough – and now must rebuild her Britishness once more.

Lauren has also faced challenges getting her home state of New Jersey to agree to a name change so she can retake her maiden name. She told me that the application actually required the signature of her ex-husband before it would be considered – an egregious violation of her autonomy, since they were divorced. Lauren said that 'spouses lose out twice over' – and she's right. These are the kinds of everyday tragedies that so often get overlooked in public outcries over migration targets. These are not simply unintended consequences, but real people left short-changed by an immigration system that must be improved.

Close relatives are negatively affected as well. Adult and elderly dependent relatives are required to apply from outside the UK for entry – while also making clear that as a result of their age, illness or disability they require long-term personal care to support everyday functions. Crucially, this care must be shown to be provided for in the UK by their sponsor – and without recourse to any public funds.

Government has brought several strings attached – hurdles to jump and, more likely, traps to reduce numbers. Bhikhu Parekh told me a clear problem was with the assumptions behind this way of thinking. He said that this supposes that dependent relatives – such as elderly parents – 'are a burden'. Everything is built around the undesirability of allowing such burdens to enter the UK for fear someone's personal costs could become shared.

Bhikhu rejects this perspective. 'Instead of thinking it is a burden to look after one's parents,' he told me, 'why not say it should be an honour or a privilege?' Children who are raised and nurtured by loving parents are not burdened by caring for them in older age.

The single biggest problem with the spousal immigration rules is simple: the rules are changing so fast that not even Home Office officials or their representatives can provide reliable advice. The outcomes are inevitable: prolonged anguish, spiralling costs, maltreatment and sometimes lives destroyed for decent people playing by the rules, while ministers skip along without noticing the damage this causes.

These problems are illustrated in the appalling treatment suffered by Peter and Maria. Their names and identifying details have been changed to protect their privacy in light of the fact they continue to endure the consequences from their experiences, but they asked me to share their story.

Peter is a British citizen who was living in Canada. He met an American named Maria and they were married about ten years ago. Maria had a teenage daughter from a previous relationship and she came to live with her mother and stepfather in Canada.

After some discussion they decided to move to Britain. But before doing so, they obtained some advice. Peter and Maria had both lived abroad before and were aware of the importance of following strict – and often complex – immigration guidelines. They met with the British High Commission, who advised Peter that Maria and her daughter could join him in moving to the UK. The High Commission said neither required any prior entry clearance. Peter asked the High Commission for a copy of its email to the Home Office confirming the advice he had been given as valid – and still has it. Furthermore, the High Commission said that his wife and stepdaughter could apply for British citizenship twelve months after coming to the UK.

Later that year, they packed their bags for Britain. They informed the immigration officer on arrival into Britain that Maria was married to Peter, who was a British citizen, and that she and her daughter intended to apply for citizenship after twelve months. The officer agreed only to grant them a visitor's visa covering a short visit, but gave assurances that permanent residency could be acquired in-country. The three later went for a holiday in Spain – although after Maria and her daughter had overstayed on their visas. When returning back to the UK, they informed the immigration officer of their intention to stay permanently. Maria and her daughter received a new visitor's visa, but they were assured yet again that permanent residency could be in reach shortly.

Maria submitted an application to acquire a spousal visa – and received not a new visa but a deportation order. The order noted that she had been an overstayer and – even worse than this – she was accused of misleading an immigration officer. This was because she intended to stay in the country permanently, but accepted visitor visas. That act was seen as entry by deception. Their lives were turned upside down.

Peter and Maria are strong people. Their marriage continues, but they are changed from this experience. Each is now on prescription medication to address ailments relating to the stress and anguish associated with their problems with the Home Office. Their legal fight was enormously costly – enough to buy a new BMW. More than a decade later and still Maria and her daughter are not citizens. But they were able to get discretionary leave to remain covering six years.

Perhaps the heaviest cost is on Maria's daughter. During this time, her visa status was often under review or her passport in a Home Office pigeon hole. She could not attend university as she was unable to afford the much higher non-EU student fees. She has been unable to drive or work. And socialising has been a problem as she still has only an American passport for identity checks at bars and restaurants – and not all accept it.

The real tragedy of this story is that here are people still living with the consequences of a High Commission that did not give them the correct legal advice. This fact, which they have in writing, was no defence against their having been in breach of the immigration rules. Incredibly, written advice from a British High Commission is not worth the paper it is printed on if a problem arises. And, still worse, this advice was seen by Peter and Maria to have been emailed to the Home Office, who should either have been waiting for them at the border or have corrected the advice they received before they returned to the UK. There was never a reason for the Home Office to be surprised. Yet they were, and they treated Peter and Maria as mercilessly 'as if we were criminals'. This is no way to treat any law-abiding British citizen making every reasonable effort to abide by a complex set of rules shifting so quickly that neither the High Commission nor two different immigration officers could keep up with something as basic as visa restrictions on the non-British spouses and children of UK citizens.

Sham marriages have been a growing concern for successive governments. The issue regularly makes the news headlines, and the scale of the problem is increasing. A Freedom of Information request for postcodes in Derbyshire, Leicestershire and Nottinghamshire for the number of suspected sham marriages or partnerships reported by registrars is fifty-three in 2012, fifty-four in 2013, but sixty-eight in only the first nine months of 2014.

Sham marriages and partnerships are not genuine relationships; they are those entered or contracted for the purpose of avoiding provisions of immigration law. In other words, to illegally sneak in by the back door. The Home Office has described these shams as 'a significant threat to UK immigration control'. Just one person let in can help open the way for other family members to follow who might otherwise all be barred.

The way this has been tackled is to make it more inconvenient to get married in this country. For church or civil ceremonies, residency in England or Wales for at least twenty-eight days and advance notice of where the wedding will take place are now required. Evidence of names, dates of birth, marital statuses and nationalities must be provided. If one of the persons is a non-EEA national, he or she is referred to the Home Office, where there is discretion to extend the notice period for up to seventy days. If refused, people tend to submit the same application – and hope for a different result. Sir John Vine, the former Independent Chief Inspector of Borders and Immigration, found that 72 per cent of refusals were repeat applications.

But the fact is that no one really knows how many sham marriages happen or what their full consequences might be. Sir John revealed to the Home Affairs Select Committee that 'the Home

Office does not really know' the scale of the problem, adding, 'The fact that we are estimating in the first place says it all.'

While the burden is on the state or other authorities to show a marriage is a sham, the checks are more thorough than many might think – when done appropriately and fairly. I know something about this because I experienced it. When my wife and I decided to marry, we wanted to have our wedding at her local church. She is very close to her family, with many living near by. While my immediate family is still in the New Haven area, much of my extended family is spread across the United States, from New England to the Pacific North West and then south to several states between North Carolina and Florida. And it was a lovely local church, too.

All we had to do was agree a date with the vicar. Or so we thought. We quickly set a date after meeting the vicar, but there was more to do. He had to visit me in my home – to ensure I really was where I said I was. Not for religious purposes. No, this was for immigration purposes – triggered by my being American.

And that was not all. Most people wanting a marriage in an Anglican church pay for wedding banns in the weeks leading up to the wedding. But not if you're a foreigner. We had to purchase a far more expensive marriage licence because I was not a British citizen.

I have met only a handful of people who have heard of this difference based on nationality – and all work in the wedding business. Another thing you only find out when you have to do it.

This could possibly explain why the Home Office-produced *A Practical Guide to Living in the United Kingdom* – aimed at migrants newly arrived in the UK – has serious mistakes, like saying banns are OK when they are not. This was one of several errors or omissions I pointed out in a report published shortly after the guide appeared – and, strangely, you hear little about it these days, although it remains in print unchanged.

The right to family life does not work the way many people think. The bare fact that someone lives in a country does not give effect to that right. What is required is a genuine and subsisting relationship with a partner in the UK who is a British citizen, or someone settled in the UK, including someone with refugee leave.

Children bring important considerations to the fore, as their best interests must be taken into account. This can sometimes help ensure a parent stays in the UK to care for their child whereas they would otherwise be forced to leave. This is true for adopted children as well – leading some to fear that adoption of non-EU children could undermine efforts to reduce net migration. When narrow pursuit of a meaningless target becomes a reason to try to prevent British couples from raising the family they could not conceive on their own, there is a real absence of common sense, fair play and perhaps humanity.

One European lawyer told me the easiest way to stay in the EU was to conceive or adopt a child. Last spring, the UK Supreme Court ruled that what matters is the stability of a child's residence in the country in question – and not the length or permanence of the residency, especially 'the more deeply integrated' they become.

The right to family life can be established with children where there is a genuine and subsisting parental relationship with a child in the UK under eighteen years old and who is also a British citizen or continuously living in the UK for seven years – and where 'it would not be reasonable to expect the child to leave the UK'. Lots of strings attached. Not all relationships can be shown to be subsisting, especially at a time when so many live apart from one another – and when divorce is more commonplace than it once was.

When headlines announce someone can stay in the UK because of a right to family life, the suggestion seems often to be that *therefore* they are obviously going to soak the rest of us. But this is not what research from the House of Commons has found. A 2013 report found that 'successful applicants are granted permission to work, but are likely to be subject to a "no recourse to public funds" condition unless they provide evidence of exceptional circumstances'. So the assumptions can often bear little relation to the reality. For most people affected, a right to stay is a right to have a go at earning a living without help from the state. This might not fit expectations, but looking below the surface to how things actually work can reveal a different picture.

The situation becomes more complex as non-British children reach adulthood – and here the government appears to have become increasingly aggressive. *Private Eye* uncovered the case of Benita and Eugene. They came from South Africa to the UK in 2008 with their three children aged between fifteen and nineteen years old. Each was in education. Benita found work as a senior systems analyst and Eugene was an educational psychologist. Benita and Eugene earned a welcome living paying the top rate of income tax. They invested heavily in their children's learning, spending over £160,000 on schooling.

When they applied for permanent residency as a family in 2013, all received it – except for their eldest daughter, Nicole. The family had been advised to have her apply separately for a student visa because she had a place at university – despite her remaining very much 'dependent' on the support of her parents. That year, extensions to her visa were rejected and in June 2014 she was served a deportation order.

Nicole went to a tribunal to appeal the decision on the grounds of her right to a private and family life. Each month she had to report to a police station. Inevitably, this took a heavy toll on her well-being, but she tried to stay positive and regularly worked as a volunteer at a local charity. A year on, an immigration tribunal found in her favour. The judge commented on her positive contribution to society, describing her as 'a worthy member of her community' who 'enhances the cultural life of the UK'.

The Home Secretary Theresa May's response is nothing short of appalling. She has sought an appeal against Nicole's successful appeal in a determined bid to see her thrown out of the country.

It is disappointing to see someone – yes, a migrant – who is contributing so much towards the Big Society receive so little in return.

Love and marriage may go together like two peas in a happy pod, but that is only until the immigration rules enter the frame. The problem is not having rules or maintaining standards, but the way in which these rules and standards are enforced. There is an increasing zeal from May and her government to use – and sometimes twist – the rules in a single-minded effort to reduce net migration one way or another. It seems that if families must pay the price, it is of little concern to the government.

There is scope for reform. It is welcome that efforts have increased to target sham marriages and partnerships. These must continue. Perhaps the time frame for informing the Home Office of the intention to have a marriage ceremony should be extended – although this could also push the problem elsewhere if couples choose marriage in another country to avoid stricter regulations in the UK.

Residency requirements might also be revisited with a view to extending them. This would provide a trade-off: people could continue to live together for a year or two longer than now, which they desperately seem to desire, but at the cost of having to remain self-subsisting without recourse to public funds. A slight increase in time commitments could make a difference in deterring sham arrangements who are not *that* committed to such a deception, but help keep loving families together – including the families of British citizens.

Falling in love need not mean having to live apart. We have too many stories of people's lives being upended for no good purpose. With a few small changes indicated, it could make a positive difference to the families affected and to wider British society.

CHAPTER 8

SEEKING ASYLUM

S peak about 'migrants' and a particular image comes to mind
for many people – typically, a refugee who seeks to claim asylum. It is not unusual for the public to overestimate the numbers
of ethnic or religious minorities in the wider population. But there
is something different – and disturbing – about the widespread
caricature of the immigrant as an asylum seeker.

This view of the imaginary immigrant is so embedded in our
public debates that talk about migration is expected to focus on
asylum seekers and other refugees. If we believed the hype, we
would think refugees by far the largest group of migrants entering Britain, coming from desperate poverty, lacking education,

and full to the brim of values incompatible with a free society like ours. And, we would think, you can tell a refugee just by looking at them.

At the 2015 Tory spring conference, Home Secretary Theresa May appealed to the many citizens sharing this image. She wanted to reinforce the point she had made earlier that the streets of Britain are not 'paved with gold'. May's focus was not on foreign entrepreneurs, economic migrants or students. No, it was on asylum claimants, and her determination to clamp down harder on them in order to help reduce net migration. This would be an important achievement for anyone believing refugees are half as numerous as popular opinion would have it – fewer refugees means much less migration.

The speech was music to the ears of the Tory faithful lining the conference hall. But it received a very different reaction from viewers at home – and especially from anyone who knew that the hype is a caricature so removed from reality this is less a straw man than a pure conjuring from a land of make-believe.

As a frequent columnist writing about immigration issues, it is safe to say I receive my share of 'spirited' reader feedback. To be fair, the feedback is far more often supportive of my arguments than attempting to 'correct' my 'mistakes' – although there is always the rare person who tells me I should leave the UK if I have anything resembling a criticism of government policies.

But I was moved by one reader who wrote to me about May's speech.

She has got it so wrong – my father was an immigrant.
He was a refugee from Hitler's Germany just before the war.
Despite being interned, on his release he worked at three
jobs in order to make ends meet. After the war he started
his own company, which must have given jobs to hundreds
of people over the thirty or so years before his death. A contribution in all sorts of ways – I feel deeply offended and
insulted by her remarks.

It is easy to see why.

Asylum seekers might appear out of place for a book about
becoming British. But they aren't. When I asked British citizens
or prospective citizens, asylum seekers and refugees were largely
absent from the discussion. While a majority of the public thinks
of migrants as refugees, most people do not think of them as
fellow future citizens. To be British is to speak English, to contribute, to pay taxes and become positively involved in everyday
British life.

This view was not shared by everyone, of course. But the dis-
senters were very much exceptions to the rule. From hundreds of
interviews and questionnaires, only one person noted that to be
British is to have 'a multiplicity of origins and backgrounds, opinions and interests, united but not homogenous'. Some people
worried about the increasing intolerance and moral panic they
believed is shown about migrants in general – and fuelled by concerns over refugees. A few people said that to be British was to

have a willingness to help those most in need, such as refugees coming to the UK.

But what is clear overall is that, in the eyes of most, British citizenship and asylum-seeking refugees don't mix. It is far more prevalent to think of them as a group that is permanently 'other' and separate – they are people 'we' might choose to assist, but *they* are not *us*. Becoming British is for others and not them.

Adopting what I would call the 'them and us' perspective, viewing refugees as separable others, makes some sense of the moral panic that grips so many. Last autumn, the *Times* columnist and ConservativeHome blogger Tim Montgomerie weighed in on the refugee crisis, claiming that Britain has 'got to be harsh to be kind to migrants'. A policy of tough love, as if refugees get too little rough treatment and too much affection.

Montgomerie took as his model the immigration policies of former Australian Prime Minister Tony Abbott, who vowed to 'stop the boats' coming to Australia with refugees. Montgomerie says: 'Some of the measures undertaken to end the traffic have been controversial. The detainment facilities at Nauru, for example, which house migrants with no obvious safe place to return, are blighted by accusations of cruelty ... But the policy has largely worked.'

So that's the position – success of a narrow policy at high moral cost. The word 'barbarian' might have once been roughly synonymous with 'foreigner', but this is no excuse to treat these foreigners like barbarians. Montgomerie longs for the day when a British Prime Minister can speak – and act – like an Australian Prime Minister and say, 'We will decide who comes to this country and the circumstances on which they come.' Not a problem if you don't mind the gap between doing the right thing and doing it in the right way.

This issue helps unmask an important fact about migration generally: the great majority of asylum-seeker claims are made not at the border, but after the refugee is already inside. Stopping the boats misses the point. The other popular image of refugees making their asylum applications at the airport is true only about 10 per cent of the time. In fact, the typical case is someone who makes an application from within the country – after having already crossed the border.

The public assumes that asylum seekers are the largest group of migrants, but actually they are about the smallest. According to the Office for National Statistics, there were 25,771 asylum applications made in the year ending in June 2015. Numbers remain low from their peak of 84,123 in 2002. The top nationals applying for asylum in the UK prior to the recent EU refugee crisis were Eritrea (3,568), Pakistan (2,302) and Syria (2,204). They are usually men. After relative size is taken into account, the UK ranks sixteenth of twenty-eight EU countries – so hardly at the top of the #refugeeswelcome list. But it's also true that the Home Office does not know the total number of refugees in the UK today.

While there are sometimes worries expressed that asylum seekers are claiming state benefits they are not entitled to, the government has only recently acknowledged that, in fact, they had no statistics at all on whether this was true. Nor does the government have any plans to permit asylum seekers waiting for their applications to be processed to engage in paid or voluntary work until at least twelve months have passed – and then asylum seekers can only start employment if their line of work is on the government's list of shortage occupations. The process can take more than a year, and sometimes much longer.

This process of assessing asylum applications through various enquiries and conducting searches is complex – and it is important to get right. One refugee told me, 'I would not make the process shorter than it is now, as that would be unfair and also cause more wrongful refusals.'

Asylum seekers receive only 'essential living needs' as their legal test for income support. The level of support is kept under constant review. It includes the cost of food stuffs, clothing, toiletries, household cleaning products, non-prescription medication and limited travel. It totals £36.95 per week for each person in the household claiming asylum. A couple might receive only £295.60 to live on for the month. They also receive accommodation as well as free access to health care, and education for any children.

This puts asylum seekers in a very difficult situation in terms of public acceptance. Not only do people resent the minimal public benefit they receive to survive, but asylum seekers are unable to do anything about it as they forbidden from lawfully supporting themselves financially. They are forced onto benefits – and then disliked by some people for their reliance on benefits. Asylum seekers cannot win. The government should stand up to protect those it claims to help. It can and should do more.

A key problem with the current asylum system is a lack of support from the beginning to the end of the asylum process – and this is a particular problem for those cases where an appeal against the Home Office's decision to deny asylum is overturned. Successful asylum seekers are people who have suffered persecution, discrimination or worse, justifying their repatriation to a place often far from their native home. The assessment can take several months, with little assistance or support. If applications are not upheld, appeals are normally only considered once they have left the UK – this significantly reduces their chances of success, as indeed the policy is designed to do.

There is too much emphasis on managing asylum on the cheap rather than getting the process fit for purpose. An example is Middlesbrough – which has been named the 'refugee capital' of Britain. The reason for the high number of asylum seekers was simple. House prices are significantly lower in the city and surrounding areas than in places like London or the south-east. The now privatised asylum-seeker management system was able to home asylum seekers in Middlesbrough for less – and it did. By comparison, wealthier constituencies like Witney, represented by David Cameron, have no asylum seekers.

There are national guidelines for limits on the number of asylum seekers permissible for different regions. This is linked in part to the size of the local community. The idea is that moving numbers of asylum seekers to a new area should be limited by the threat it may pose to social cohesion. If too many are permitted, this can undermine a community's solidarity – and lead to tensions between local people and vulnerable asylum seekers living in a legal limbo as they await a decision on whether they can stay in the country or whether they will be deported.

The problem in Middlesbrough was that the rules were broken. Far more refugees were placed in the cheaper accommodation available than were allowed under the national guidelines. Instead of one asylum seeker per 200 people, Middlesbrough was found to have one per 180 people. This led to avoidable tensions in the local community: there were pressures on school places, public transport and more that were out of proportion to expectations given by the government.

The government's response has been more akin to a plaster than a proper fix. Emergency funding was provided to help deliver temporary relief for the pressures faced by public services. But there was no fine for the private firm responsible for violating national guidelines and causing the problem in the first place. There appear to be insufficient assurances in places to ensure situations like this will not happen again – and the people who were housed in Middlesbrough were not given an opportunity to move elsewhere if they wanted to, either. The potential cost to social cohesion was apparently a price worth paying. The story gets worse.

In January 2016, it was discovered that 155 front doors across 168 properties in two wards housing asylum seekers in Middlesbrough had been painted red. The red doors left some asylum seekers feeling as if they had been marked out as targets for abuse, with reports that doors were smeared with dog excrement and graffiti. Eggs and stones were thrown at homes, too. Shortly afterwards, asylum seekers in Cardiff reported being harassed after they were required to wear red wristbands.

The government was taken by surprise when these events came to light – and it is easy to see why. The Home Office had contracted out the work of managing accommodation for asylum seekers to private firms; in the case of Middlesbrough, this work was then subcontracted out to a second private firm. These companies can play an important role in an efficient, well-managed system for refugee support. The problem is that the Home Office can agree contracts for others to manage the daily operations of this support system, but it cannot subcontract out the government's responsibility for it. Areas affected were not examined properly by ministers – and they received a lot of egg on their faces, figuratively speaking, when these embarrassing revelations were exposed. And there remains no clear punishment for private firms that pack asylum seekers into communities in excess of national guidelines, taking advantage of refugees while taking control of public funds.

It is especially disappointing to see the current government fail to make any clear defence of the current asylum system it has in place. Instead of addressing public concerns by making the argument for why Britain should continue to honour its international obligations to provide asylum, ministers like Theresa May play to mistaken fears about the number of refugees and the threat they pose to social cohesion – deliberately fanning the flames of animosity towards vulnerable people whose true stories few citizens will hear. Not only is this a coward's game in failing to stand up for the government's policies, but it also has a dark side in its targeting already heavily marginalised people.

Securing Britain's borders is not as easy as some think. The UK might be an island nation, but people enter and leave the country by more means than just a boat from authorised ports. However impressive Britain's naval history, we must scrap such outdated models of what Britain is and get firmer control of the challenges Britain faces in the twenty-first century. Migrants enter by land, sea and air – and modern modes of travel must be taken into account. No country is an island any more when seen through this perspective.

Border controls – paradoxically – are often exercised not at the UK's boundaries but after people have already entered. Millions of people travel across the border each year – there were more than 123 million journeys made over twelve months in 2015. Tourists, foreign football teams, international musicians, film stars, doctors, teachers and refugees – these are some of the many different kinds of people who choose to enter Britain each year. The overwhelming majority leave shortly afterwards, travelling on their time-restricted visitor's visa or similar status. While border controls have their place at refusing entry to people – 17,279 people were refused entry at port in 2015 – they are largely directed at people already resident in the UK.

Critics are highly vocal in their insistence that the asylum process is not rigorous enough, providing an alternative route to residency for those lacking real employment prospects. This view can be summarised as: if you can't stay by other means, apply for asylum and get your citizenship. Theresa May clearly appeals to such detractors.

In practice, there are stringent tests used before an individual is recognised as an asylum seeker. The UK is a party to the Convention relating to the Status of Refugees 1951 and its 1967 Protocol. The convention established an important legal principle of *refoulement* – that no state can return (*refouler*) a refugee who 'owing to a well-founded fear of being persecuted for reasons of race, religion, nationality, membership of a particular social group or political opinion, is outside the country of his nationality and is unable or, owing to such fear, is unwilling to avail himself of the protection of that country'.

The Home Office uses a variety of measures to determine whether to accept an application for asylum. It provides a list of select countries where there is generally believed to be no serious risk of persecution – and applications from citizens of these countries are normally refused. While there is much discretion, this is limited in Home Office guidance by the need for compatibility with the European Convention on Human Rights.

What this means in practice is that someone must continually apply – successfully – for restricted leave to remain for maximum periods of six months at a time.

There have been problems – especially with how asylum claims have been handled. In the words of former Home Secretary Charles Clarke, there was 'a dreadful legacy of asylum claims made before 2005'. He refers to claims that had been left unexamined and unclosed for several years – including 'roomfuls of files which were never opened'.

The backlog is still a problem. About a year ago, the Home Office confirmed it had nearly 23,000 applications since April 2006 still pending a decision – whether an initial decision, an appeal or a further review – nearly ten years later. This is a 34 per cent increase on the previous year and set to become much worse.

Part of the cause is cuts to frontline staff. The Office for National Statistics claims it is 'due to a decrease in staffing levels following a restructure initiated by the UK Border Agency', adding: 'Since 2014, the Home Office has taken steps to reallocate resources to this area.' This restructuring saw the UK Border Agency split in two: a UK Visas and Immigration and a separate Immigration Enforcement unit.

This came on the heels of a budget cut of up to 20 per cent aimed at reducing staff by 5,200. The delays faced are a serious issue: the longer an asylum applicant must wait before a decision is made, the greater the cost to taxpayers. Equally serious are the terrible personal costs to those directly affected. At a time when many need safety and security, they are placed in limbo. Margaret Hodge, the former chair of the Public Accounts Committee, found that the failure of major IT projects designed to help streamline the process may cost taxpayers the 'gobsmackingly awful figure' of up to £1 billion.

Some people I spoke with who work closely with the Home Office told me that it is 'a victim of many reforms – and a target for improvisations'. Staff are hardworking and professional, but under huge pressure from targets that make a very difficult job even more demanding. People who claimed asylum successfully told me that 'the communication between applicants and the Home Office is still very poor'.

If a claim is successful, people granted asylum no longer receive automatic permanent settlement, but instead five years' residency in the UK. At the end of this time, they can apply for permanent residency. Anyone who receives asylum or humanitarian protection and then becomes a British citizen can only sponsor family to come to the UK like any other British citizen – they could no longer do so under the category of Refugee Family Reunion.

But most people get turned down. Sixty per cent of all applications are rejected. This decision can often take close to a year or more for many people. In 2010, official statistics found 3,158 applications took under six months to decide and 4,081 applications took longer than this. By 2015, there were 11,269 asylum decisions made in less than six months, but 11,629 taking longer.

If someone's claim for asylum is rejected, there are other options available to stay in the UK – something I am often asked about. Most rejected asylum seekers lodge appeals – because they can stand a reasonable chance of success. Consider these figures from 2014: of the 70 per cent that made an appeal, 28 per cent were allowed to pursue it while the others were either dismissed or withdrawn. Of appeals that made it past this hurdle and were considered, 45 per cent – nearly half – were granted and the applicant could stay in the UK. That is a lot of Home Office decisions gone wrong.

Successive governments have struggled to reduce the time it can take to hear appeals and deport failed asylum seekers. Recently, the courts have struck down the government's short-lived fast-track appeal system. The government tried to limit the window for submitting an appeal to no more than twenty-two days after a claim for asylum was denied. But as I told the online BBC magazine, the Court of Appeal declared the system unfair and 'unlawful'. The reasoning was simple: the period of time that people had to make a claim was far too short to put together any meaningful case. Given that the risks of getting it wrong are potentially so great, sufficient time is necessary.

Not all appeals are made by refugees. A surprising number come from the Home Office. After a written Parliamentary Question by Jeremy Corbyn, now Leader of the Labour Party, the Home Office admitted that it had lodged 1,964 appeals – but only 730 (or just over a third) were allowed.

Other than asylum, the Home Office can grant either

'humanitarian protection' or 'discretionary leave' visas. These were introduced in 2003 to cover cases of people who are genuinely in need of protection or where there are compelling reasons permitting their staying inside the UK and outside of the immigration rules despite not being declared an asylum seeker.

The steep rise in applications for asylum in Britain are dwarfed by what we find in other European countries. During 2015, Germany received 431,000 asylum seekers and the UK only 39,000 – Britain had the ninth most asylum applications in the EU. This has not been without costs. Germany was faced with at least 200 confirmed attacks on refugee accommodation during the first six months of 2015 and there were reports of widespread sexual assaults by refugees in Cologne on New Year's Day 2016.

It is commonly – but falsely – believed that all refugees wishing to claim asylum must declare it in the first European country they arrive it. Like most myths, this is based on a half-truth. EU member states did agree something called the Dublin Regulation – a common asylum policy they decided to implement at a meeting in the Irish capital.

The Dublin Regulation is an agreement among EU countries – including the UK – that the first safe EU country a person arrives at is where his or her asylum application should be processed. This was designed to prevent asylum seekers 'shopping around' different EU countries, submitting multiple claims in the hope that one might be accepted. The EU established a system to help identify which country was the entry point for asylum seekers.

If someone were to enter one country but claim in another, the system is meant to identify the first country entered so that he or she can be sent there to have their claim processed.

This regulation is not always policed as well as it should be. Human traffickers might help people illegally enter an EU country – and then help them arrive at a different country to make their claim. The Schengen Agreement between most EU countries permitting relatively few border controls is thought to help facilitate these activities.

Calais is regularly taken to be an example of where the Dublin Regulation breaks down. A growing number of refugees can be found in camps called 'The Jungle' near the entrance to the Eurotunnel. Since at least September 2014, the situation had been described as a crisis as the numbers of refugees crept towards an estimated four thousand people.

For many British citizens, the scenes of refugees attempting to break into freight lorries heading to the UK looked like a failure of Europe. It was thought that if asylum seekers should seek refuge in the first safe country they arrive at, then either this should have been much earlier or it was the responsibility of the French authorities to process known refugees in their territory.

But the situation is more complex, as I told television viewers regularly during the summer of 2015. I was asked to do three or four live interviews a day for several weeks on this topic with the BBC, ITV and Sky, as well as several foreign stations including France 24, Al Jazeera and Turkey's TRT World channel.

When the Eurotunnel was built, the UK and France agreed a deal. Each would start entry to their border on the other side of the tunnel. This meant that anyone wanting to enter the Eurotunnel to get to France enters the French border control on the UK side. Similarly, the UK's border would start on the French side – in Calais. It is a reciprocal agreement.

The French had been reluctant to act to process any asylum-seeker claims for fear of the high costs and potential risk of sparking tensions – especially when just about all the refugees were there so they could leave France and enter the UK.

What eventually happened was what I call the Calais Compromise, signed by Home Secretary Theresa May and her French counterpart, the Interior Minister, Bernard Cazeneuve. They agreed that Britain would help fund 'dedicated facilities' in Calais as part of a multi-million-pound package designed to fast-track asylum-seeker claims in France. Essentially, much of the compromise entailed helping cover the costs to the French for processing more of the people in the area in order to reduce numbers.

The government has spent £9.46 million between July 2014 and April 2016. These costs were primarily to install fencing along the approach road to protect freight entering the tunnel, but also covered improved detection technology and 'boosting our dog-searching capability by £1 million'. This was no medium- or long-term solution. It merely tried to address the immediate situation on Britain's doorstep. If every person could be moved out of the Jungle camps, this would do nothing to stop more travelling across Europe to take their places.

Enforcement of the Dublin Regulation has sometimes flared into violence. When refugees travelling from Serbia into Hungary were screened and their fingerprints taken in summer 2015, it led to angry protests. Refugees were soon met by Hungarian security forces firing tear gas as 200 refugees attempted to leave the country's main processing centre in Röszke. These protests erupted because many of them were entering Hungary on foot because it was on the Serbian border, but they wanted to go to countries like Germany, Sweden or the Netherlands – and they would be prevented from doing so if fingerprinted. This is because the Eurodac fingerprint database would quickly inform another EU country they had arrived first in Hungary – and so they would be returned there instead of being allowed to stay in the country they wanted to be in.

There is an important principle behind the Dublin Regulation. It is that refugees fleeing civil war or persecution require urgent safety – and so wherever they can be harboured safely first should be the primary port of call. If the first safe place is somehow unacceptable or worth passing by, some might think this undermines the claim to asylum by that action.

But this rule is more aspirational than enforced – and it is too frequently overlooked. Asylum seekers have a right to make a claim for asylum anywhere they like outside their home country. This means they could apply in the first, second or tenth country arrived at. People fleeing civil war or persecution urgently need not only a safe haven, but some place where they feel safe. This may not always be the first country they arrive at.

But the Dublin Regulation does provide cover for EU countries that want to lower the number of asylum seekers who can claim asylum in Europe. The Home Office has made clear that it takes 'full advantage' of the rule to return migrants to the EU country they set foot in first. This is one EU rule the UK says it likes a lot. While in 2013 there were 827 people returned to the first EU country they entered (known as 'Dublin transfers' after the regulation), only 252 people were returned similarly in 2014.

However, if Britain left the EU, this might end the UK's ability to make Dublin transfers, as the Dublin Regulation is an agreement by EU member states for the management of asylum seekers in the EU. Leaving the EU could mean exiting this agreement and so not having it to fall back on when trying to reduce asylum seekers entering the country. The UK can already opt out of EU asylum policy. For those who think reducing numbers of asylum seekers a worthy goal, this becomes more difficult if there is a Brexit.

In October 2015, 300 leading former judges – including Lord Phillips, the former head of the UK Supreme Court, and Lord Macdonald, ex-Director of Public Prosecutions – criticised the government for its 'slow and narrow' response to the refugee crisis. It is worth pausing to reflect on the fact that such figures are so often hesitant to make any public statement like this.

The reasons are all too British: unlike the heavily politicised

American court, the British judiciary has a tradition of leaving politics to the politicians. This uncharacteristic outpouring of disappointment and exasperation from retired legal experts is one of the most remarkable – and striking – such statements in recent years.

Crucially, many who joined them in speaking out are those who have dealt with immigration cases relating to refugees – these are people on the judicial front line. They cannot be fobbed off as being unaware of the system, lacking knowledge of specific cases or ignorant about the consequences of their actions, however much the government – surely shamed by such dissent – might wish to dismiss them. The government's reply? A pathetic claim to be 'at the forefront of the global response'.

The British government offered to accept 'up to' 20,000 refugees from Syria over five years in an Australian-styled solution to the EU refugee crisis – echoing the views of Tim Montgomerie at the start of this chapter. Of course, 'up to' can mean one – or none. Even if it ends up being the full 20,000, this response is thousands less than Britain's other European partners. The UK has only admitted 4,980 Syrian asylum seekers in total since 2011 at the time of writing – and there is a long way to go before 20,000 will be processed. This raises serious questions about the seriousness of the government's commitment – not least its capability to make good on the meagre promise it has made.

Cameron wants to see established refugee camps outside the European Union, building asylum centres in the Balkans, Turkey, the Middle East and Africa. This plan is meant to discourage economic migrants with no chance of asylum – about a third of claimants. If refugee camps were set up in close proximity to the refugees' countries of origin, this would make their return easier and cheaper.

A special advisor and international development expert in Westminster told me just after visiting refugee camps along the Syrian border that many of the people in the camps are peasants. Dealing with them meant handling whole families at a time, not one or two individuals. Many were unable or unwilling to travel further – they wanted to return to their homes.

The government wants to accept refugees from these camps instead of refugees already in Europe. This is meant to help send a signal that refugees should go to these camps and avoid risking life and limb to reach Britain. But, with most other EU member states doing something very different, it is unclear how or why the government think its lone-wolf policy will work given the lack of any EU-wide agreement.

The European migration crisis brought chaos to the EU's common asylum policy. Not all countries enforced the Dublin Regulation – and some struggled to get a grip on the situation. Since February 2016, the European Commission has clamped down on countries turning a blind eye to the Dublin Regulation, but it has also made clear its recommendation that the regulation should be replaced. The issue is that the overwhelming majority of migrants are entering countries along the EU's border, like

Greece, Italy and Hungary. Returning every asylum seeker for processing in the first safe EU country they entered places more significant burdens on these border countries than on the others. Some compromise will likely be agreed – and soon, as the EU migration crisis looks set to worsen in 2016.

About £8 million has been allocated by the European Commission to deal with the migration crisis, including setting up 'hotspot' processing centres to speed up the assessment of asylum claims in high-volume areas. This has had beneficial effects already. Greece was found to have fingerprinted and documented only 8 per cent of migrants arriving from Turkey in September 2015, but this figure had increased to 78 per cent by January 2016. Big strides have been made, although there remains much more to do, including establishing a European Border and Coast Guard to better secure the EU's coastline from illegal human traffickers.

The crucial issue for the UK is what former Home Secretary Charles Clarke rightly calls 'the EU's broken asylum system'. By remaining outside the Schengen area, the UK cannot share in the EU's Visa Information System because Britain does not share its visa policy. This system is designed to detect bogus visa applications using biometric technology that Britain cannot tap into. The benefits of joining such a system – and therefore improving Britain's border security – drive Clarke's view that Britain should join and the Schengen Agreement and help improve it from within, as well as strengthening Frontex, as a revitalised EU border agency.

The current refugee crisis concerns more than Europe alone,

but there is certainly more that Britain can do in Europe as a starting point. At a keynote speech to the Institute of Directors, former Foreign Secretary David Miliband, now the president of the International Rescue Committee, said that the way we respond to the refugee crisis must first take account of who refugees are – and we must correct mistaken and outdated imaginations. Refugees are not all the same.

Refugees cross borders for different reasons. Hosam was a civil engineer from Khartoum in Sudan. He travelled thousands of miles with the aim of entering the UK. Hosam paid about £7,000 to illegal people traffickers who helped him reach Calais.

Hosam's story has a tragic ending. Over two months, he attempted to board a freight train travelling through the Eurotunnel to England, but without success. That is, until he finally was able to run across the tracks and jump on board a freight train's last carriage. But, during his daring attempt, he suffered a massive head injury and died.

After his death, his reason for wanting to come to the UK came to light. Hosam did not choose Britain from out of nowhere. He did not risk his life to sponge off the British welfare state. No, Hosam was trying to reach his brother, who was living in the UK.

There are increasingly desperate scenes of refugees climbing barbed-wire fences and scrambling to break into lorries at Calais so they can set foot in Britain. Like Hosam, several people are known to have died making their attempt – people are literally dying to enter Britain.

All of the refugees I spoke with who had applied for asylum in the UK had entered Britain first. While they found the British asylum process offered them support while their application was being considered, they were mixed on the fairness of the process and found it difficult to understand on the whole.

It can be surprising for some British citizens to learn this, but not all asylum seekers list the UK as their first choice. I heard from one refugee from the war-torn former Yugoslavia – whom I will call 'Milan' as he did not want to be identified – that he tried desperately to get his family to other countries first. Milan queued for several days and nights outside various consulates in Zagreb so he could get visas for him, his wife and his daughter. He tried Germany, Denmark, Sweden, the United States, Australia – 'even' (in his words) Canada. 'But', Milan told me, 'it was impossible to get any kind of visa for persons fleeing from war.'

They eventually contacted a relative who had become a British citizen to help them travel to Britain. Things were as close to the wire imaginable. Milan was not able to fly to London until the very last day before his passport expired.

However, he got to the UK, was cleared for legal entry, and started rebuilding his life and that of his family. It took a long ten years for all hurdles to be jumped, but Milan and his family eventually became British. From refugee to UK citizen. And now? Milan has lived in the UK for over twenty years. He said that he was 'very grateful to the government and the country' for his new citizenship. He is proud to be British.

Milan is not alone. Jacqui Smith told me that many asylum seekers who move to the UK 'find it very important to become a British citizen – it really means something special'. I agree – virtually everyone I spoke to found becoming British a moving experience. So should we all.

Not everyone resident in a country has his or her official papers like Milan did. There is widespread concern that many either lack papers or have fraudulent papers, including stolen passports. It can be very difficult to detect where people have citizenship if their papers are missing or false. A presenting officer for the Home Office at tribunals told me that insufficient documentation was one of the biggest problems faced. Tony Blair remarks in his memoirs that Britain has inherited an old, creaking system from the Second World War: 'The presumption was plainly false; most asylum claims were not genuine. Disproving them, however, was almost impossible … once someone got into Britain and claimed asylum, it was the Devil's own job to return them.'

And the government appears continually wrong-footed. When the Tory peer Lord Blencathra asked Lord Bates, then Minister of State for the Home Office, what steps were being taken 'to detect people from Iraq, Pakistan, Palestine and Albania using stolen Syrian passports to enter the United Kingdom' – as many Syrians were being fast-tracked – Lord Bates could only reply that 'a range of methods' were used, including 'advanced technology' and 'a network of overseas liaison officers'. Thirty-one people have been convicted for failing to present a passport at immigration control at UK ports in the year up to March 2015. This information was not recorded previously.

The social justice community group Citizens UK has launched an important campaign called 'Save Lives by Helping Resettle Refugees'. This offers welcomes to refugees in local communities through finding a safe home. The programme makes an explicit link between the offer of a roof over someone's head and the life-saving and potentially life-transforming experience that migrating to another country can represent for refugees.

It sounds simple to host an asylum seeker in your home, but there are complications. One is that if someone has a mortgage they may be required to inform their bank should there be an asylum seeker living long-term in the home. Single people welcoming asylum seekers would lose their 25 per cent discount on council tax. There may also be increased tariffs from insurance providers. But these are very minor problems compared to the need to reassure the Home Office that the home is satisfactory for someone claiming asylum. This is because there is a potential duty of care for refugees making asylum claims. At the very least, some form of risk assessment must be undertaken to avoid a greater likelihood of lawsuits.

Some concerns about refugees are based on more pragmatic issues. As the Conservative peer Daniel Finkelstein notes, 'Trying to solve the problem of the world's poor and oppressed people... is like trying to empty the ocean with a bucket.' This is not a call for inaction, but a realisation of how difficult the task is.

Of course, many of the refugees who make it to Europe are those who are most able. They bring skills and often enough they are graduates. They represent a crucial national import of people and talent, but also a cause for concern. This brain drain can make a country in trouble even worse off as it loses the people it needs most. As the economist Paul Collier has said, 'A talent transfer from poor societies to rich ones is not necessarily something that should be cause for global celebrations.' This is not to say any migration from such countries should be stopped, but it is an argument for controlling migration better so that poorer societies do not become substantively worse off.

Britain can do better – and change cannot be led by a government too squeamish to stand up for principles worth defending. It should either defend its asylum process or change it. Ministers should not be afraid to correct false impressions about the number of refugees that come to Britain, the support they receive and the challenges faced in securing Britain's borders.

This need to come clean is crucial to help rebuild public trust – and partnership. As the government will soon find out, if they do not know this already, they are becoming increasingly reliant on their citizens to assist them in ensuring that immigration rules are followed. It may be tempting to tell people only what they might want to hear, but peddling myths that risk the danger of inflaming tensions does a disservice to everyone – to refugees, to the government and, not least of all, to the public.

Finally, Britain exists in a world that is more interconnected than ever before. Going it alone can only get you so far. There is strength in numbers – that is, in working closely with other countries to share intelligence about migrants to ensure the system is not being abused or visas claimed through deception. A natural ally – the European Union – is on Britain's doorstep. There are clear advantages to working more closely with the EU, improving Britain's capacity to secure its borders. But it is still unclear whether the current government possesses the political will to see such change through.

CHAPTER 9

ENDING BRITISHNESS

It is hereby ordered, in pursuance of the notice of decision dated [insert date] that [insert name], born in [insert town and country of birth] on [insert date of birth] be deprived of his/her [delete as appropriate] British citizenship.

In accordance with the terms of sections 40(3) of the British National Act 1981 I certify that I am satisfied that the naturalisation as a British citizen of [insert name] was obtained by means of fraud, false representation or concealment of material fact.

N ow that is a letter you never want to receive from the Home Secretary. It is one of several used by the British government to inform British nationals their citizenship has been stripped, and is followed soon after by an order for their deportation. It is enough to make receiving even a hefty credit card bill sound appealing.

Being British is not only something a person can become – it is also a status that can end by choice or coercion. The state giveth, but it can also taketh away. This is concerning for many people: one person told me that she dislikes the idea of depriving others of their citizenship because it is 'destabilising and undermines the meaning of citizenship as a shared status'. The right to end someone's British citizenship remains controversial even if it has existed for much longer than most people recognise.

Of course, ending Britishness is something citizens can choose for themselves. It had long been the case that a British woman married to a non-British man would lose her British citizenship on her wedding day. If she had any children, they might lose their Britishness too. These days are now over. Nonetheless, people still choose to give up being British for a variety of reasons. Not all countries accept dual nationality – and so taking on citizenship elsewhere could mean having to end citizenship in Britain.

The process is surprisingly easy – the guidance on how to do it is only eight pages long. Easier than programming a television. Renouncing British citizenship requires completing a form and maybe enclosing some documents before submitting it in the post. Individuals must be eighteen or older and be of sufficiently sound mind that they understand the potential consequences of their actions. Any British passport must be submitted with the application, along with a letter from the country the applicant wants to join, confirming that they will grant citizenship once their Britishness ends. And that's it.

But, while Brits may choose to be citizens no more, losing Britishness is not always a free choice. The state can act to end someone's British citizenship and see them deported. This has always been controversial as a significant deprivation of a person's rights and legal identity – to be stripped of one's Britishness is to have one's rights as a citizen torn away. Unfortunately for anyone affected, appeals against decisions to revoke citizenship are especially difficult.

US Chief Justice Earl Warren once described deprivation as 'a form of punishment more primitive than torture'. The power to end Britishness is not to be used lightly – although there are concerns that it does not receive the extra consideration and careful scrutiny it demands. For example, it has been discovered fairly recently that the HM Courts and Tribunal Service is so swamped with current immigration appeal hearings that they have been pushed back by several months. The service has agreed a list of priority cases 'to ensure the most urgent issues are dealt with' – giving 'bottom billing' to cases involving deportation. This suggests that deportation cases lack the urgency that are often claimed for them – so the removal of formerly British people stripped of their citizenship ranks lower still.

The least controversial justification for stripping someone of their British citizenship is where it was obtained by fraud, false representation or the concealment of material circumstances. This is not a power that can be exercised against most British citizens – only people who became British through naturalisation are potentially affected. Becoming British transforms an individual into a UK citizen, but it does not erase the path taken to get there.

If someone receives a letter like the one starting this chapter above, there are some options they may be able to pursue. The first is to plead mitigation. This can take the form of claiming that someone else acted on their behalf or that they were advised wrongly by an interpreter.

The second is to pursue a claim for asylum. In fact, the letters sent by the Home Secretary stripping British nationals of their citizenship include a note that the person may want to make a claim for asylum. The letter says that if someone was a refugee to the UK before becoming a British citizen then – under the Geneva Convention – they no longer fit the definition of a refugee and so will be automatically rejected. You are only once – and not twice or three times – a refugee as far as British citizenship is concerned.

There are several immigration advisory services across the UK providing free and independent legal assistance to anyone who has been deprived of their British citizenship. However, their locations are far from ideal. The 'Northern Region and Scotland' has but one office to visit – in Salford – and no email address is provided to contact them.

The government attempts to remove ex-British citizens in a

two-stage procedure. First, they strip them of their citizenship before serving them with a deportation order. This is to minimise claims that rights under the European Convention on Human Rights have been breached – the government's view is that 'this cannot be the case in the absence of a decision or directions for your removal from the UK'. Essentially, people are to lose their citizenship first and then be deported afterwards.

Contrary to the name, permanent residency – or 'indefinite leave to remain' – is no permanent, indefinite right. It can be revoked for several reasons, including living outside the UK for two or more years. The rationale is that this shows that someone lacks the required intention to make their future in Britain, after living abroad for so long.

If permanent residency is lost for some reason, it is possible – but likely extremely difficult – to acquire it again in future. Should someone with permanent residency be served with a deportation order that later becomes null and void, the annulment does not revive the permanent residency. Someone in this situation must apply again for the permanent residency he or she should have had still. An application could be made quickly, but there would be increasingly high application fees and the need to convince UK Visas and Immigration that there was no good reason to question his or her good character in relation to the terminated deportation order.

Between 2006 and 2014, there have been thirty-seven individuals deprived of their British citizenship under the royal prerogative power. There were several grounds used for ending their UK citizenship, including that it was conducive to the public good to do so and that their citizenship was obtained by means such as fraud or deception.

None were only British and all were considered by the UK government to have had an alternative nationality – this means that the UK must be satisfied that a person to be stripped of his or her British nationality could readily possess citizenship from somewhere else. It does not matter whether a person actually is a citizen, and the state does not require a guarantee from another country they would grant someone citizenship if their Britishness expired. This can be an issue, because, as we saw above, many countries do not recognise dual nationality and so one citizenship might only take effect after another has ceased. Nonetheless, the courts have ruled recently that it is unlawful to assume a person would possess a citizenship he or she does not have.

The process of rescinding someone's British status is understandably difficult, as such cases attest – and often doesn't go according to plan. In 2014, the Home Secretary Theresa May stripped 'Mostafa' (not his real name) of his British citizenship as a national security risk because of his alleged links to al-Qaeda, including acting as a courier for them. Mostafa had come to Britain as a child and became British in 2011. May is able to revoke the citizenship of dual nationals – and some foreign-born Britons – she deems a national security risk. Such persons would not be rendered stateless and a successful appeal is very difficult to make.

Abu Qatada was a Jordanian living in London – and a known associate of Osama bin Laden. It's fair to say that Theresa May tried desperately to see him expelled. Qatada was wanted to stand trial in Jordan, but a significant hurdle arose concerning the worry that he could not be deported from the UK if evidence obtained through torture was to be used at his trial.

After living in Britain for over a decade, he was finally deported to Jordan – but only after Jordan and the UK ratified a formal agreement on evidence that could be used in his trial. While Qatada still lives in Jordan and is barred from entering the UK, he was cleared of all charges he faced in Jordan.

Typically, citizenship is revoked while the person is abroad. There is then usually an exclusion order made that bans the newly rendered ex-citizen from re-entering Britain. This is what had happened to Mostafa. The Home Office claimed he made two suspicious trips to Afghanistan in 2013 and 2014 – and Mostafa learned he had lost his British citizenship while in Afghanistan.

Mostafa wanted to be back in the UK – and he used his Afghan passport to return to London within weeks of having his British citizenship terminated. While his British passport was cancelled, he still had his Afghan passport and this had an indefinite leave to remain visa denoting permanent residency. He was soon caught – in an effort to appeal the decision made against him – and a lengthy process to deport him began.

At his four-day court hearing of the Special Immigration Appeals Commission, Mostafa sat in the public gallery as much of the proceedings took place in a different room. He could not hear the government's evidence in open court because the reason for stripping his citizenship was on national security-related grounds, and the evidence was therefore kept secret from the public, from Mostafa and from his lawyers.

Mostafa claimed he had travelled to Afghanistan for family reasons on both occasions. The evidence against him was described as 'fairly flimsy', but his case is not yet over. The Home Office argued that he had entered the country illegally because his permanent residency was cancelled with his being served a deprivation order ending his British citizenship.

After an initial placement in a detention centre, Mostafa was freed at a bail hearing and has been residing in London since, subject to a number of restrictions: he must wear an electronic tag, he can only speak to people pre-approved by the Home Office, and he is allowed to leave his accommodation only at certain times of the day.

His case continues without any clear idea about how much longer it might take – a Home Office spokesperson said, 'It would be inappropriate to comment while legal proceedings are ongoing,' when pressed for a time frame. Previous appeals of this sort have taken up to seven years to resolve.

Mostafa is not the only person whose removal has not gone according to plan. 'Ibrahim' (not his real name) came to the UK as a student from Libya in 1981. He has lived in Britain for much of the time since. Ibrahim became an alcoholic and this contributed to serial offending – he was found to have committed seventy-eight offences on fifty-two different occasions. After the Home Secretary sent him five letters warning that serious consequences could follow from his criminal activities, Ibrahim was served with a deportation order in 2008.

This order was the first of many – and all were appealed. Most recently, the Upper Tribunal of the Immigration and Asylum Chamber dismissed the government's appeal to deport Ibrahim to Libya. In their judgment, his 'history of addiction is such that he cannot abstain from consuming alcohol when alcohol is available'. This would expose Ibrahim to a serious risk of ill treatment – including beatings – if he were found with alcohol in Libya, should he be returned. This led to the judgment that deporting Ibrahim to Libya would breach the European Convention on Human Rights. The issue was not whether he chose to drink, but whether he was an addict and therefore unable to abstain. A case where someone's personal vice was his saving grace, stopping his deportation.

A common route to challenging deportation is to claim rights in the European Convention on Human Rights, especially Article 8 concerning rights to private and family life. The UK Supreme Court has ruled that the best interests of the child must be a primary consideration if potentially affected by a decision to remove one or both of their parents from the UK. The fact that a child is a British citizen is not to be considered a 'trump card' although its importance is pressing, as any rights bestowed on the child through this citizenship could be lost if they were deported from the UK with their parents. Parents who might otherwise be deported could be spared if the courts find the interests of their children to stay in Britain sufficiently strong.

Deportation is no simple task – and recent governments have been keen to reform procedures. The coalition government's Immigration Act 2014 was meant, in part, to simplify the process to deport individuals lacking lawful continued residency in the UK. Problems were highlighted early on that this legislation simply did not go far enough. An official impact assessment noted that 'the law currently requires a removal decision to be made in addition to a separate decision to refuse leave or curtail a migrant's leave to remain. This is unnecessary and means migrants can challenge both decisions, delaying their removal from the UK.'

The process would work like this. Suppose there is a woman named Mischa who applies to remain resident in the UK. Her application is refused and she can appeal against that – and all of this takes time, allowing Mischa to stay in Britain. If she loses her appeal, there must still be a separate removal decision – and Mischa can appeal against that too.

The process would be more efficient if these two decisions were merged into one – to find Mischa should not remain resident is to find she should be removed by a certain date, if she was not already out of the country. Conversely, to decide Mischa can remain resident is to decide she should not be removed.

If ministers want to curb appeals, this is one area that demands closer scrutiny and a rethink.

As with any debate, there is also another side. Critics rightly point out that the Home Office does not have a very good track record on getting its decisions right. Too often it has been mired by inefficiency and has generated poor decision-making, leading to a high number of successful appeals against Home Office decisions. A lawyer's advice for any client up against the Home Office might be: if in doubt, appeal – and appeal again until you succeed.

Because of these problems, a merger of these two decisions could run a serious risk of wrongfully removing individuals who would have fewer opportunities to challenge bad decisions. This is a very important concern, not least because of the profound – and potentially life-threatening – consequences for people affected by losing their residency and even their citizenship.

But we should not be complacent, simply accept our institutions are broken and throw in the towel. We are not defeatist, but British. It does not take the spirit of Dunkirk to find the resolve to better support a department that has struggled to keep up with its caseload. The public has every right to expect a professional and competent service managing applications, whether at the Home Office or the DVLA.

If the reason for keeping procedures more inefficient than they need to be is because this provides some protection against the relatively high number of poor decisions made by an overstretched and overworked Home Office, the answer should not be to keep things broken but to fix them. We must demand better decision-making from the start. Inefficiency in one area should not be relied upon to correct incompetency in another. Such a system is tantamount to managing cases literally by trials and errors. We deserve better. Maybe it means another reorganisation or new procedures, or maybe more staff should be made available to handle casework. This is not just about improving a service for migrants: British citizens will benefit directly too and this should count for much more than it does.

In recent years, there have been some controversial developments. The first is that the rules established for targeting terrorists and hate preachers have been stretched to target others for deportation and removal.

The best-known example concerns an Australian named Trenton Oldfield. He made headlines worldwide for 'protesting' against the elitism of the annual Oxford–Cambridge boat race by jumping in the water to try to interrupt it. These actions led to his being imprisoned for seven weeks.

In what seemed like a case of very bad timing, Oldfield applied for permanent residency not too long afterwards. The Home Office had not forgotten his earlier stunt, and refused his application on the grounds that his continued presence in the UK was 'undesirable' – a provision in the immigration rules meant to address terrorism-related concerns. Things were not looking good for Oldfield.

But he appealed – and did so on the grounds that his wife, who is of Indian descent, would be at risk if he was forced to return to his native Australia, claiming it is 'a particularly racist country'. A tribunal found in his favour and Oldfield remains in Britain – and the decision paves the way for a future application for citizenship. This helps illustrate that rules can be applied in cases perhaps not originally intended. If he was from another country or had a different spouse, the government might have been able to see Oldfield removed from the country after all.

A second controversial development has been the increase in attempts to deprive British nationals of their citizenship and so render them stateless. As we have seen, the case of dual citizens is generally more straightforward: if they lost British citizenship, then they would still have another nationality – like in the case of Mostafa discussed above. Not that the government has any idea of how many people are dual nationals – they don't.

But there have been an increasing number of cases where the Home Secretary has looked to deport suspected terrorists – many of whom had citizenship elsewhere but gained UK passports through naturalisation or asylum.

The former Home Secretary Jacqui Smith moved to make stateless a former Iraqi refugee named Hilal. He had been a terrorist suspect and had been stripped of his British citizenship while he was with his family in Turkey. Hilal fled Iraq in 1992 and came to the UK, earning British citizenship in 2000. This automatically ended his Iraqi citizenship because Iraq did not recognise dual nationality for its citizens – Hilal went from being an

Iraqi citizen to being a British citizen to being neither. Following his internment in Iraq by US forces on suspicion of his targeting coalition troops, Smith ended Hilal's British citizenship, claiming it 'would be conducive to the public good'.

The case went before the UK Supreme Court, and the current Home Secretary, Theresa May, argued that Hilal would have regained his Iraqi citizenship through an Iraqi law in place between 2004 and 2006. The Special Immigration Appeals Commission agreed – and on two separate occasions. But the Court of Appeal did not, which paved the way for a landmark decision in the UK Supreme Court.

The court unanimously found in Hilal's favour – and dismissed the appeal by May. Their judgment said, 'It is clear that the question is simply whether the person holds another nationality at the date of the order depriving him of British citizenship.' It was irrelevant whether it was likely – or even certain – that another country could or would grant Hilal citizenship. The only thing that mattered was whether another country had done so. Since none had, Hilal could not be rendered stateless by the Home Secretary.

Part of the problem for the Home Secretary was the Home Office guidance used, which had incorporated word for word the United Nations High Commissioner for Refugees' 'Guidelines for Statelessness'. As long as Britain is bound not to render persons stateless, it is difficult to see how the situation could be changed so that someone in Hilal's position would lose his case.

One possibility would be to change the relevant guidance so that it does not cite chapter and verse the 'Guidelines for Statelessness'. Instead, it could develop a clear and demanding test that sets a high bar to be crossed in order to deem otherwise stateless persons as not stateless. The test should require something close to certainty that the person in question satisfies all criteria for citizenship elsewhere and would gain it if deprived of their British nationality – although again it is difficult to see much change on this issue.

A third and final controversy concerns an extreme expression of depriving British nationals of their citizenship: the lethal targeting of British citizens with drones. This issue made headlines after the deaths by drone strike of two British citizens-turned-Islamic State jihadists named Reyaad and Ruhul. The strike was operated from an airbase in Lincolnshire after a decision was made to attack by Michael Fallon, the Defence Secretary, in consultation with other members of the Cabinet.

The legal basis for such an attack is shaky at best. The United Nations Charter permits states a right of self-defence, but any armed attack must be imminent or actual. Moreover, according to leading international lawyer Philippe Sands QC, the need for a pre-emptive attack in self-defence must be 'instant, overwhelming, and leaving no choice of means, and no moment of deliberation'. Whether or not these criteria have been satisfied is a matter of debate, as the government has not unambiguously made clear its reasons for the strike.

Being British is important. Some people are born British and many others earn it. What is created or given can be destroyed or taken away. This need not always be a problem – some citizens will choose to become nationals of another country which might not permit dual citizenship and so some will want to choose an end to their Britishness.

The main concerns are with attempts by the government to end a citizen's Britishness through coercion. The Home Secretary has the discretion to strip away someone's citizenship and deport them. But this is not without several strings attached. It is surely a very good thing that such safeguards are in place. The gaining or losing of citizenship comes with real potential consequences – it is not a decision to be made lightly or without caution.

But the problem has been that too often such caution has not been exercised. The goal of removing certain individuals permanently from the country is rushed. This has had the effect of making some positive headlines – which have their own impact, which should be recognised, in forming public opinion. Yet, there is also the risk that things can unravel if not performed with sufficient care – the short but sweet rush of initial public support soon gives way to a long crash and a painful headache.

Perhaps the best way to handle the problems of how and when to deprive persons of their citizenship is not to have them in the first place. Many terrorist suspects are home-grown – this is no less true for the recent terrorist attacks in France and Belgium. Stripping them of their citizenship and deporting them to foreign countries may be even more difficult to do than it sounds. For those who became British through naturalisation, the government might seek to restrict further the conditions under which naturalisation can happen. But this would be a fairly heavy price to pay in order to ever so slightly strengthen the state's hand in ending Britishness. Not least when the Home Office so often gets decisions wrong or finds itself unable to act anyway. For these reasons, we might put a greater emphasis on strengthening the future of British citizenship for the many, rather than seeking novel ways of ending it for the few.

CHAPTER 10

A FUTURE FOR BRITISHNESS?

Britishness has undergone radical changes over the past few centuries. It has never been about a single people, a single custom or a single tradition. Britishness expanded with the British Empire, bringing together new citizens of the United Kingdom and Colonies – and then began a long contraction that continues today. This has meant that Britain has come to the modern citizenship game fairly late. British subjects became citizens at last. Playing catch-up in a fast-moving globalised world is never easy. When it concerns citizenship and immigration, it becomes all the more difficult.

Britain's unique history is important because it helps explain its unique challenges. Britain started as a political union of England with Scotland – and so diversity was at its heart from the beginning. This has grown as Britain's global reach expanded. A consequence is that peoples from all over the world have been subjects of a British monarch, and many held British passports. Many of the people who seek permanent residency or citizenship today could have had one if not the other by right in a previous generation.

This complex, global history renders 'Britishness' impossible to pin down to any single way of looking, being or even worshipping. But to locate Britishness is not to find nothing – to crack open a golden shell only to find an empty cavity within – but to discover something important about citizenship more generally for a modern world.

Being British is about adopting certain values, such as fair play, democracy, the rule of law and a respect for cultural differences. These values might not seem applicable to Britain alone – and that is probably right. Fairness and equality are values that are cherished in Britain, but not unique to it – they can also be found in the United States, France and many other countries.

What makes these values British is that they are understood and applied in a British way. Democracy may be about popular elections, but there is more than one way to conduct elections. The British application of this value is in our Westminster model of parliamentary democracy. This is how a British value is realised in a British way.

Similarly, a respect for cultural differences is just that – a recognition that more than one culture has importance for fellow British citizens and that they are equally worthy of our respect. This is understood and applied in a British way. Respecting cultural diversity need not demand that every view receives the same attention or prominence – only the opportunity for people to enjoy participating in their cultural customs under the same rule of law for all.

It is commonplace to consider cultural differences in an antagonistic way, like the West versus the non-West, or in Islamophobic terms. But culture is more than that. It is about celebrating the cultural diversity of people from outside the UK who have made a life in Britain, whether in this or in earlier generations, but it is also about honouring the diversity of the rich history behind Britain's nations of England, Scotland, Wales and Northern Ireland, including its regions, from Cornwall to Yorkshire and beyond.

Being British can mean different things depending on who you ask – as I found out in speaking with people born British, those who became British, those who want to become British and others up and down the country. This is not to say that we should have an overly nostalgic view of what Britishness is, and we should resist defending any idyllic conception that few – whether born or naturalised – can live up to. Samantha, a Briton in her twenties living in the West Midlands, said that 'the UK is put on a pedestal'.

This view of what Britishness is about is meaningful – and it should be accorded its rightful importance. This means taking British citizenship seriously.

British citizenship matters to British citizens. They expect their children to have an automatic right to citizenship as individuals born to British parents and within a British community. Their knowledge about life in the United Kingdom, forged through personal experience and relationships, provides an understanding about how life is lived in Britain – and how British values are applied in British ways.

British citizens are generally welcoming of newcomers – and much more so than is often believed. But they also have at least two broad fundamental concerns about contribution and integration.

The first concern is that immigration should be controlled to ensure that migrants contribute to British society. There is understandably little public support for paying out benefits to whoever sticks out their hand – especially if they have only just set foot in the country. Some fear that the system is essentially one where citizens give and migrants take. Migrants are perceived sometimes as benefit scroungers and health tourists, enjoying public benefits at the expense of the taxpayer.

There is little basis in fact to support this view of migrants. But the stats do little to stem the potency of the widespread public image – and neither does the cowardice of the current government, which makes little if any effort to set the record straight.

The need for newcomers to contribute – and the importance of making a contribution before becoming a British citizen – is a view held across the political divide. Even some of the most left-wing people I know – sometimes to my surprise – reaffirm that anyone wanting to become British has to offer some contribution to Britain. The contribution could take more forms than only economic, including cultural and public involvements and influence. One person I spoke with made this point: 'There are more ways to contribute than by improving the economy – academics and medics, to mention a couple, would add to the overall good of UK plc.'

While I found most citizens open-minded about what form this contribution might take, they were relatively unforgiving about people who could not satisfy this broad test. This is where I uncovered the most concerns about refugees – the worry was they were almost by definition unable to make a suitably satisfactory contribution to British society. When asked about whether it mattered if these same refugees were trained engineers, medical doctors and other skilled workers, this helped bring out a more positive response. Public debates too rarely focus on who refugees are and what they might bring. As in so many other areas, the more that people come to learn about who refugees are, the less worrying these concerns about contribution might seem.

New citizens are expected to pay their full share of tax, avoid criminal convictions and support themselves without relying on public benefit for several years minimum. These points are broadly covered by existing regulations – but not exactly. Anyone wanting to become a citizen is expected to gain permanent residency first. The form for residency asks about current and past bank accounts: this means financial checks can be made to see if taxes have been paid and bankruptcy avoided, as per the current rules.

But the form in place for applying to become a British citizen is very different. It asks for the applicant's tax office reference number, but it does not ask about current or past bank accounts. This is surprising: the standard for becoming a resident should not be more difficult than the standard for becoming a citizen. Furthermore, failure to have paid all due council tax payments is no barrier to becoming a British citizen.

This should be corrected as a matter of urgency. The current situation can give the impression that paying taxes lacks importance – not least for migrants wanting to become British. This false picture is not helped by poor Home Office record-keeping – for example, it admitted that it did not know how many people had disclosed financial fraud in their applications for citizenship. Moreover, most migrants applying for citizenship will have met this test when granted permanent residency. So this is a change that better meets public expectations and raises a bar for entry that many of those currently applying should meet.

Financial requirements are in place to control migration numbers. These take the form of a pay threshold and a cap on non-EU skilled migration subject to people working in a job listed on a shortage occupation list. The shortage list's problem is more its length than its brevity, as it tends to add new occupations without sufficient reviews on whether all existing jobs should remain on the list. These jobs range from engineers and medical practitioners to animators, ballet dancers and chefs. These requirements can have a profound impact on who can come to live and work in the UK and thus on who can become British.

Wealthy individuals can apply for what is called a Tier 1 investor visa. These are designed to attract entrepreneurs to Britain to invest while offering a faster track to citizenship than for people on other visas. Such investment is important and the UK is not alone in offering these terms. But they rarely talk publicly about how this works in practice. In 2013, these visas were issued to 187 Chinese nationals, 126 Russians, twenty-six Americans, nineteen Indians and fourteen Kazakhstanis, among others. Changing the specific financial requirements can attract different numbers of migrants – and those from different nationalities – in a complex balancing act.

The government makes its decisions on these financial factors on the recommendation of the Migration Advisory Committee, a group of five economists. This group undertakes important work. Their reports are well researched and presented – and they provide a welcome evidence-based intervention at the heart of immigration policy. While providing independent advice that is published freely online, they take their cue from government, examining the economics and likely consequences of adopting different policies.

The Migration Advisory Committee can be improved further by expanding its membership to include non-economists. No single discipline has a monopoly on valuable advice, and a wider range of expertise might not only assist the committee in formulating its reports, but also help it become more flexible and capable of addressing issues more robustly than at present, bringing to bear the benefits that interdisciplinary approaches – when done well – can offer.

The second broad concern many citizens have is that newcomers should integrate. Integration is almost always presented as a problem for the foreigners – they are the ones who need to adapt to the values and cultural traditions of their new land. But too rarely is it recognised that integration works both ways. Newcomers come to understand and identify with a new community that, in turn, comes to understand and identify with them as new members.

A key worry about integration is the fear that migrants might undermine the local culture, leading to British customs becoming second class to imported cultural practices. The problem is not the different cultures that migrants come from, but rather the perception that local culture is somehow losing out.

No culture exists in a vacuum; no culture is chiselled in stone. Each develops alongside others – and they feed off each other. This is clear when looking at past photographs or old magazine covers. What it means to be British has changed over time. Who had a political voice, what it meant to be an equal citizen, what it meant to be free from discrimination, what made the list of the nation's favourite foods and what counted as 'posh'. Elite universities are often the oldest, but not always – England's three most ancient universities in Cambridge, Durham and Oxford often rank alongside much younger arrivals like Bristol, the LSE and Warwick. Change happens. Culture – even British culture – is no exception to this ancient rule. This includes its universities.

But there should be no doubt that integration into a new culture is far from easy. This came across very strongly in interviews. Malcolm, a British citizen in his fifties living in the south-east, highlighted to me how few really grasp how difficult it can be for people moving to a new country, even thinking purely in terms of what they leave behind. This view was also expressed by Mary, a British citizen from London, who told me how changing her citizenship would be like 'changing my DNA – a huge decision' that she could not contemplate doing herself. Those who do undertake it overcome higher hurdles than are regularly acknowledged.

One way in which integration is assessed for citizenship is to consider whether someone has 'good character'. This requirement is divided into several criteria, such as the full payment of taxes owed, no unspent convictions, no civil judgments leading to a court order are in force, no cautions or reprimands on someone's criminal record either in the UK or abroad, not listed on the sex offender register, not charged with any offence and no involvement in terrorism, genocide, crimes against humanity or war crimes.

These requirements can and should be tightened. At present, anyone with a prison sentence of four or more years is normally refused citizenship. The government should consider several reforms. First, normally refusing citizenship to anyone with more than two years served in prison. This would change the rules slightly, which currently look only to the sentence imposed and not the time served. A typical four-year prison sentence might have only two years served and so this change would not rule out for citizenship everyone who might be eligible on this criterion. Many past offenders in England and Wales can benefit from the Rehabilitation of Offenders Act 1974 and subsequent relevant legislation because it prevented lifelong disclosure of criminal convictions. This legislation is restricted to job applications, obtaining insurance and in civil proceedings – and so the law need not be changed as disclosure remains warranted for naturalisation purposes.

But this change should be coupled with a possible termination of permanent residency. Currently, someone who earns 'indefinite leave to remain' can live in the UK permanently. Yet, this can be stripped if they live abroad for two or more years. The reason, as we have seen, is that foreign residence is regarded as evidence that they did not intend to make Britain their permanent home when applying to become a resident.

Similarly, there is a good-character test for indefinite leave to remain that must be satisfied – and serious criminal convictions are considered grounds by the Home Office for stripping someone of their permanent residency under this requirement too. The test should be sufficiently stringent – such as for anyone convicted of specific serious offences like grievous bodily harm or a sexual offence. Not only would this likely have public support, but it would be evidence of someone not having the good character claimed for permanent residency. This change would end an anomaly whereby someone could be sentenced for a serious offence and so denied citizenship, but allowed to reside in Britain permanently. This should end.

We might wonder how robust existing good-character checks are, too. The immigration minister James Brokenshire has recently confirmed that they are not conducted by external agencies – but it is unclear how they might be done without them. One of the checks is into a person's financial history in Britain, but there are also to be checks for any past criminality in Britain or abroad. The previous Independent Chief Inspector of Borders and Immigration Sir John Vine found that these checks were often not taken at all. There is difficulty in making them, especially when looking into someone's possible criminal record abroad – the onus is on the Home Office to find that someone is not of good character.

But there is now a move towards this responsibility being shifted to individuals, whereby they must show some documentary proof from their home country that they have no criminal record. This is probably a move in the right direction. However, it increases the prospects for more documentation getting lost or being faked – where one problem becomes less prominent, another can take its place.

So we can and should do more to improve and strengthen existing requirements for citizenship. But no controls are cost free. Immigration controls, including citizenship requirements, are often thought to be about raising the bar for migrants. But actually they also impose costs on British citizens too.

Checks to ensure that only people lawfully resident in the UK can do the things that law-abiding citizens do – from having a driver's licence and opening a bank account to renting a property – clearly create burdens on immigrants, who must regularly confirm their legal status to live in the UK. However, they also impose costs on British citizens, who will find themselves having to confirm frequently not only their identity, but their nationality – not only *who* they are, but *what* they are. This is a change that could have negative consequences for how individuals relate to the state.

For example, the government's 'right to rent' policy requires private landlords to rent properties only to individuals lawfully resident in the UK. Landlords must verify their tenants' residency status or risk fines of up to £3,000. One concern is that the policy may make some landlords refuse to rent properties to renters who appear to be non-British to avoid the risk of renting to someone who is in the country fraudulently. This could lead to racial discrimination against renting to British citizens and others with a right to rent. A second concern is that British citizens or foreign nationals who are in the country lawfully but lack the required documentation may find themselves made homeless despite their having a right to rent. These examples show that British citizens may suffer more than mere inconvenience from this policy. It may have serious negative consequences, as evidenced by research that found 42 per cent of landlords were less likely to rent a property to someone without a British passport.

It is crucial that the government gets the public on board with its plans in a robust sense. Front-page headlines and focus groups are no substitute for engaging directly with people on the street. We are already seeing the first signs that leaving it to landlords to ensure they rent only to people allowed to be in the UK is having the predictable outcome of some people being discriminated against because of how they sound or appear. Shadow Home Secretary Andy Burnham has likened these checks to saying 'no dogs, no blacks, no Irish'.

Improving checks to reduce illegal immigration requires goodwill and support from the public. This is not only because they are affected too, but because the state will require their help. It is not only migrants who must convince landlords of their residency status, but British citizens as well – a rule for one becomes a rule for all.

Many so-called 'border controls' come into play far from the water's edge. We no longer live in a maritime world where people only entered countries from boats. Now we come by land, sea and air. A border is more than an external boundary found on a map. The border is everywhere people are.

Our understanding of migrants unlawfully in the UK should be revised, too. It is common for people to believe that illegal migration is primarily about stopping people from illegally crossing the border – but this perception is incorrect. Most people in the UK illegally overstayed their entry visas, whether for work, visiting or study. This fact about overstayers helps explain the government's increasing focus on tackling illegal immigration by effectively trying to 'smoke out' those who are in the country unlawfully. Recent policies enacted include increasing fines for businesses hiring people in the country illegally and restricting who can open a bank account or possess a driver's licence – making it ever more difficult to find work, drive and live a 'normal' British life. The Organisation for Economic Co-operation and Development estimated five years ago that migrants working in the UK illegally probably represent about 1 per cent of total employment in Britain. So these measures to help drive 'illegal' migrants out of work are addressing a relatively select group of people – not nearly as large as many assume.

The most controversial proposal by the government to tackle illegal migration is to target landlords who rent properties to migrants. If someone lacks a valid visa or passport allowing them to stay in the UK while they rent a property, their landlord can be hit with significant fines and potentially even prison. The idea is that this will also help bring to light people living in the country illegally.

Unfortunately for the government, this is one of those plans that sounds good in theory but is not good at all in practice. The Home Office conducted a pilot in which landlords were fined if they were found to have rented properties to migrants not living lawfully in the UK. But the results were modest – if this is the government's great new hope for reducing net migration by something like 200,000 or more, then this policy is only a drop in the bucket. Worse still, we have learned that only 'two full-time equivalent members of UK Visas and Immigration staff' have been set aside to help all British landlords to ensure compliance with these regulations. That's right – two. Which makes you hope no one needs to make a call.

What is worrying about this is that it turns everyday civilians into specialist border agents without the training or expertise. Most people simply don't know what to look for. Neither do ministers – including those with responsibility for this area! A powerful example concerns former immigration minister Mark Harper. He was found to have employed a migrant living illegally in the UK as his cleaner, leading to a swift resignation from government. But the question that must be asked is simple: if the government's own immigration minister cannot conduct proper checks, why do they think the general public will do better? And why then subject the public to possible prison? Such a sanction was never imposed on the minister. Why should citizens be punished more?

We do not know how many people are living in Britain illegally. The economist Jonathan Portes notes that the last serious estimate was in 2009, using data from the end of 2007 – so several years out of date. These figures estimated there were between 420,000 and 860,000 migrants in the UK illegally, with a central estimate of the still commonly quoted figure of 620,000 people. The government does deport hundreds of people each year – over a thousand were returned to their country of origin by July 2015 at an average cost per person returned of £5,209 and a cool 49 pence.

Immigration crimes, including people living in the UK without valid residency, are causing the government considerable problems. To start with, the government does not know how many immigration offenders there are overstaying their visas. The absence of exit checks at airports and ports does not make it easier figuring out the total number. Other visa checks are very difficult to obtain. Student visas are only valid when properly registered at an approved education institution – and become invalid in cases where the student might quit studying at their institution. Spousal visas are only valid while the couple are married – and become invalid when they are divorced.

Yet ex-students and ex-spouses have their visas in their passports – and no change is made to either their visas or passports to confirm their change in status, which is a breach of the condition of their visa's validity. It is not like the necessary information is impossible to find. Colleges and universities will know the nationalities of their students and whether they remain registered at them. Divorce is a legal matter, with records kept, and where people are often represented by a lawyer. The Home Office should know who has what visa in which passport – and if it does not now, then it must do soon. If ministers want to clamp down on overstayers, this is a problem that must be faced, perhaps by better record-keeping but also by being more aware of how this problem works, so we can say with visas that what you see if what you get.

While the government has tried to recruit the help and support of citizens to uncover immigration crimes, this has rarely led to deportations. During 2013, the Home Office received 76,075 allegations of immigration crimes, including 987 of smuggling. Only 6 per cent of these allegations led to an enforceable arrest, and less than half led to removal: a total of 1,991 people. That's less than 3 per cent of all reported immigration crimes leading to deportation.

No doubt the gaps between allegation, arrest and deportation of people for immigration crimes might be explained – at least to some degree – by prejudice, where someone questions another's residency status based only on appearance. As a white native English speaker, this has never happened to me. But it could be very different if I looked less 'English' – and it goes to show that to say someone 'looks' like an immigrant is mistaken at best.

If the Home Secretary finds it 'conducive to the public good for the person to be excluded or removed from the United Kingdom' he or she can deprive a British citizen of their residency in the UK and deport them. Enforced removals fell by 6 per cent from 13,311 in 2013 to 12,460 in 2014 – and not through any lack of trying to bring these numbers up. The government has had more success refusing entry at ports and deporting people – the figure increased from 14,722 to 16,519 in the year ending June 2015. This is partly because of restrictions on people with criminal records, such as the boxer Mike Tyson, who was excluded in December 2013.

When someone receives a deportation order, immigration offices are required to outline their reasons for it. This can include the gist of evidence behind its decision. While there is some discretion in deciding who should be deported, reasons must be given, although they need not be very detailed – and there must be reasonable evidence to form a sound judgement in light of the relevant published policies. Should a decision depart from these policies then it must say why this is so. For the Court of Appeal, these safeguards are important to ensure decisions have been made fairly.

More must be done to help relieve pressures on public services caused by migration. Jacqui Smith launched a Migration Impacts Fund in 2009 that helped provide financial support of about £70 million over two years. It was funded neither by taxpayers nor by the European Union but by a levy on immigration applications, providing an invaluable source of new funding to reduce migration-related pressures on local services. The fund covered a range of programmes including English language training, extra support teachers and improving emergency services.

The coalition government stopped support for the fund because it found it 'ineffective', but provided no alternative in its place. Then communities minister Baroness Hanham CBE said: 'The purpose of the Migration Impacts Fund was to alleviate the impacts of immigration on local public services … In light of the overall fiscal position the government concluded that it was not a priority funding stream.' Or a stream worth having at all. The extra income the fund's application levy continues to bring in was diverted to other spending programmes. Today, the government is forced to find money elsewhere – including from emergency funding – for a programme that should never have been scrapped.

The coalition government introduced a migrant 'health surcharge' they claimed would raise £200 million per year and recoup up to £1.7 billion over the next ten years 'to help pay for the cost of NHS treatment given to temporary migrants'.

The health surcharge is based on a similar idea to the Migration Impacts Fund. It is a surcharge added to all immigration applications – £200 per year or £150 annually from students – payable up front. Dependents must pay the same as a main applicant. That means a family of four would need to pay £700 per year if they have two children in education. James Brokenshire has said, 'The health surcharge will play a vital role in ensuring Britain's most cherished public service is provided on a basis that is fair to all who use it.' But does it?

Thus far, it has not earned the funding promised – only £50 million was collected between April and August 2015. More a funding flop than a flagship programme. The Department of Health has confirmed they are working on proposals that will substantially raise the costs for migrants to access the NHS, which will mean 'non-EEA visitors who use the NHS will be charged 150 per cent of the cost of their treatment'. Thus someone from the US or Nepal would each be charged £150 for £100 of treatment – after already forking out £200 in an annual fee estimated to cover their full expected costs before a pound has been spent. This will all be on top of National Insurance contributions and other taxes paid.

This is not a policy aimed at relieving the pressures on the health service caused by migration. No, this is about getting migrants to plug funding gaps they have not caused. An exercise in milking foreigners for a problem they are not a party to.

But there is more. The health surcharge is paid up front and goes in full to the local NHS services. Yet people move. The funding would not be moved to a new location if the migrant who paid for it left the area. A Canadian who pays the surcharge when moving to Birmingham but then moves to Manchester a week later will see the former get the extra funding – but not the locality where the migrant actually lives. This is a mistake.

Plus, the funding relief is concentrated narrowly on the NHS alone. This ignores the fact that pressures on public services from migration are wider – not only on health care, but also on school places, public transport and housing. Yet there is nothing to support these vital services.

It is time ministers resurrected the original scheme in the form of something like a Migration Impacts Reduction Fund. A £25 levy on immigration applications could support an extra

£11.7 million or more. This could provide urgent support without increasing costs for hard-working taxpayers, improving public services for all. The funding raised can then go to where it is needed most. The health surcharge does not allow for this. A Migration Impacts Reduction Fund would more effectively target services and better track need.

Ideally the levy could be found – and ring-fenced – in the current application fees. These were originally set to include such a levy and for this purpose. It is right that migrants help pay to reduce related pressures on public services, but it is less clear that even more should be demanded from them financially in having to pay ever more extortionate application fees than currently charged, usually hundreds of pounds if not a couple of thousand.

Jacqui Smith told me that she was surprised to see the original Migration Impacts Fund scrapped, and as fast as it was. She called the fund's launch 'a reform in the right direction'. She is absolutely right – and it is time we saw its return. The fund is not perfect – the money it raises can be very modest and it tends to see non-EU citizens paying the costs for non-EU and EU citizens – but it is much better than the health surcharge or doing nothing at all.

I should note a personal interest in the Migration Impacts Fund. It is not simply a policy that I endorse. This is something I have done – I paid it when I was applying for my permanent residency. So I do know how difficult it is to put together visa applications and how expensive the process can be, and I share the strong view of many migrants who have become British that the fees are currently higher than they need to be. Nonetheless, this is one policy that I experienced and still support.

However, if brought back, there should be some public recognition that local bus services receiving funding paid for by migrants themselves reduces the impact of migration. Likewise for other public services receiving this money. This could go some way towards convincing the public that something is being done by a government that listens to their concerns and make clear that migrants do contribute. If only it was noticed.

Becoming British is important – so it is time we treated it accordingly. Citizenship has become too much of a form-filling, box-ticking exercise. I found that more than half the migrants I spoke to were either undecided about becoming a British citizen or were opposed. Sometimes, the reason was that they were European citizens who did not require British citizenship. However, the high costs and constant negative messages from the media were also turn-offs for many.

But of those that did go ahead, few were inspired by the idea of Britishness. The prime motivation was that they lived and worked here – and wanted to continue living and working here. For many, the experience of becoming British was fairly negative.

One naturalised British citizen told me the application process is 'a thing to be endured'. It is an alienating experience undertaken individually with little or no support surrounded by a public discourse and media bordering on outright hostility to migrants in their midst.

People who naturalised and became British found the requirements they had to pass did nothing to help integrate them into
British society – many felt integrated before they started, but then
felt more like an outsider the further they went down the road
towards becoming British. Lauren, an American living in the
Midlands, observed that migrants are 'being integrated into an
immigrant world, not the British world'. Migrants do not share
more in common with British citizens in general through becoming British, but to other immigrants only.

Personal security was a common response to my questions
about why people chose to become British. Ekaterina, a Russian
living in the south-west who plans to apply to become British,
said:

> Yes, I do want to become a British citizen, and it's important
> to me for personal and professional reasons. My partner is
> British and I have been studying British history and poli-
> tics for most of my adult life. So the transition to becoming
> a British citizen seems to be quite natural to me.

This is not unique to the UK. The British actress Emily Blunt
became an American citizen after several years living in Los
Angeles. She is married to an American actor, John Krasinski.
Blunt said, 'I'm not sure I'm entirely thrilled about it … People
ask me about the whole day. They were like, "Oh, it must have
been so emotional." I was like, "It wasn't! It was sad!" I like being

British.' When asked later about why she did it, Blunt said it was 'mostly for tax reasons'. Welcome to the globalized world of 21st-century citizenship.

The same comments could be made about many a new British citizen, too. People like Ekaterina have set up residence in Britain, fallen in love with British citizens and taken a personal interest in British society. The desire to become British is not about wanting to change who they are, but rather getting the personal security that citizenship brings. They have forged a life in Britain, paying their own way, and want to continue it without the threat of having it torn away through deportation. One British citizen said to me that the process for becoming British is so unwelcoming that often after people have passed the last hurdle and receive UK citizenship, they then left the country for new lives elsewhere. If ever there was a damning verdict of the system, this anecdotal comment is it.

Becoming British has become a solitary exercise conducted between the individual and the state. It misses out the general public in the middle. This must be corrected.

Sir Bernard Crick's Life in the UK Advisory Group led a national conversation on what it means to be British. Not all of his ideas were accepted. They argued that new citizens should sit a 'programme of study' rather than a one-off test. This would have allowed migrants to meet each other and share their experiences of becoming British. The group argued that the test handbook should be made freely available at all airports and seaports as a useful resource for citizens and prospective citizens alike. They recommended that there should be mentors – such as naturalised citizens who had become British – to help support integration. And, finally, they wanted the government to create an Advisory Board on Education for Naturalisation that would meet twice a year and advise the government on how best to implement existing regulations. The lack of such a body has meant that government policies can rest on too little evidence – and typically no feedback at all from migrants with crucial first-hand experience of the system.

Migrants lack that extra support to help encourage their integration. A mentor who had come to the UK and become a British citizen would be well placed to provide concrete, first-hand experience to help new potential citizens integrate into British society better. This is to the benefit of everyone. Such integration classes in Europe come with penalties for failure to attend or progress, such as a cut in any benefits. This is to help ensure full compliance with a programme that is seen as important. But nothing like it exists in Britain. Migrants are simply expected to get on or go off.

There is a strong case to be made for a new requirement for becoming British. Earned citizenship was the idea that migrants could earn points for certain activities that would allow them to become British citizens more quickly. The idea is built on a model of active citizenship. David Blunkett and Matthew Taylor have argued in a jointly written essay that 'active citizenship is vitally important ... Active citizenship is therefore not some sort of optional extra but an essential part of revival and the glue which holds society together.'

But there were problems designing an earned citizenship pathway. Charles Clarke told me he had sympathy with it, 'but it became too bureaucratic' and increasingly difficult to manage. Furthermore, critics objected to the voluntary service at the heart of earned citizenship, because they argued no one should be forced to do voluntary work.

The earned citizenship ideal touches on something important – the value of people making a contribution to British society and trying to help improve and transform it into something even better. But it ran into problems when it became overly managerial.

From its ashes, I recommend that all new British citizens pass a new *contribution* test. The public is generally sceptical about the contributions that new migrants bring to the United Kingdom. They are often unconvinced that migrants bring much-needed skills and experiences to benefit the British economy and society.

The contribution test attempts to overcome this challenge. Individuals wanting to apply for British citizenship must deliver several hours of voluntary service aimed at improving the employability skills or training of British residents. The hours set should be no more than can be undertaken in one day. If every new citizen performed five hours, this could contribute over 1 million hours of additional support aimed at making Britain more skilled and more competitive. Not all new citizens may be qualified trainers and so the scheme would require some support measures in place where appropriate. But the focus is on getting new migrants to share their skills and experience for the benefit of existing British citizens.

There should be flexible opportunities made available for delivering this service. It could take place at Jobcentre Plus, colleges and universities, and perhaps religious places of worship. Many of these places are already on existing registers for accepting migrants for work or study and so are already registered with the Home Office.

The public should benefit from being able to reskill and retool. They could receive direct advice on how they might find work in certain industries or service sectors, or other practical knowledge like preparing for interviews, working with businesses from a migrant's native country or foreign language instruction. The idea is not that new citizens should replace career advisors and educationalists, but that migrants can support them.

Migrants would also benefit from the additional work experience; they could say they had led training or a seminar on their curriculum vitae; and they could forge new contacts they would not have if this were not required. Migrants could develop a new passion for contributing to their local communities in this way – and this could lead to their delivering further training in the future because they want to and not because they have to. An active, positive, contributing citizen is born.

Most importantly, the public could see – and seeing can often mean believing – migrants not as people out to take their jobs or opportunities (when not leaching off the state), but as people who can help them enter work or earn a new promotion. Migrants could be seen to contribute – not only working for their own personal benefit or their employers', but delivering a public good shared with local communities.

The contribution test is not a policy consistent only with Labour values. It also connects with an ambition of the previous coalition government. In 2012, then immigration minister Damian Green MP said that the UK should move from a points-based system to 'a contribution-based system'. He said:

> Whether you come here to work, study, or get married, we as a country are entitled to check that you will add to the quality of life in Britain. There are people who think that all immigrants are bad for Britain. There are also people who think that all immigrants are good for Britain. To move the immigration debate on to a higher level, let's take it as read that they are both wrong, and that the legitimate question in today's world is how we can benefit from immigration.

I agree – and he's spot on. The contribution test can mark an important step forward in shifting the debate, which could go some way towards improving the public's confidence in the system and their view of migration in Britain.

So much has changed – some might say everything has changed – since Crick's Life in the UK Advisory Group last met.

Ten years later, net migration has reached record levels and immigration has become the number one concern for many voters. Well over a million people have sat the citizenship test and taken part in citizenship ceremonies. But there has never been a single, substantive consultation with anyone who became British to gain their perspectives on how these measures aimed at supporting their integration helped them achieve that goal.

It beggars belief that the current government ignores the people who are subjected to immigration restrictions, rather than trying to understand whether these measures are working or can be improved. This group of citizens has been found to be the most trusted source of information about immigration. It is time for government to hear their important voices – and begin a serious review of its handling of citizenship and immigration policies.

Becoming British should not mean getting a veto on what immigration policies the government implements, but the government's failure to consult substantially *at all* with those citizens who can provide the most invaluable insight into how government aims can be achieved speaks volumes about its priorities.

But it is not too late. There is something that can be done. The system can be improved. British citizens care intensely about how it works – and people who have become British are keen to help. I have been frankly overwhelmed by the outpouring of stories that came in flooding in when I began speaking to people prior to writing this book. Citizenship matters and it should be afforded the importance it deserves. New citizens – like me – love our adopted home and are ready to contribute to make Britain even better. The government should embrace their goodwill and positive energy – listening to their concerns in a new, bold, national conversation about Britishness and what it means for citizens today.

Despite the major political and demographic changes of the past decade, little has changed fundamentally in terms of how citizenship has been understood and regulated. It is time there was an honest debate about how this might change in light of background context and the known evidence. A new citizenship advisory group is both timely and necessary to review current regulations and highlight how they can be made fit for purpose, and how they can improve public confidence. The journey to becoming British has evolved. So too must our understanding. And the time is right now.

FURTHER READING

A few words about the sources used. Statistical information is taken from one of several sources: the Office for National Statistics, the Home Office, the National Audit Office and from written Parliamentary Questions. I benefited enormously from hundreds of interviews over the past decade and discuss only a select few of these in the chapters. Names, where used, are occasionally changed to ensure anonymity for interviewees who did not want to be identified. Some readers might want to further examine data, facts, quotations and wider research specifically highlighted in individual chapters. These are referenced below by chapter in the general order they appear, with links provided where possible.

Chapter 1: Immigration Rising

Information about data from the last national census that took place in 2011 can be found from the Office for National Statistics Digital, '1 in 7 people in England and Wales in 2011 were born outside of the UK', ONS Digital (30 July 2015), web: http://visual.ons.gov.uk/migration-census. Long-term migration figures are from the Office for National Statistics, 'Long-term international migration, October 2013 to September 2014 (provisional estimates)', ONS (26 February 2015), web: http://www.ons.gov.uk/ons/rel/migration1/migration-statistics-quarterly-report/february-2015/info-long-term-international-migration.html. Information about the Organisation for Economic and Co-operation and Development report can be found in Beulah Maud Devaney, 'So many Brits now live abroad that they're causing immigration debates. Oh, the irony', *The Independent* (5 November 2015), web: http://www.independent.co.uk/voices/so-many-brits-now-live-abroad-that-theyre-causing-immigration-debates-oh-the-irony-a6723006.html.

The poll conducted by *The Economist* and Ipsos MORI is August 2015 Economist/Ipsos Mori Issues Index (21 August 2015), web: https://www.ipsos-mori.com/researchpublications/researcharchive/3614/EconomistIpsos-MORI-August-2015-Issues-Index.aspx. The research by Scott Blinder on public perceptions of immigration refers to 'Imagined Immigration: The Impact of Different Meanings of "Immigrants" in Public

Opinion and Policy Debates in Britain', *Political Studies* 63 (2015), pp. 80–100.

The quote by Enoch Powell is from his 'Rivers of Blood' speech delivered on 20 April 1968 and it is worth citing the passage in full to avoid any ambiguity:

> I stress the words 'for settlement'. This has nothing to do with the entry of Commonwealth citizens, any more than of aliens, into this country, for the purposes of study or of improving their qualifications, like (for instance) the Commonwealth doctors who, to the advantage of their own countries, have enabled our hospital service to be expanded faster than would otherwise have been possible. They are not, and never have been, immigrants.

So there we have it: students in the UK earning qualifications 'are not, and never have been, immigrants'. That even *he* said this should give anyone wanting to include students in immigration statistics serious pause for thought.

The quote by Tony Blair is from *A Journey* (London: Arrow, 2011), p. 523. The references to Paul Collier refer to comments made in *Exodus: How Migration is Changing Our World* (Oxford: Oxford University Press, 2013) and his 'Immigration's "dark side": a challenge for the left', Policy Network online (4 December 2014), web: http://www.policy-network.net/pno_detail.aspx?ID=4788&title=Immigrations-dark-side-a-challenge-for-the-left.

See also Ciaran Devlin, Olivia Bolt, Dhiren Patel, David Harding and Ishtiaq Hussain, 'Impacts of migration on UK native employment: an analytical review of the evidence' (London: Home Office and Department for Business, Innovation and Skills, 2014).

The report cited by Jonathan Wadsworth is 'Immigration and the UK Labour Market' (London: Centre for Economic Performance, 2015). The comments about nurses in Newcastle are from Craig Thompson, 'Shortage fear as foreign nurse visas are blocked', *The Journal* (11 September 2015), p. 5. On EU citizens and benefits, Lord Patten and Lord Freud, Social Security Benefits: Immigrants, HL Deb, 24 June 2015, cW. The reference to Jonathan Portes is to 'A budget for hard-working Poles', NIESR Blog (9 July 2015), web: http://www.niesr.ac.uk/blog/budget-hard-working-poles#.VfxxK8-FPIU. The Migration Observatory at Oxford University has confirmed Portes's analysis. See Tom Brooks-Pollock, 'EU migrants coming to UK for higher wages but no evidence of "benefits tourism", report shows', *The Independent* (13 April 2016), web: http://www.independent.co.uk/news/uk/politics/why-eu-migrants-are-really-heading-to-britain-and-where-they-come-from-a6981781.html. Findings about immigration and jobs noted the economic report that US President Barack Obama commissioned in 2013 are discussed and quoted in Kevin R. Johnson, Raquel Aldana, Bill Ong Hing, Leticia M. Saucedo and Enid Trucios-Haynes, *Understanding Immigration Law*, 2nd edition (New York: Lexis Nexis, 2015), p. 20. Similar findings were found in an economic report for US

President George W. Bush in 2005: 'A comprehensive accounting of the benefits and costs of immigration shows that the benefits of immigration exceed the costs', also reported in Johnson et al., *Understanding Immigration Law*, p. 20.

The information about ethnicity in the UK around 4000 BC is from Barry Cunliffe, *Britain Begins* (Oxford: Oxford University Press, 2012), p. 128. The research by Bobby Duffy is reported in 'Perceptions and Reality: Ten Things We Should Know about Attitudes to Immigration in the UK', *Political Quarterly* 85 (2014), pp. 259–66. The quote from Lord Green of Deddlington is from David Barrett, 'Britain is home to one in five new European citizens', *Daily Telegraph* (1 July 2015), web: http://www.telegraph.co.uk/news/uknews/immigration/11711922/Britain-is-home-to-one-in-five-new-European-citizens.html.

Citizenship statistics come from sources including the Home Office, Migration Statistics: Immigration Statistics July to September 2014, tables cz_01 and Scott Blinder, *Briefing: Naturalisation as a British Citizen: Concepts and Trends*, 3rd edition (Oxford: Migration Observatory, 2015).

Chapter 2: From Subject to Citizen

The quote by Gary Slapper comes from 'Parliament, the Law Courts, and the Interpretation of Statutes', *Student Law Review* 74 (2015), p. 14. The first legal support for the principle that anyone born in the Crown's realm was a subject of the monarch is *Calvin's*

Case [1608] 7 Co. Rep 1a; 11 Digest 496, 2. This was later established in the British Nationality and Status of Aliens Act 1914. On the 'right of abode', see Immigration Act 1971, British Nationality Act 1981 and Immigration, Asylum and Nationality Act 2006. Other legislation cited includes the Act of Union 1707, the Naturalization Act of 1790, the Hugh Maxwell (Naturalisation) Act 1975, the Aliens Act 1905, the British Nationality Act 1948 and the Commonwealth Immigrants Act 1962.

The quote by the Chartist commentator is from Robert Winder, *Bloody Foreigners: The Story of Immigration to Britain* (London: Little, Brown, 2004) cited in David Miller, 'Immigrants, Nations, and Citizenship', *Journal of Political Philosophy* 16 (2008), pp. 371–90 at 373. The quote by Mahatma Gandhi is from *An Autobiography: Or, the Story of My Experiments with Truth* (London: Beacon Press, 1993), p. 212. The question noted from the Life in the UK citizenship test is taken from the Home Office, *Official Citizenship Test: Study Guide* (London: TSO, 2007), p. 24. This was the official study guide for the second edition of the citizenship test and no longer valid since 2013.

The quote from Gina Clayton is from her scholarly *Textbook on Immigration and Asylum Law*, 6th edition (Oxford: Oxford University Press, 2014), p. 9. See also p. 31 for the quoted comment about immigration rules being in the language of administrators rather than lawyers – an implication of this is that the rules should be interpreted less strictly than standard legal texts. See *Alexander v IAT* [1982] 2 All ER 766 and *Mahad and Others v*

ECO [2009] UKSC 16. Margaret Phelan and James Gillespie's *Immigration Law Handbook* is the 9th edition (Oxford: Oxford University Press, 2015). The Home Office's online points calculator can be found at web: https://www.points.homeoffice. gov.uk/gui-migrant-jsf/SelfAssessment/SelfAssessment.faces. Quotes from Sophie Barrett-Brown are from Edward Fennell, 'UK "loses control" of immigration', *The Times* (17 April 2014): 61. On claims by Nigel Farage there is a 'flood' of migrants, see Ben Riley-Smith, 'Thousands of Isil fighters could use migrant crisis to "flood" into Europe, Nigel Farage warns', *Daily Telegraph* (4 September 2015), web: http://www.telegraph.co.uk/news/ politics/nigel-farage/11844290/Thousands-of-Isil-fighters-could-use-migrant-crisis-to-flood-into-Europe-Nigel-Farage-warns.html.

The quoted speech by Theresa May is 'An immigration system that works in the national interest', 12 December 2012, web: https://www.gov.uk/government/speeches/home-secretary-speech-on-an-immigration-system-that-works-in-the-national-interest. Quote from Kamila Shamsie found in her essay 'I never felt safe', *The Guardian* (4 March 2014), web: http://www. theguardian.com/uk-news/2014/mar/04/author-kamila-shamsie-british-citizen-indefinite-leave-to-remain. Fee information on three-year Tier 2 visas is from 'Home Office Immigration and Nationality Charges 2016', web: https://www.gov.uk/government/uploads/system/uploads/attachment_data/file/510922/ Fees_Table_for_website_2016-17_v0.2.pdf. Further information on these visas and their extension is found in 'Tier 2 (General) visa', web: https://www.gov.uk/tier-2-general. The cost per passenger arriving in Britain is from Home Office Border Force, 'Border Force Transparency Data Q4 2015' (London: Home Office, 25 February 2016). The cost per migration application decision is from the Home Office, 'Temporary and Permanent Migration: UK Visa & Immigration Transparency Data Q4 2015' (London: Home Office, 25 February 2016).

Chapter 3: What is Britishness?

The quote by Tony Wright and Andrew Gamble is from 'The End of Britain?', *Political Quarterly* 71 (2000), p. 1. The British National Party website is http://www.bnp.org.uk. The speech by Enoch Powell is the 'Rivers of Blood' speech delivered on 20 April 1968. The piece commented on by Anila Athar is 'If you believe British and Islamic values are incompatible, why do you want to live in the UK?' *The Nation* blog (14 July 2015), web: http://nation.com. pk/blogs/14-Jul-2015/if-you-believe-british-and-islamic-values-are-incompatible-why-do-you-want-to-live-in-the-uk. The reference to a 'clash of civilisations' is to Samuel Huntington, *The Clash of Civilizations and the Remaking of World Order*, updated edition (New York: Simon & Schuster, 2011).

The references to David Goodhart are to his 'Discomfort of strangers', *The Guardian* (24 February 2004), web: http://www. theguardian.com/politics/2004/feb/24/race.eu and his *The British Dream: Successes and Failures of Post-war Immigration*

(London: Atlantic, 2013), pp. xxvi, 117, 261. On the hunker-down thesis, see Robert D. Putnam, '*E pluribus unum*: diversity and community in the twenty-first century: the 2006 Johan Skytte prize lecture', *Scandinavian Political Studies* 30 (2007), pp. 137–74. Criticisms by Jonathan Portes refer to 'An Exercise in Scapegoating', *London Review of Books* 35 (20 June 2013), pp. 7–9 and by James Laurence to '"Hunkering Down or Hunkering Away?" The effect of community ethnic diversity on residents' social networks', *Journal of Elections, Public Opinion and Parties* 23 (2013), pp. 255–78.

The quote by David Blunkett can be found on the BBC News website (15 December 2004), web: http://news.bbc.co.uk/1/hi/uk_politics/4099799.stm. Some great examples of Englishness – presented with humour – referred to come from Kate Fox, *Watching the English: The Hidden Rules of English Behaviour* (London: Hodder, 2004). The quote by David Gervais is from Michael Kenny, *The Politics of English Nationhood* (Oxford: Oxford University Press, 2014), p. 7. On the *Times* reader poll, see Greg Hurst, 'Maverick streak makes mockery of hunt for a British motto', *The Times* (22 November 2007), web: http://www.thetimes.co.uk/tto/news/politics/article2024244.ece.

On quotes by Bhikhu Parekh and the Parekh Report, see Bhikhu Parekh (ed.), *The Future of Multi-Ethnic Britain: Report of the Commission on the Future of Multi-Ethnic Britain* (London: Profile, 2000), pp. ix–x; Bhikhu Parekh, *Rethinking Multiculturalism: Cultural Diversity and Political Theory*

(Basingstoke: Palgrave Macmillan, 2006), pp. 201–2, 231–3; and Bhikhu Parekh, *A New Politics of Identity: Political Principles for an Interdependent World* (Basingstoke: Palgrave Macmillan, 2008), p. 69. The Denham and Crick reports are John Denham et al., 'Building Cohesive Communities: A Report of the Ministerial Group on Public Order and Community Cohesion' (London: Home Office, 2001) and Bernard Crick et al., 'The New and the Old: The Report of the "Life in the United Kingdom" Advisory Group' (London: Home Office Social Policy Unit, 2003).

The government White Paper referred to is HM Government, 'Controlling our borders: Making migration work for Britain – five year strategy for asylum and immigration' (London: Home Office, 2005). The quote by Mark Easton is from 'Define Britishness? It's like painting wind', BBC News (2 March 2012), web: http://www.bbc.co.uk/news/uk-17218635. The quotes by Crick and Gordon Brown are from Bernard Crick, 'Identity Politics' in Bernard Crick and Andrew Lockyer (eds), *Active Citizenship: What Could It Achieve and How?* (Edinburgh: Edinburgh University Press, 2010), pp. 193–4. The quote by Daniel Finkelstein is from 'Here's what we really think about migrants', *The Times* (23 September 2015), p. 23.

Chapter 4: Testing Citizenship

The Nationality, Immigration and Asylum Act 2002 brought the citizenship test into being. Its shape was influenced by several reports, including Bhikhu Parekh (ed.), 'The Future of

Multi-Ethnic Britain: Report of the Commission on the Future of Multi-Ethnic Britain' (London: Profile, 2000); John Denham et al., 'Building Cohesive Communities: A Report of the Ministerial Group on Public Order and Community Cohesion' (London: Home Office, 2001) and Bernard Crick et al., 'The New and the Old: The Report of the "Life in the United Kingdom" Advisory Group' (London: Home Office Social Policy Unit, 2003).

The first edition of the citizenship test handbook is from the Home Office, *Life in the United Kingdom: A Journey to Citizenship* (London: TSO, 2004). The second edition test handbook is from the Home Office, *Life in the United Kingdom: A Journey to Citizenship*, 2nd edition (London: TSO, 2007). Its accompanying practice question guide is Home Office, *Official Citizenship Test Study Guide* (London: TSO, 2007). The current edition is Home Office, *Life in the United Kingdom: A Guide for New Residents*, 3rd edition (London: TSO, 2013). Accompanying official study books are Michael Mitchell, *Life in the United Kingdom: Official Practice Questions and Answers* (London: TSO, 2013) and Jenny Wales, *Life in the United Kingdom: Official Study Guide* (London: TSO, 2013).

My comprehensive report is Thom Brooks, 'The "Life in the United Kingdom" Citizenship Test: Is It Unfit for Purpose?' (Durham: Durham University, 2013). Earlier work on the test is Thom Brooks, 'The British Citizenship Test: The Case for Reform', *Political Quarterly* 83 (2012), pp. 560–66. My interview on BBC Radio 4 was on the *You and Yours* programme airing 10 October 2011 and can be found from twenty-three minutes in at this still-live website: http://www.bbc.co.uk/programmes/b015mzl2 (and just after Chris Tarrant on the use of pauses on TV and radio). David Cameron's speech confirming changes to the current test is 'Prime Minister's speech on immigration', 10 October 2011, web: http://www.number10.gov.uk/news/prime-ministers-speech-on-immigration.

Statistics on citizenship tests taken, passed or failed in addition to the success or failure of naturalisation applications comes from 2015 data by the Office for National Statistics. Further data comes from James Brokenshire MP, British Nationality: Assessments, HC Deb, 2 December 2014, cW. The data on the record of sixty-four failed tests is from both Louise Sassoon, 'British citizenship test slammed after applicant is allowed to re-sit exam 64 times before he passes', *Daily Mirror* (4 July 2015), web: http://www.mirror.co.uk/news/uk-news/british-citizenship-test-slammed-after-6000864 and Philip Davies MP, British Nationality: Assessments, HC Deb, 2 July 2015, cW. Statement by James Brokenshire from Andrew Rosindell MP and James Brokenshire MP, Immigration, HC Deb, 11 February 2016, cW.

Information about the Australian citizenship test can be found at Australian government, Department of Immigration and Citizenship, 'Citizenship Test', web: http://www.citizenship.gov.au/learn/cit_test. The American test can be found at US Citizenship and Immigration Services, 'Learn about the United States: Quick Civics Lessons for the Naturalization Test', M-638 (rev. 01/13), web: http://www.uscis.gov/citizenship.

Chapter 5: The English Question

The Eric Pickles quote is from Richard Ford, 'Quarter of councils have areas where little English is spoken', *The Times* (5 July 2014), p. 14. The former regulation on English language proficiency is Part 1(33B) of Immigration Rules (HC 395). Requirement of English proficiency is found in section 2 of the British Nationality and Status of Aliens Act 1914, s41(1) (ba) of the British Nationality Act 1981, s40(3) of the Borders, Citizenship and Immigration Act 2009 and British Nationality (General) (Amendment) Regulations 2013. Today, the standard of English required is B1 of the Common European Framework of Reference for Languages or higher, or equivalent.

The Scots Gaelic and Welsh languages held 'equality' with English in schedule 1–(1)(c) of the British Nationality Act 1981 ('that he has sufficient knowledge of the English, Welsh or Scottish Gaelic language'). This is no longer the case and terminated for naturalisation purposes in the British National (General) (Amendment) Regulations 2013. Information about tests taken in Welsh or Scots Gaelic, Lord Roberts of Llandudno and Lord Bates, British Nationality: Assessments, HL Deb, 6 January 2015, c118W. On Parliamentary Questions by Lord Roberts, see Lord Roberts of Llandudno and Lord Bates, British Nationality: Assessments, HL Deb, 6 January 2015, c118W; Lord Roberts of Llandudno and Lord Bates, Naturalisation, HL Deb, 6 January 2015, c179W and Lord Roberts of Llandudno and Lord

Prior of Brampton, Nurses: Qualifications, HL Deb, 18 June 2015, cW.

On ESOL with Citizenship, see 'Citizenship Materials for ESOL Learners', web: http://www.niace.org.uk/projects/ esolcitizenship. On ESOL learner statistics and pass rate, see Lord Greaves and Lord Popat, English for Speakers of Other Languages, HL Deb, 29 August 2013, c352W. On ESOL qualifications and funding info, see Pip Kings and Helen Casey, 'ESOL Qualifications and funding in 2014: Issues for consideration' (London: National Research and Development Centre for adult literacy and numeracy (NRDC), October 2013).

On government plans to tighten up English language requirements, see BBC News, 'British citizenship test tightened to include English test', BBC News Online (17 April 2013), web: http:// www.bbc.co.uk/news/uk-politics-22158482 and Home Office, 'Knowledge of language and life in the UK for settlement and naturalisation: statement of intent, changes to the requirement from October 2013' (London: Home Office, April 2013). On NIACE workshop report, http://www.niace.org.uk/current-work/ esol-provision-and-the-home-office-statement-of-intent.

On UK NARIC, see web: http://ecctis.co.uk/naric/Individuals. On Lord Roberts's Parliamentary Question, see Lord Roberts of Llandudno and Lord Bates, Naturalisation, HL Deb, 6 January 2015, c179W. On the government's answer to Graham Brady's question about fraud or abuse in English language testing, see James Brokenshire MP, Entry Clearances: English Language, HC Deb,

5 January 2015, cW. The statement by James Brokenshire MP about his reasons for reducing the number of approved English test providers is HC Deb, 26 March 2015, cW. The Bibi case is *R (Bibi) v Secretary of State for the Home Department* (2015) UKSC, *The Times* (16 December 2015), p. 55; [2013] EWCA Civ 322.

The *Times* investigative report is Richard Ford, 'Quarter of councils have areas where little English is spoken', *The Times* (5 July 2014), p. 14. David Cameron's speech on extremism can be found at 'Extremism: PM speech', 20 July 2015, web: https://www.gov.uk/government/speeches/extremism-pm-speech. On the American English test, see US Citizenship and Immigration Services, 'Study Materials for the English Test', http://www.uscis.gov/citizenship/learners/study-test/study-materials-english-test.

On literacy rates, see National Literacy Trust, 'How many illiterate adults are there in England?' http://www.literacytrust.org.uk/adult_literacy/illiterate_adults_in_england. David Cameron's statement on ESOL support and tackling extremism is '"Passive tolerance" of separate communities must end, says PM', Prime Minister's Office, 18 January 2016. For criticism, see Thom Brooks, 'Cameron's immigration strategy is to govern through gimmicks', LabourList (19 January 2016), web: http://labourlist.org/2016/01/camerons-immigration-strategy-is-to-govern-through-gimmicks and see earlier essay: Thom Brooks, 'The Government's strategy for tackling extremism is more Little Britain than Big Society', *The Journal* (22 October 2015), web: http://www.chroniclelive.co.uk/news/north-east-news/

governments-strategy-tackling-extremism-more-10309211. On
Germany's integration system, see http://www.bamf.de/EN/
Willkommen/DeutschLernen/Integrationskurse/integration-
skurse-node.html. On France's integration and welcome contract,
see http://travail-emploi.gouv.fr/IMG/pdf/cai_anglais.pdf.

On the noted Demos report, see Ally Paget and Neil Stevenson, 'Making ESOL policy work better for migrants and
wider society...' (London: Demos, 2014). Welsh policy: Lly-
wodraeth Cymru/Welsh Government, 'English for Speakers
of Other Languages (ESOL) policy for Wales' (Bedwar: Welsh
Department for Education and Skills, June 2014).

Chapter 6: The Free Movement Myth

The free movement myth is the false belief that European
Economic Area (EEA) citizens can travel freely – and without
restrictions – to and from any member EEA state. Most of the
EEA is the EU, but it also includes Iceland, Lichtenstein and
Poland. Quotes by Jack Straw are from Alice Philipson, 'Labour
made a "spectacular mistake" on immigration, admits Jack Straw',
Daily Telegraph (13 November 2013), web: http://www.telegraph.
co.uk/news/uknews/immigration/10445585/Labour-made-a-
spectacular-mistake-on-immigration-admits-Jack-Straw.html.
Statistics about Polish migration to the UK from James Slack
and Ian Drury, 'Rise of the Polish Brits', *Daily Mail* (31 January
2015), web: http://www.dailymail.co.uk/news/article-2933970/

Rise-Polish-Brits-Number-given-UK-citizenship-soars-1-200-just-five-years.html. Some of the statistical information used is from Office for National Statistics data – ONS, 'Overseas Travel and Tourism – Monthly Release, Provisional Results for June 2015' (released 21 August 2015), web: http://www.ons.gov.uk/ons/rel/ott/overseas-travel-and-tourism-monthly-release/provisional-results-for-june-2015/index.html.

The Electoral Commission report referred to is Electoral Commission, 'Referendum on membership of the European Union: assessment of the Electoral Commission on the proposed referendum questions' (London: Electoral Commission, September 2015). I am cited at 4.19:

> Another key factor that explained concerns about this was the use of 'no' to represent a change. Professor Thom Brooks of Durham University was concerned about the lack of consistency when compared to previous referendum questions: 'There is a convention that the answer "no" should be reserved for a verdict of no change – and "yes" for a verdict of change. The problem with the current question is that a "yes" vote is a verdict of no change. This is inconsistent with referendums on AV nationally and on independence in Scotland.'

On EU free movement law, see the Treaty on the Functioning of the European Union 2012, the Immigration (European Economic

Area) Regulations 2006. The law relating to part-time workers discussed refers to *Levin v Secretary of State for Justice* [1982] ECR 1035. The law concerning the six-month rule discussed refers to *R v IAT, ex p Antonissen* [1991] 2 CMLR 373. The law concerning self-sufficient persons discussed refers to Article 8(4) of the Directive 2004/58 EC. The law concerning the relation of EU law and the British law discussed refers to the European Communities Act 1972. The law on Citizens of the UK and Colonies refers to the British National Act 1948. The law that Ireland is to be considered a foreign country refers to the Ireland Act 1949.

The statement by Migration Watch can be found on the website FAQ here: http://www.migrationwatchuk.org/faq. The quote by David Goodhart is from his *The British Dream* (London: Atlantic, 2013), p. 35. The speech by David Cameron is 'David Cameron's EU speech: full text', BBC News (28 November 2014), web: http://www.bbc.co.uk/news/uk-politics-30250299. On permanent residence cards for non-EEA family of EEA nationals, see Frank Field MP and James Brokenshire MP, Visas, HC Deb, 18 June 2015, cW.

Quote by Chuka Umunna from Peter Dominiczak and Matthew Holehouse, 'Labour could create tough EU free movement policy, Chuka Umunna hints', *Daily Telegraph* (10 January 2014), web: http://www.telegraph.co.uk/news/worldnews/europe/eu/10563395/Labour-could-create-tough-EU-free-movement-policy-Chuka-Umunna-hints.html and further commentary from Jason Beattie, 'Labour toughens up on immigration as shadow cabinet minister calls for end to free movement of EU

jobseekers', *Daily Mirror* (10 January 2014), web: http://www.
mirror.co.uk/news/uk-news/chuka-umunna-immigration-
labour-toughens-3009396. An excellent source on EU citizenship
and its restrictions is Robert Schütze, *An Introduction to European
Law*, 2nd edition (Cambridge: Cambridge University Press,
2015), pp. 268–94. The figures on migrants in work and on
Jobseeker's Allowance are found in Anoosh Chakelian, 'What
are EU migrants entitled to in terms of benefits and housing, and
when?', *New Statesman* (28 November 2014), web: http://www.
newstatesman.com/print/node/142975. On non-UK referees,
see David Hanson MP, British Nationality, HC Deb, 5 January
2015, cW and James Brokenshire MP, British Nationality, HC Deb,
5 January 2015, cW. On the government's admissions about health
tourism, in-work and out-of-work benefits, see Sir Greg Knight
MP and Alistair Burt MP, Health Services: Foreign Nationals, HC
Deb, 26 October 2015, cW and Lord Kinnock and Lord Freud,
Immigration: EU Nationals, HL Deb, 4 January 2016, cW. Home
Office guidance on the removal of EU and EEA citizens can be
found at Home Office, 'European Economic Area administrative removal: consideration and decision', version 1.0 (London:
Home Office, 2016). Data on EU and EEA citizen removals and
re-entry are from Christopher Chope MP and James Brokenshire
MP, Repatriation: EEA Nationals, HC Deb, 11 April 2016, cW.

The quote by Steve Peers and comment on Dano case is
from Steve Peers, 'Benefits for EU Citizens: A U-Turn by the
Court of Justice?' *Cambridge Law Journal* 74 (2015), pp. 195–98,

EU Citizen's Rights Directive (Dir. 2004/38, OJ 2004 L 158.77) and see *Dano*, ECLI:EU:C:2014:2358. On Roksana Mirga case, see *Mirga v Sec of Stet for Work and Pensions*, UKSC, *The Times* (8 February 2016), p. 49. Quote by Jonathan Portes is from his 'What would UK immigration policy look like after Brexit?', National Institute of Economic and Social Research blog (14 September 2015), web: http://www.niesr.ac.uk/blog/what-would-uk-immigration-policy-look-after-brexit. The pamphlet by Charles Clarke referred to is 'The EU and migration: a call for action' (London: Centre for European Reform, 2011). On Theresa May and James Brokenshire's claims of full, 100 per cent border checks, see Jim Shannon MP and James Brokenshire MP, Criminal Records: EU Nationals, HC Deb, 13 January 2016, cW; Theresa May, Port Security, HC Deb, 22 February 2016, c5 and Philip Davies MP and James Brokenshire MP, Immigration Controls: Criminal Records, HC Deb, 7 March 2016, cW.

The post-election speech by David Cameron is 'PM speech on immigration', 21 May 2015, web: https://www.gov.uk/government/speeches/pm-speech-on-immigration. On David Cameron's proposed 'emergency brake', see European Council, 'Decision of the Heads of State or Government, Meeting within the European Council, Concerning a New Settlement for the United Kingdom within the European Union', EUCO 4/16 (2 February 2016). Information about National Insurance numbers and the quote by Jonathan Portes can be found in Antony Seely, 'National Insurance numbers (NINOs): House of Commons Library Briefing Paper Number 04281' (London: House of Commons, 8 September 2015). The speech by Yvette Cooper is 'Labour's approach to immigration', 18 November 2014, Labour Party website, web: http://press.labour.org.uk/ post/102953239474/yvette-cooper-speech-labours-approach-to. The comments by Lord Green of Deddlington on identity cards and migration are in Andrew Green, 'We're too soft. Bring in the army and ID cards', *The Times* (13 August 2015), p. 24. On identity cards, see also Nicholas Soames MP and Frank Field MP in Immigration System, HC Deb, 11 January 2016, c553–54. Data on the numbers who have failed passport interviews annually since 2010 can be found at Lord Roberts of Llandudno and Lord Bates, Passports: Interviews, HL Deb, 11 December 2015, cW.

Chapter 7: Love and Marriage

The laws relating to marriage and citizenship discussed include the Naturalisation Act 1844, the Naturalisation Act 1870, the British Nationality and Status of Aliens Act 1914, the British Nationality Act 1981, *Quila and Bibi v Secretary of State for the Home Department* [2011] UKSC 45 and Saint Prix [2014], ECLI:EU:C:2014:2007 Case C-507/12. Family visa statistics are from the Home Office, Freedom of Information release published 18 December 2014 and Office for National Statistics, 'Statistical News Release: Immigration Statistics', ONS (26 February 2015). On income thresholds, see *MM (Lebanon) & others, R (on the application of) v*

Secretary of State for the Home Department [2014] EWCA Civ 985 and James Brokenshire, Family Visas, HC Deb, 22 February 2016, c3. Quote by Manjit Singh Gill is from Jessica Elgot, '"Absurd" visa rules on income force UK citizens into exile, court told', *The Guardian* (22 February 2016), web: http://www.theguardian. com/uk-news/2016/feb/22/absurd-minimum-income-visa-rules-forcing-uk-citizens-into-exile-court-told. The story of Katy James is from BBC News, 'Home Office to reconsider visa for American mother to stay in UK', BBC News (8 April 2016), web: http://www.bbc.co.uk/news/uk-england-sussex-35997066 and Peter Lindsey, 'Eastbourne family "over the moon" after Home Office reverses decision', *Eastbourne Independent* (14 April 2016), web: http://www.eastbourneindependent. co.uk/news/14427187.Eastbourne_family__over_the_moon__ after_Home_Office_reverses_decision.

Story about Reyna Khosla is from Jennifer Newton, 'Businesswoman born and bred in UK with a British father must take citizenship test to get a passport thanks to legal loophole', *Daily Mail* (26 August 2015), web: http://www.dailymail.co.uk/ news/article-3211818/Businesswoman-born-bred-UK-British-father-citizenship-test-passport-thanks-legal-loophole.html. The story about Harley is from Emily Dugan, 'I feel like I have been let out of prison', *The Independent* (2 February 2015), web: http://www.independent.co.uk/news/people/ harley-miller-i-feel-like-i-ve-been-let-out-of-prison-it-was-like-i-was-under-house-arrest-10019228.html.

The UK Supreme Court decision on the habitual residence of children referred to is *In re AR (Children: Habitual Residence)* UKSC 3 June 2015. On the right to family life, see Melanie Gower, 'Article 8 of the ECHR and immigration cases', House of Commons Library Note SN/HA/6355 (London: House of Commons, 18 October 2013). On adoption, see *FAS v Secretary of State for the Home Department* [2015] EWCA Civ 951. On the van Niekerk family, see 'May daze', *Private Eye* 1397 (24 July 2015), p. 35.

On sham marriages, see *Rosa v Secretary of State of the Home Department*, Court of Appeal (12 February 2016): 55 and Home Affairs Select Committee, 'The Work of the Immigration Directorates (October–December 2013)' (London: Home Affairs Select Committee, 25 July 2014), web: http://www.publications.parliament.uk/pa/cm201415/cmselect/cmhaff/237/23703.htm. On the Home Office 'public statement' form for reporting ex-partners, see Thom Brooks, 'Government wants us to rat out those we once loved – but doesn't even tell us how', *The Journal* (17 December 2015), web: http://www.chroniclelive.co.uk/news/news-opinion/government-wants-rat-out-those-10616605 and Thom Brooks, 'Breaking up is hard to do – especially when you have to fill out a government form', *The Conversation* (7 January 2016), web: http://theconversation.com/breaking-up-is-hard-to-do-especially-when-you-have-to-fill-out-a-government-form-52783.

On the *Practical Guide*, see Jenny Wales, *A Practical Guide to Living in the United Kingdom* (London: TSO, 2014). For more report on it, see Thom Brooks, *A Practical Guide to Living in the United Kingdom: A Report* (Durham: Durham University, 2015).

Chapter 8: Seeking Asylum

Comments about the law on asylum seekers and refugees refer to the Asylum and Immigration Act 1996, the Nationality, Immigration and Asylum Act 2002, the UN Convention on the Rights of the Child and the 1967 UN Protocol Relating to the Status of Refugees (generally known as the Geneva Convention).

On Theresa May's comments, see her 'A borderless EU harms everyone but the gangs that sell false dreams', *Sunday Times* (30 August 2015), p. 21 and her conference speech of 6 October 2015 can be viewed at web: http://www.bbc.co.uk/news/uk-politics-34452966. Quotes by Tim Montgomerie are from his 'You've got to be harsh to be kind to migrants', *The Times* (17 September 2015), p. 29.

The figures on refugees come from the Office for National Statistics. Report by Frances Gibb is 'Asylum appeals fuel "growth industry" as judicial reviews soar by 86% in six years', *The Times* (7 September 2013), p. 22. On asylum checks, Frank Field MP and James Brokenshire MP, Asylum, HC Deb, 15 January 2015, cW. OECD statistics from Dan Andrews, Aida Caldera Sánchez and Åsa Johansson, 'Towards a better understanding of the informal economy', OECD Economics Department Working Papers, no. 873 (Paris: OECD).

For the BBC figure on immigration checks and landlords, see 'Illegal immigration: Minister pledges crackdown on "rogue employers"', BBC News (10 August 2015), web: http://www.bbc.co.uk/news/uk-33844047. On illegal residents asylum seekers, see Jonathan Portes, 'Is illegal immigration really "getting worse"?', *New Statesman* (23 April 2014), web: http://www.newstatesman.com/politics/2014/04/illegal-immigration-really-getting-worse.

The government's acknowledgement that it lacks data on what payments, if any, have been made to asylum seekers not entitled to state benefits is from Lord Roberts of Llandudno and Lord Bates, Asylum: Finance, HL Deb, 5 October 2015, cW. The government's acknowledgement that it has no plans to allow asylum seekers to take up paid or voluntary work earlier than currently permitted comes from Lord Roberts of Llandudno and Lord Bates, Immigration: Appeals, HL Deb, 5 October 2015, cW. Information on cash support for asylum seekers is from 'Asylum support', web: https://www.gov.uk/asylum-support/what-youll-get.

On asylum seekers in Middlesbrough, see 'Middlesbrough revealed as England's asylum seeker capital, with 982 making the town their home', *Daily Mirror* (8 October 2014), web: http://www.mirror.co.uk/news/uk-news/middlesbrough-revealed-englands-asylum-seeker-4403722 and 'Middlesbrough has largest proportion of asylum seekers of anywhere in England', *Evening Gazette* (8 October 2014), web: http://www.gazettelive.co.uk/news/teesside-news/middlesbrough-largest-proportion-asylum-seekers-7899474. The red doors in Middlesbrough incident is discussed by Andy McDonald, Asylum Seekers: Middlesbrough, HC Deb, 20 January 2016, c1426. For information on asylum support and review, see Lord Bates, Asylum Support (Amendment No. 3) Regulations 2015, HL Deb, 28 July 2015, cW. On Charles Clarke's views on the UK and asylum quoted, see his 'The EU and migration: a call for action' (London: Centre for European Reform, 2011), pp. 4, 5, 15, 42 and 49. On statistics about those failing to produce passports at airports, see David Davies MP and James Brokenshire MP, Immigration: Prosecutions, HC Deb, 10 September 2015, cW. Information on the return of people by commercial flights and costs: James Brokenshire MP, Asylum: Deportation, HC Deb, 28 July 2015, cW.

Figures on UKBA are from HC Deb, 22 November 2010, c75W and HC Deb, 24 November 2010, c301W. On the legality of fast-track rules, see R (Detention Action) v First-tier Tribunal (Immigration and Asylum Chamber) and Others, Court of Appeal, 29 July 2015 reported in The Times. Judgment by Lord Dyson, Master of the Rolls. On appeals data, see Jeremy Corbyn MP and Shailesh Vara MP, Immigration: Appeals, HC Deb, 7 January 2015, cW. The government admits it does not know the number of refugees in the UK at Fabian Hamilton MP and James Brokenshire MP, Refugees: China, HC Deb, 4 November 2015, cW.

On cited Calais costs, see David Hanson MP and James Brokenshire MP, Illegal Immigrants: France, HC Deb, 21 September 2015, cW and Lord Patten and Lord Bates, Undocumented Migrants: Calais, HL Deb, 5 October 2015, cW.

For my interview with BBC News magazine, see Camila Ruz, 'What happens to failed asylum seekers?', BBC News magazine (13 August 2015), web: http://www.bbc.co.uk/news/magazine-33849593. For information on the number of people removed from the UK under the Dublin Regulation since 2010, see David Hanson MP and James Brokenshire MP, Asylum: Reportation, HC Deb, 15 June 2015, cW. On the criticism by senior judges about the EU refugee crisis, see BBC News, 'Migrant crisis: UK response criticised by senior former judges', BBC News (12 October 2015), web: http://www.bbc.co.uk/news/uk-politics-34502419. On the Cologne attacks, see Victoria Richards, 'Cologne attacks: What happened after 1,000 women were sexually assaulted?', *The Independent* (11 February 2016), web: http://www.independent.co.uk/news/world/europe/cologne-attacks-what-happened-after-1000-women-were-sexually-assaulted-a6867071.html.

The tragic story of Hosam Osman Alziber can be read in 'Tragic end to Hosam's quest for a better life', *The Times* (12 August 2015), p. 8. On Lord Blencathra and Lord Bates's question and answer, see Undocumented Migrants, HL Deb, 22 September 2015, cW. On potential costs to housing asylum seekers, see Jill Insley, 'Could your home be a haven for refugees?', *Sunday Times* money section (13 September 2015), p. 1. Quote by Daniel Finkelstein is from his 'Here's what we really think about migrants', *The Times* (23 September 2015), p. 23. On the EU migration crisis, see European Commission, 'Communication on the

State of Play of Implementation of the Priority Actions under the European Agenda on Migration' (10 February 2016) and Thom Brooks, 'The EU Migration Crisis: What Next?', *Netherlands Quarterly of Human Rights* 34 (2016), pp. 4–7. Quote by Paul Collier is from his *Exodus: How Migration is Changing Our World* (Oxford: Oxford University Press, 2013), p. 117.

Chapter 9: Ending Britishness

The law referred to throughout includes the British Nationality and Status of Aliens Act 1914, the Immigration Act 1971, the British Nationality Act 1981, the Immigration and Asylum Act 1999 and the Immigration Act 2014. Case law discussed includes *H (Tanzania) v Secretary of State for the Home Department* [2011] UKSC 4; *Thapa v Secretary of State for the Home Department*, Queen's Bench (11 March 2014), *The Times* (18 April 2014), p. 67; and *R v Secretary of State for the Home Department*, UKSC 1 June 2014, *The Times* (2 June 2014), p. 51. The quote by US Supreme Court Chief Justice Earl Warren is from *Trop v Dulles* (1958) 356 US 86, see p. 101.

For the quote on the backlog of cases, see John Hyde, 'Immigration appeal hearings delayed up to nine months', *Law Society Gazette* (12 October 2015), web: http://www.lawgazette.co.uk/news/immigration-appeal-hearings-delayed-up-to-nine-months/5051475. article?utm_source=dispatch&utm_medium=email&utm_campaign=GAZ121015. On the Home Office statistics on the number of people entering UK, see Home Office, 'A Short Guide to the Home Office' (London: National Audit Office, June 2015). For information on the number of people deprived of British citizenship, see Home Office, 'Individuals deprived of British citizenship since 2013', FOI release (18 December 2014). On Mike Tyson's ban from entering the UK, see James Meikle, 'Mike Tyson banned from UK over rape conviction', *The Guardian* (10 December 2013), web: http://www.theguardian.com/uk-news/2013/dec/10/mike-tyson-banned-uk-rape-conviction.

On the case of 'Mostafa' (not his real name – he is identified in court papers as 'M2'), see Victoria Parsons and Alice Ross, 'UK government faces long legal battle after man stripped of citizenship returns', *The Guardian* (20 August 2015), web: http://www.theguardian.com/uk-news/2015/aug/20/uk-government-legal-battle-man-stripped-citizenship-returns. On the case of the Libyan 'Ibrahim', see *H U v Secretary of State for the Home Department*, UKUT (IAC) (1 April 2015) Appeal Number: DA/02122/2013, unreported. On the government not knowing how many people are in the UK illegally, see David Hanson MP and James Brokenshire MP, Entry Clearances, HC Deb, 23 February 2015, cW. On the government's not knowing the number of dual citizens, see Sadiq Khan MP and James Brokenshire MP, Dual Nationality, HC Deb, 29 October 2015, cW.

On the case of the Iraqi Hilal, see Paul Gallagher, 'Humiliating defeat for Theresa May in Supreme Court appeal over "stateless" former terror suspect stripped of British

citizenship', *The Independent* (9 October 2013), web: http://
www.independent.co.uk/news/uk/crime/humiliating-defeat-
for-theresa-may-in-supreme-court-appeal-over-stateless-former-
terror-suspect-8868951.html. On capital punishment, see Thom
Brooks, *Punishment* (London: Routledge, 2012). For the quote
by Philippe Sands QC, see Ewen MacAskill and Richard Norton-
Taylor, 'How UK government decided to kill Reyaad Khan',
The Guardian (8 September 2015), web: http://www.theguardian.
com/world/2015/sep/08/how-did-britain-decide-to-assassi-
nate-uk-isis-fighter-reyaad-khan-drone-strike.

Chapter 10: A Future for Britishness?

On the salary threshold for permanent residency, see Melanie
Gower and Ben Politowski, 'The £35,000 salary requirement to
settle in the UK', House of Commons Briefing Paper CBP-7264
(London: House of Commons, 2015) and Migration Advisory
Committee, 'Analysis of the Points Based System Settlement Rights
of Migrants in Tier 1 and Tier 2', November 2011 and HC Deb, 29
February 2012, c34WS. For the quote by Andy Burnham, see Dan
Bloom, 'Theresa May's landlord immigration checks "like saying
no dogs, no blacks, no Irish" claims Andy Burnham', *Daily Mirror*
(11 October 2015), web: http://www.mirror.co.uk/news/uk-news/
theresa-mays-landlord-immigration-checks-6612553.

On good-character requirements, see S41A of the British
Nationality Act 1981 and Home Office, 'Guide AN: Naturalisation

as a British Citizen – A Guide for Applicants' (London: TSO, October 2013). For David Hanson's question on financial fraud, see James Brokenshire MP, British Nationality, HC Deb, 5 January 2015, cW. On Tier 1 applications in China, Home Office, 'Tier 1 entrepreneur visa applications processed in China from April 2013 to March 2014', FOI 32259 (5 January 2015). On good character not being checked outside the Home Office, see Michael Crockart MP and James Brokenshire MP, British Nationality, HC Deb, 12 January 2015, cW. On there being only two full-time 'equivalent' members of UKVI to help landlords with any questions with immigration regulations, see Gavin Newlands MP and James Brokenshire MP, Home Office: Staff, HC Deb, 26 October 2015, cW.

On the Migration Impacts Fund and Migration Impacts Reduction Fund, see Melanie Gower, 'Migration Impacts Fund', House of Commons Library Note (15 October 2010); Patrick Wintour, 'Fund to ease impact of immigration scrapped by stealth', *The Guardian* (6 August 2010), web: http://www.theguardian.com/uk2010/aug/fund-impact-immigration-scrapped and Thom Brooks, 'Migration Impacts Reduction Fund', Durham Law School Briefing Document, Durham University, web: https://www.dur.ac.uk/resources/law/research/Brooks_Migration ImpactsReductionFund.pdf. On health surcharge, see Home Office, 'Migrant "health surcharge" to raise £200 million a year', gov.uk (19 March 2015), web: https://www.gov.uk/government/news/migrant-health-surcharge-to-raise-200-million-a-year and

Thom Brooks, 'New migrant "health surcharge" – an election stunt full of loopholes', LabourList (22 March 2015), web: http://labourlist.org/2015/03/new-migrant-health-surcharge-an-election-stunt-full-of-loopholes.

Quote by Emily Blunt from David Lawlor, 'Emily Blunt regretted becoming US citizen after Republican presidential debate', *Daily Telegraph* (15 September 2015), web: http://www.telegraph.co.uk/news/worldnews/northamerica/usa/11867442/Emily-Blunt-regretted-becoming-US-citizen-after-Republican-presidential-debate.html. The other story on Emily Blunt is from Andrew Pulver, 'Emily Blunt: I became a US citizen "mostly for tax reasons"', *The Guardian* (5 October 2015), web: http://www.theguardian.com/film/2015/oct/05/emily-blunt-i-became-us-citizen-mostly-for-tax-reasons.

On Labour's plans for earned citizenship, see UK Border Agency, 'The Path to Citizenship: Next Steps in Reforming the Immigration System' (February 2008); UK Border Agency, 'Earning the Right to Stay: A New Points Test for Citizenship' (3 August 2009) and Home Office, 'The Home Secretary's immigration speech' (5 November 2010).

On the David Blunkett quote, see David Blunkett and Matthew Taylor, 'Active Citizenship and Labour' in Bernard Crick and Andrew Lockyer (eds), *Active Citizenship: What Could It Achieve and How?* (Edinburgh: Edinburgh University Press, 2010), p. 28. On Damian Green quote, see Damian Green MP, 'Making immigration work for Britain', 2 February 2012, web: https://www.gov.

uk/government/speeches/damian-greens-speech-on-making-
immigration-work-for-britain. On the Life in the UK Advisory
Group report, see Sir Bernard Crick et al., 'The New and the Old:
The Report of the "Life in the United Kingdom" Advisory Group'
(London: TSO, 2003) and Thom Brooks, 'Labour must not be
"squeamish" about immigration', LabourList (18 June 2015), web:
http://labourlist.org/2015/06/labour-must-not-be-squeamish-
about-immigration. On the government's plan to run no review
of immigration procedures, see Margaret Ferrier MP and James
Brokenshire MP, Immigration, HC Deb, 2 November 2015, cW.

For a full list of my columns for LabourList, *New Statesman*,
Progress Online, the *Journal* newspaper in Newcastle and others
where I have defended immigration reforms in the past that contribute to the arguments of this book, see my website: http://
thombrooks.info.

ACKNOWLEDGEMENTS

This book is a product of experience, interaction and research. My thanks to the generous support from Durham Law School and Durham University for research leave that helped facilitate my work on this project. I am grateful to Scott Shapiro and the Yale Center for Law and Philosophy at Yale University's Law School for welcoming me as a visiting fellow and providing me with such an excellent space to complete my writing. I must also thank Frank Michelman and Harvard University's Law School for supporting my work on this book too and for the productive environment made available to me.

I have benefited enormously from conversations and feedback from Bruce Ackerman, Orkun Akseli, Hilary Benn, David Blunkett, Catherine Briddick, Alan Campbell, Matt Cavanagh,

Simon Child, Melanie Cooke, Gareth Dant, Cathrine Degnen, Lisa Diependaele, Maria Dimova-Cookson, Don Flynn, David Hanson, Andrew Harrop, Matt Henderson, Peter Jones, Harley Miller, David Miliband, Ed Miliband, Tariq Modood, Martin Nickson, Martha Nussbaum, Chi Onwurah, David Owen, Erica Rackley, (Lord) Roger Roberts, Martin Ruhs, Philippa Scutt, Robert Schütze, Anqi Shen, Avital Simhony, James Simpson, (Baroness) Angela Smith, Luke Sullivan, Jessica Toale, John Tribe, Astrid von Busekist, Patrick Weil and everyone I interviewed for the experiences and insights they shared.

Special thanks must go to Charles Clarke, Harvey Redgrave, (Baroness) Angela Smith, Jacqui Smith and Phil Woolas for extensive discussions. I owe further thanks to Phil Wilson, my good friend and local Member of Parliament for Sedgefield. We spent time campaigning on the 2015 election trail where immigration was an issue on the doorstep and I benefited from these conversations.

Perhaps the most significant influence on my thinking on these and other matters is (Lord) Bhikhu Parekh. He and I have been close friends for over a decade. Every meeting is like a reawakening for me where what is opaque becomes much clearer. When I think about my model of someone becoming British, he stands head and shoulders above the rest.

I offer special thanks – in a book like this – to Alan Johnson, who was Home Secretary when I received my indefinite leave to remain, and to Theresa May, who served as Home Secretary when I became a British citizen. Becoming British clearly made a deep impression on me and I'm honoured to have crossed the bridge before it became too great a barrier.

Further thanks must go to my editor, Caroline Wintersgill. I have wanted to work with her for some time. This book would never have come to be if not for her steady and strong support from the beginning, but also – no less importantly – for her constructive criticisms and really pushing me to improve each draft. My thanks also to the Biteback team, who have been a sheer joy to work with, including Victoria Gilder and Sam Jones. I am indebted especially to managing editor Olivia Beattie, who has helped me develop the final product far beyond its first draft. I could not have had better support.

Finally, my greatest debts are to my family and especially my wife Claire – and it is to her that I dedicate this book. I have learned much of what I know from her, not least how surprisingly different American English is from British English – there never cease to be new north-east words I have not heard once before and which continue to amaze me. We became British in different ways, but arrived at the same place, and I could not be happier for that.

About the Author

Thom Brooks is an author, columnist and senior policy advisor – and a leading authority on immigration law and policy. He appears frequently in the media, often commenting on citizenship and migration-related topics, including with BBC One, BBC News, ITV, Sky News, Al Jazeera, CNN, France 24, BBC Radio 4, BBC 5 Live and leading newspapers. Brooks is a regular contributor to LabourList and the Newcastle *Journal*. He is originally from New Haven (US), but lives in Sedgefield (UK) and holds dual American and British citizenship. He became British in 2011.

Brooks is Professor of Law and Government at Durham University's Law School where he is an award-winning author and teacher. He is also a visiting fellow at Yale University's Law

School. He has held visiting appointments at the University of Oxford, the University of St Andrews, Uppsala University and previously worked at Newcastle University. He is a Fellow of the Academy of Social Sciences, Higher Education Academy, Royal Historical Society and Royal Society of Arts. His books include *The Legacy of John Rawls* (2005), *Punishment* (2012), *Ethical Citizenship* (2014) and *Rawls's Political Liberalism* (co-edited with Martha C. Nussbaum, 2015).

Thom Brooks can be contacted via his website – http://thombrooks.info – or on Twitter @thom_brooks.